4/99

HOOPS
NATION

HOOPS
NATION

**A Guide to
America's Best
Pickup Basketball**

CHRIS BALLARD

ILLUSTRATED BY BOB PORTER

AN OWL BOOK
HENRY HOLT AND COMPANY
NEW YORK

**To my parents and my brother, Dustin, for their support . . .
and to Alex and Chuck, for letting me run it back**

Henry Holt and Company, Inc.
Publishers since 1866
115 West 18th Street
New York, New York 10011

Henry Holt® is a registered
trademark of Henry Holt and Company, Inc.

LIBRARY OF CONGRESS CATALOGING-IN-PUBLICATION DATA
Ballard, Chris.
Hoops nation : a guide to America's best pick-up basketball /
Chris Ballard. — 1st ed.
p.   cm.
"An Owl book."
Includes index.
ISBN 0-8050-4877-4 (pbk. : alk. paper)
1. Basketball courts—United States.   I. Title.
GV887.75.B35   1998   97-28106
796.323'025'73—dc21   CIP

Henry Holt books are available for
special promotions and premiums.
For details contact: Director, Special Markets.

First Edition 1998

Designed by Kathryn Parise

Printed in the United States of America
All first editions are printed on acid-free paper. ∞

1   3   5   7   9   10   8   6   4   2

Contents

Acknowledgments

When I put out an open casting call for the best basketball courts in America, I had no idea so many people would be willing to provide nominees. To thank everyone who gave me an assist—from rec directors, to parks and rec officers, to the thousands who wrote into our web site—would take a whole book in itself, but there are a few people who deserve special mention.

First and foremost I must thank Alexander Wolff and Chuck Wielgus, the two itinerant hoops junkies who paved the way for me back in 1979 when they dreamed up the *In-Your-Face Basketball Book* and, five years later, the *Back-in-Your-Face Guide to Pick-up Basketball*. I grew up with a dog-eared copy of *BIYF* in my gym bag, and I have these two gentlemen to thank for feeding my basketball jones as a young baller. They were generous with their time and wisdom throughout the writing of this book.

Of course, the research for this book—seven months and 30,000 miles of ballplaying throughout 48 states—would not have been possible without the rest of the Hoops Nation team: Eric Kneedler, Craig Harley, and my brother, Dustin Ballard. I feel blessed to have found three guys who didn't mind putting their lives on hold for half a year so that they could sleep in a van, eat microwave meals, and spend all day searching for basketball hoops. I especially can't thank my brother enough for his assistance in this project; not only did he come along on the tour but he read through endless rewrites of this manuscript, did side research, and provided valuable moral support. I am also deeply indebted to Craig Welsh, our link to the outside world during the tour.

Craig designed our web site, worked to get us publicity and sponsors, and was a steadying presence from the start.

Off the court, I couldn't have done any of this without my agent, John Ware, who believed in the idea from the start and is the definition of a professional. I am also grateful to my team of editors at Holt: Jonathan Landreth, David Sobel, and Eric Wybenga; they provided solid advice and made sure the book didn't get lost in the shuffle. For reading over my early work and encouraging me, I owe a lot to Erik Larson. The man behind all the icons and funky cartoons is Bob Porter, who is that hardest of things to find—an artist who is also a gym rat.

Others whose assistance was vital include Jodi Silverman of the Philadelphia 76ers, Dick Schaap and the ABC news crew, the many NBA players who talked with me, Robin Uris, Power Bar for fueling a labor of love with over 1,000 energy bars, Baden basketballs, Mike Budenholzer for the many sandwiches, Bob Welsh, Tom Konchalski, Rick Telander, Frederick Marx, Earl "The Goat" Manigault, Fred Sontag, Clark Kellogg, Terry Murphy, Cecil Watkins, John Rhodes, Steve Kijak, Dan Greenstone, Tom Mulhern, Steve and Cap Lavin, the Roxborough YMCA afternoon crew, Sarah Prehoda, Franklin Caesar, Ken Graham, Larry Bird, Master Rob Hokett, Vinny Malozzi, Mike McLaren, Phil Schaaf, and all those who took us into their homes during our crazy journey.

Last but certainly not least, I must thank my parents for their peerless support and enthusiasm throughout the project. I might even let you win a game of H-O-R-S-E one of these days, Dad.

Foreword

When Chris Ballard first told us about his plans for this book, we couldn't help but get nostalgic. Back in 1979, when we barnstormed the country in search of the best pickup games, Michael Jordan was an unknown high-schooler, Earl Manigault hadn't yet been the subject of an HBO docudrama, and top collegians and pros still found their way to pickup games on outdoor concrete slabs. Two decades later, it's hard to recognize the hoops landscape. Street basketball has gone from 135th and Lenox to Madison Avenue and Broadway. We see the backwash from the schoolyard culture everywhere—in movies, TV, magazines and books, as well as in advertising, fashion, and politics. Phrases like "in your face" recur in everyday speech. And to protect their knees and egos, the best players rarely run with the common folk, and almost never do so outdoors.

But even as mass culture has co-opted the outward trappings of the playground game, something inalterable and down-to-earth remains inside the lines. There's still no better proving ground for a ballplayer than some Y, rec center, town park, or chain-link-enclosed schoolyard. And as *Hoops Nation* shows, the essence of the pickup game still rests in a crazy quilt of customs and language, a culture that's both dynamic and immutable. Now more than ever, there's no misunderstanding anyone who refers to playing "ball." It's unmistakably hoops—not baseball or football or any other cheap imitation.

Like many other aging baby boomers unwilling and unable to give up the game, we now put our faith in stretching exercises, sport drinks, and the spot-up jumper. But to do justice to today's game

requires young legs and youthful passion, not creaky wheels and mel-
lowed sensibilities like ours. We're delighted that Chris Ballard has
captained a new generation determined to chase and chronicle the
game we love. *Hoops Nation* ably claims and puts back the rebound of
our old shot. We know you'll want to run with it.

> In your face,
> Chuck Wielgus and Alexander Wolff
> Authors of *The In-Your-Face Basketball Book*

Introduction

Having played at Ohio State and in the NBA with the Indiana Pacers, I have a healthy respect for organized basketball—a coach orchestrating the action, thousands of cheering fans, a direct, orderly pursuit of victory—but there is something fundamentally real and authentic about pickup basketball. Give me the bent rims (preferably with nets), the tilted courts, the hecklers leaning against the fence talking junk. Take away the refs, the coaches and the clock. What remains is the essence of the game.

Growing up in East Cleveland, playing ball was my passion. There was an outdoor court a mere three hundred yards from my house, and they'd be running daylight to dark during the summertime. Every day after school I'd head down there, practicing my ball-handling on the way. When I got older, I'd bum rides around the city, to the P.O.C., to Cain Park, searching out the best games, testing myself against older players. Back then, there weren't many big men handling the rock, so if I tried to go rack to rack with the ball, my coach would have had my butt on the bench before I made it to half court. But in a pickup game? I could take off and go behind-the-back three times without worrying—part of the gaining of respect on the playground is being able to do special things. That's how you got your props, if you had some flavor in your game.

As a CBS college basketball commentator, I now spend most of my time watching organized basketball, but I make sure I head down to the park or local gym occasionally to watch the has-beens and might-bes hooping and hollering. There's nothing quite like the atmosphere, culture, and language of the pickup game: the court comedians bestowing unwarranted nicknames, the old, crafty guys teaching the younger players the tricks of the trade, and the running dialogue. Players argue and try to one-up each other in describing something. Guards aren't just faking you out, they're "breaking ankles" with their crossovers. I remember guys on defense would say "off," and if the shooter knew the ball was going in, he'd come right back with "awfully good."

In this book you'll find a celebration of that culture as it is played out all across the hoopscape of America. Remember your friend in high school who drove to the other side of the city and came back raving about the "best game in the city, bar none"? Well, Chris Ballard has gone to every major city in the country and come back with hundreds of such courts. He's got games for hotshots, games for the ladies, and games for the little fellas lacing up their first pair of high-tops. He's got a streetballer's dictionary, tales of playground legends, and even tips on throwing down with authority (something my two sons will doubtless reference one day when they reach flushing height). Whether you read it for the stories or just flip through and find a destination for your Saturday afternoon game, I know you'll enjoy *Hoops Nation*.

—Clark Kellogg

HOOPS
NATION

1

The Hoops Nation

A summer day at a park anywhere in America . . .

The rhythmic smack of a basketball on asphalt echoes across a crowded court. A fierce midday sun bastes shirtless players, their sweaty bodies shimmering in the light. Ten men sprint down the dusty blacktop, hurtling themselves forward in pursuit of a battered leather ball. The man controlling the ball bobs and weaves like a boxer, slipping through defenders while searching for cutters or a path to the bucket amidst all those legs, elbows, and grasping hands. He looks in toward the basket, where the physics of position are being played out in a jumble of heavy bodies, interlocking arms, and tree-trunk legs. Seeing no one open, he abruptly halts his forward motion, elevates into the air, and releases a soft jump shot. The other nine players tense up simultaneously, their eyes following the arc of the ball as they try to gauge the direction of the rebound.

On the sideline, those who have "nexts" sit or stand. Some watch sullenly, brooding over their performance in the previous game. You can see it in their eyes—"I should have hit that turnaround"; "I could have rebounded better"; "Why won't Frank pass the damn ball!" Others move around, following the game action, animated by the drama unfolding before them. "Ohhhh man! Good shot, G!" they yell out. "Traaavel! Damn, that boy walked bad!"

Players and spectators alike are absorbed in the game. For some, it is an intensely personal experience; they strive to shoot better, play better defense, or score more points than the day before. For others, it is less about personal performance and more about the camaraderie of

The joys of pickup basketball include swatting away
would-be layups like this one in Ft. Lauderdale

the basketball court, an everyman's country club where friends can
hang out, joke around, and enjoy life.

Regardless of their reasons, millions of people gather every day at
parks, schoolyards, and gyms to play pickup basketball. Out on these
courts, all of society's distinctions and stereotypes disintegrate. It
doesn't matter if you're a highly paid executive, a construction worker,
or a burger-flipper at the local fast food chain; what you do off the
court quickly becomes irrelevant once you're on it. Your teammates
could care less that you're two months behind on your rent and just
got dumped by your fiancée; all they care about is whether you can
stick a jump shot, snare a rebound, or make a no-look pass. And that is

the beauty of playing pickup hoops: it lets you forget the rest of your life and focus on a single challenge—can you and your squad beat the five guys with the bowling ball biceps who've held court all day? If you can't, see ya later, because in this game you've got to win to stay on the court.

Once the day's games are over, you have to make the cruel transition back to your other life. You have to shower, walk the dog, sleep, wake up, and go back to the real world. At least until tomorrow afternoon, when once again you can put on your smelly gym shorts, spend a couple seconds in a hasty attempt to stretch your oh-so-tight quadriceps, and start sprinting up and down the court. Out on the blacktop or the hardwood floor, you're back in a familiar world where picks and bounce passes are much more important than taxes or tollbooths.

For those who play basketball, that is how it is. Trying to describe this to someone who does not play the game is futile. "You're playing basketball again. But honey, didn't you just play yesterday?" The answer, of course, is yes. But for the ballplayer, this has absolutely no bearing on whether or not he or she needs to play today. Each day there is that internal debate: Can I make it to the gym and back dur-

NBA dreams have to start somewhere

All you need is a ball and a hoop: lunch break at Preston's Tires in Charlotte, NC

ing lunch break? Shouldn't I spend tonight working on that proposal? I really should rest my knee, but what if I don't play today and it feels even worse tomorrow?

Rationalizing that decision becomes easy: "If I play this afternoon, it will make me more productive tomorrow morning"; "if I don't play in the league game the guys will think I let them down,"; and, of course, "if I hit my next jumper, my shot is officially back."

How did all this happen? How did basketball become a national obsession, played by close to 50 million people in the United States? Weren't people just referring to baseball as the national pastime? Or maybe they meant baseball is "past its time," because basketball is now the American sport.

The sport's top players, household names like Michael Jordan, Grant Hill, and Shaquille O'Neal, are now multimillionaire superstars who act in movies, record rap albums, publish books, and smile out from our TVs while selling us everything from hydraulic sneakers to microwave popcorn. March Madness, the college game's frenetic spring tourney, now rivals the Super Bowl and the World Series as the sporting event of the year. The women's game has taken off as well, with the success of the 1996 Olympic team serving as a springboard for two new women's leagues.

It's not happening only here in the United States, either; NBA inroads abroad have turned the sport into a global phenomenon, with Europeans learning how to say "I luv zees game" at an early age. And get this: According to a study done by the Asian Basketball Confederation and the American Basketball Council, there are more basketball players in Asia than there are *people* in the United States. "Aih Johdan" is right.

Back stateside, America's popular culture has embraced basketball. Movies such as *White Men Can't Jump* and *Hoop Dreams* have introduced the non-fan to the raw, colorful game of streetball, and the language of the court has infiltrated our daily lives. Today's businessmen walk around saying things like, "That was a *slam-dunk* proposal, Ned," and, "This project wouldn't have been possible without an *assist* from the good folks at Wilson and Weasel Incorporated."

Not only are they talking hoops; these businessmen are playing the game. All around the country, in schools, tourneys, driveways, gyms,

A telephone pole does double duty in upper Manhattan

health clubs, and parks, people are playing basketball. This book is for those people. To write it, I went out in search of the game.

Accompanied by fellow hoop junkies Craig Harley, Dustin Ballard, and (for two months) Eric Kneedler, I hit the road in April 1996 in a blue Chevy van with 68,000 miles on it. Half a year later, the odometer read 99,000 miles, the van was on its third transmission, and we had visited all forty-eight contiguous states, stopping and popping at over 1,000 basketball courts in 166 cities in the process. Every day on the trip we played ball, and every day we steered our van down the highway. For six and a half glorious months, all that mattered was basketball. Breakfast? A healthy serving of hoops, with some orange juice on the side. Entertainment for tonight? Here's an idea—let's play some roundball. One day it was Texas, the next Oklahoma, but always that white line and the horizon, and always the chance that we'd find the ultimate pickup game that day.

We went looking for it, but we never found that one ultimate game. Instead, we found games, plural. We found games in run-down recreation centers where the rims are bent down like old men, we found games at city parks where spectators lounge on the sidelines clutching

The Hoops Nation research team (from left): Chris Ballard, Eric Kneedler, Craig Harley, and Dustin Ballard

brown paper bags. We found games at luxurious health clubs where you can see your reflection in the polished wood floor, and we found games everywhere in between.

In Worcester, Massachusetts, we found a game at Newton Square Park, where we met an eleven-year-old kid with the Dream. He was sitting on a wooden bench next to an empty basketball court at three-thirty in the afternoon. We approached, carrying a ball. "Hey, can I play?" this little stringbean asked. We said sure, and the four of us shot around.

"I come here every day," he told us. "My dad goes to work at a spaghetti restaurant and he drops me off here."

Drops him off there. At noon. And, the kid tells us while practicing his between-the-legs dribble, he picks him up again every night. He does this all summer, all day, *every* day.

"The older guys let me play with them in the games. I'm pretty good, you know, and I've got big feet," he tells us with pride. "My doctor says I'm gonna be pretty tall. I hope to play college ball someday."

On the other end of the country, in Florida, we met a group of men who have started a hoops club. They call it the Sixth Man Club, and they meet three times a week to play basketball. They rent out gyms and play for two hours at a time, rotating in players. They play fast and hard; there's no time for whining, complaining, or arguing. They need to get back to their families, back to the office. Playing basketball for them is about exercising, but it's also about making connections. Jeff, a lawyer, has Bill as a client. Bill, a marketing executive, handles J.T.'s company's account. They trust each other because they have played basketball together. That is enough.

In Burlington, Vermont, we played with a bunch of locals at an outdoor court. Even in bucolic Vermont there was a lot of arguing and yelling. Everyone wanted to change the score, and everyone wanted to kick somebody's ass. If you didn't know better, you'd think ass was going to be kicked. Later that night, we went out to a bar to soak up the local atmosphere (as well as some cold beer). Whom do we see walk in but the guys from the park, the same guys who'd been intent on whupping each other earlier in the day, now laughing and high-fiving.

Through the Internet we met Pete, a thirty-nine-year-old Asian-American flight attendant who lives in Honolulu. For the last fifteen

Seems you can find rack and twine just about anywhere, even on a farm in northern Oregon

years, he has carried his gym shoes with him wherever he travels. If the layover is long enough, Pete will head out into a city and search for a game, whether it be at a YMCA or a college gym. He has played all across the United States, he has played in China, and he has played in "some great games" in Auckland, New Zealand. In addition, Pete has been meeting three buddies of his, all flight attendants from different states on the mainland, every year for the last eleven years at a tournament held in Dallas, Texas. They call their three-on-three team "the Jet Set."

In New York City we met a woman who regularly plays in an all-male league, spending most of her time guarding male players. This doesn't bother her, though; she says she enjoys the competition from all that testosterone. She enjoys it so much that she has started her own monthly newsletter, which contains, among other things, tips for women ballplayers. A self-described "feminist basketball player," her motto is one I wish more people had: "Quit your yapping and play ball!"

And in Jackson, Mississippi, we met the morning crew at a gym on the outskirts of the city. When we walked in and signed up for the next game, one of the teams on the floor included two current NBA players. We stretched out and watched the game, apprehensive about guarding guys who played in the League. We never got the chance, though, because the squad with two NBAers got beat by five NMIers ("Never Made It") who weren't intimidated in the least by a 6′ 10″ Raptor or a starting shooting guard from Motown.

During our travels across the United States, we noticed that as the landscape changed, so did the game. Streetball is played with the most passion in the five big basketball cities: New York, Los Angeles,

Sunset from above the rim in Southern California or: The late afternoon sun illuminates a rim-hanger's climactic moment

Chicago, Philly, and Detroit. It is played just as loyally in musty gyms in Greeneville, South Carolina, and Eugene, Oregon—just with a different flavor.

On the East Coast, the game is flashier and more physical; come hard or don't come at all. On the West Coast, players don't hesitate to shoot jumpers on the playground, and "finesse" isn't a dirty word (though "pass" often seems to be). On the courts of Indiana's small towns, kids actually want to play defense, as evidenced by the half-court games that are played "loser's outs" (as opposed to the offense-reliant "make-it, take-it" system). In the South, we often saw more team ball, in part because of the dearth of slick ball-handlers to dominate the rock. In the mountains of the West, television has brought the game to rural areas, and the pickup play reflects this influence; short white kids will go flying toward the hoop in hopes of replicating that Penny Hardaway move they witnessed during the NBC Game of the Week. In the Southwest, the asphalt-softening heat forces the game indoors, and as a result we came up against numerous deadeye shooters who'd grown up in breezeless gyms and could burn you with soft 20-footers. And in hoops hotbeds like Memphis, Tennessee, and Jack-

The Hoops Nation van: our home away from home for half a year

son, Mississippi, where the devotion to the game runs deep, basketball is like a job for many of the men who show up every day at noon to punch the clock at the local rec center.

What follows is a celebration of the game of basketball as it is played in America. For rookies, there is a chapter on the basics. For those ready to go play, courts are listed in every major city in the country, with pertinent info on each. For those interested in the human side of the game, I've included features on basketball's colorful characters and devotees, as well as a chapter on the potential decline of the street game. For those with an appreciation for the culture of pickup ball, there are chapters, called "Flavor of the Game," that clue you in on important issues like court fashion, dunking, and hoops lingo. And for those who wonder what it's like to be on the road for seven months playing ball, I've included "Tales from the Road," excerpts from a diary that eventually filled 300 pages.

Writing this book was a labor of love involving countless hours of phone calls, interviews, and typing, but I had a great time doing it because I love the game of basketball. After all, life's pretty good when your job is talking about and playing hoops. I hope you have as much fun reading it as I had writing it.

2

Pregame Warm-up

A PICKUP PRIMER

Basketball is a no-assembly-required type of activity. If you want to go shoot some hoops, you don't need to call ahead and reserve a court or get a tee time, and you don't need to invest in any racquets, clubs, or embarrassing plaid shorts. All you gotta do is head down to the park and get it on. It helps to have nine other guys, but you can just as easily play with five, three, or even just your shadow. All you really need is a ball and a hoop.

That said, it does help to go into blacktop battles prepared; knowing the turf, the competition, and the local customs can mean the difference between a full day of games and a long day of sitting on the sideline. This chapter covers the basics of pickup ball, from how to get into a game to dealing with that nasty ankle sprain.

Kicks and a Rock:
Game Gear

Most likely, your only two hoops investments will be shoes (a.k.a. kicks) and a ball (a.k.a. the rock, the pill, or the orange).

SHOES

Finding hoops shoes doesn't take much effort—just head down to the athletic-shoe store at your local mall. Most of these stores, with names like Big Al's House of High-tops, will have hundreds of shoes to choose from (of course, none of them will be available in your size on the day you show up). These shoes can be broken down into two distinct categories: (1) exciting new high-tech shoe endorsed by a big-name NBA player, and (2) the same shoe, just without the NBA player endorsement and the straps and gizmos. The difference in price: approximately $2,000. Well, not quite that much, but the price difference is substantial, so if you aren't interested in the latest style or "hot" new shoe, you'll be just fine purchasing a more mundane sneak or one of last year's models (often discounted considerably). Your only concern, in the interest of preventing injuries and reducing future medical bills, should be to make sure your shoes are well cushioned and provide ankle support and shock absorption.

If fancy shoes don't help you jump higher, you can always lower the rim . . .

THE BALL

Like shoes, your choice of balls runs the gamut, from red, white, and blue rubber to NBA leather. For outdoor play, your basic rubber or synthetic leather, usually denoted by an "indoor/outdoor" label on the ball, will suffice. For indoor play, the game will benefit if a leather ball is used. These days, many players are choosing indoor balls that are made with a composite and have deeper grooves, which gives them a better grip and feel when shooting. They are also easier to palm, allowing for more attempted Dr. J around-the-backboard moves.

Once you find a good ball, treat it with care and respect and it will reward you with many made jump shots and flawless crossovers. If you've got a ball you like, bring it with you to new courts and suggest it be used in games. This way, even if you're on foreign turf, at least the ball will be familiar.

A word of warning: If you do travel with your rock, make sure to keep an eye on it and write your name on it in big letters with indelible ink. Chances are, if you think it's a great ball, so will the dude at the court who's looking to upgrade his pill.

From Driveways to Domes: Where the Game Is Played

Be it the squeaky floor of the gym or the cracked concrete of the public park, the arena you choose for your game is a matter of personal preference, but this doesn't stop players from having strong opinions regarding which is the better game. When I asked a former college player in Atlanta about the best outdoor places to play in the city, he looked at me as if I'd asked him for money and replied, "I *don't* play outside."

This sentiment is echoed by many top college and pro players, who are reluctant to risk injury outdoors. "I haven't played outdoors since grade school," said Laker Frankie King. Chicago Bulls sharpshooter Steve Kerr agrees. "I never liked playing outside," Kerr said after a Bulls game played inside a draftless arena. "I hate shooting because your destiny is with the wind. You can take a perfect shot that can become an airball because a gust of wind can come and knock it off. Plus, the asphalt's tough on the knees."

On the other hand, some swear by the peculiar charms of outdoor ball. In New York, the Entertainers League, the best summer league in the country, plays at Rucker Park, an outdoor court in Harlem where pros such as Allen Iverson, Joe Smith, and Kevin Garnett have mixed it up on the asphalt in recent years. On the West Coast the best games can often be found by the beach, be it Laguna or Venice, where the lure of the surf, sun, and tan bodies is stronger than that of wood floors and glass backboards.

The choice is up to you; it's hard to go wrong either way. As Shawn Kemp told me, "I just enjoy playing basketball—it doesn't matter if it's in the street or in the gym. I'll play basketball all over."

Here are the basic options.

OUTDOORS

For atmosphere, you can't beat the outdoor game. Curveball-inducing winds make every jumper an adventure, the warm sun divides teams into shirts and skins, bent netless rims and tilted backboards force the adjustment of shooting angles, and the crowd lets you know if you suck. Weekends at the park bring out the whole community, and with them the sweet smell of barbecue, a box thumping out tunes, and coolers full of drinks.

If you head down to the park, leave that mid-range jumper at home. Playing the outdoor game is all about taking it to the rack; the closer to the basket you shoot it, the fewer environmental obstacles there are to the ball going in. Of course, the closest you can get is when you're stuffing the ball through the rim, so if you got it, by all means flaunt it—no gust of wind is going to knock a two-handed jam out of the hoop.

The two places you're most likely to find people playing outdoors are public parks and schoolyards. Parks offer the nicer scenery whereas schoolyards are more plentiful in cities. A third option is the backyard or driveway hoop, the time-honored arena for family games of H-O-R-S-E. Countless young suburban tykes have grown up challenging their siblings in intense one-on-one driveway battles where

Outdoor ball means shirts, skins, and dusty asphalt

the hedge is the out of bounds and Mom's dinner call signals the end of the game.

INDOORS

Where outdoor ball is unpredictable, gym ball is reliable and familiar. The controlled environment means you needn't worry about rain, winds, or other weather-related factors, and there is often a court monitor or rec director to handle disputes, keep a sign-up list, or run a game clock. A wood floor is a lot easier on the knees and joints than concrete, and glass backboards and breakaway rims are easier to shoot on than the half-moon metal backboards and double rims prevalent outdoors. A three-point line lets you fire from deep and, if used in the scoring system, takes the emphasis off of the big guys inside.

Because of these advantages, the majority of leagues are run indoors, where no one has to worry about checking the weather channel before heading to the court. As a general rule, you'll also find the majority of older players (those over the ripe basketball age of thirty-five) playing indoors to prolong their playing days.

The Recreation Center

Rec centers are city- or county-funded community centers that are usually free. Most will have one gym, often with six baskets that can accommodate one full-length game or two side-by-side short-court games. Rec centers can vary greatly in quality and competition. Some, like the Fondé Recreation Center in Houston, where Hakeem Olajuwon plays during the summer, have great facilities and even better competition. Others have linoleum floors, bent rims, and a collection of unskilled adolescents yelling and kicking basketballs.

At most rec centers, basketball is just another activity sharing the facility with day care and advanced walking classes, so you've gotta take your open-gym time when you can.

The YMCA

The YMCA is the great constant in hoops. Every major city in the country has a Y with a gym, so if you're a member you can travel anywhere and find a game. As with rec centers, the quality and competition vary, but there are a few things you can expect at the Y. Number one: old guys. Older players flock to the Y, where an unintimidating

Rec centers, while inconsistent, can host some good runs

atmosphere and set schedule make it easier for them to play. Number two: basketball does not come first. With a few exceptions (such as the Riverside Y in Jacksonville and the Central Y in Charlotte), YMCAs, like rec centers, don't put hoops at the top of their priority list. Translated, this means that you have to come at specified hours or you're liable to find the gym full of tae kwon do, jazzercize, or sweaty people jumping on boxes.

The Health Club

Health club memberships generally cost more than those of YMCAs, but they often have a gym set aside just for hoops. Depending on the club, this "gym" may be a converted racquetball court or it may be three full courts with glass backboards. In general, the biggest and most expensive club in a city will provide the best facility, with at least one high-quality court.

The competition at health clubs will be an upscale version of that at the Y; businessmen and well-to-do older guys often make up the majority of the players. In large cities, celebrities often stop in to play ball at health clubs; Denzel Washington, for example, will visit a local health club while filming on location in a city. Former college players and pro guys sometimes have memberships, but rarely will they play full out in pickup. The best competition is usually in the club leagues.

The Basketball-Only Gym

The wave of the future. When you buy a membership or pay a daily fee, usually $5–$10, at one of these hoopfests, you aren't paying for a swimming pool or aerobics instructors, just basketball. The successful gyms, like the gargantuan Run N' Shoot in Atlanta and the Hoop gyms in the Pacific Northwest, provide six or seven full courts and topflight equipment. Most of these facilities are open late (the Run N' Shoot is open twenty-four hours a day) and are a great place to drop off the kids for a few hours. Timed games keep things moving, and an attendant discourages fights and arguments.

The College or School Gym

Colleges and high schools have some of the best gym facilities in the country. Generally, major universities have student recreation cen-

BEAT THE PRO

We've all been there: You show at the park with your ball looking for a little competition and there's not a soul in sight. Next time you find yourself flying solo, instead of practicing your running three-pointers, try playing Beat the Pro. The game works as follows: Choose an NBA player or some other hoopster you'd like to beat the crap out of (your high school coach for example) and challenge them to a little shooting contest. Start with a free throw. If you hit it, you're up 3–0 on the pro; if you miss the free throw, he's got an early lead of 3–0 on you. Then proceed to take shots from wherever you feel comfortable, say 15- to 20-foot jumpshots. Each shot you hit is worth one point for you, each shot you miss is worth two points for the pro. The first to thirteen points wins. For example, if you start out by hitting your free throw, missing a shot, and then hitting a shot, you'll be up 4–2 on the pro. As you can see, to win you have to hit about two-thirds of your shots.

Once you've mastered beating Gary Payton with your baseline set shot, you can try changing up the game by taking only the shots that the pro would shoot. For example, if you bring Kareem out of retirement to give him a whupping, you'll be doing it with sky hooks. If you're matched up against Steve Kerr, you'll be launching them from twenty-five feet. To make it easy on your ego, you might want to start off taking on point-blank range shooters like Felton Spencer and Greg Ostertag before graduating to Glen Rice and Reggie Miller. Once you decide to take on Jordan, as every Beat the Pro player eventually does, don't feel compelled to dunk from the free throw line.

ters, and high schools will open their gyms in the summer months for pickup play. The problem with colleges is that you usually have to be a student to play (exceptions include the University of Iowa, where all are welcome). There are ways of getting around this, but it's getting tougher every year with the prevalence of electronic ID card readers, and in the case of the Duke University rec center, iron gates that make you feel like you're entering a prison. If you can get into a collegiate gym, you'll find what are, on average, the best pickup games anywhere. Drawing on a large body of young athletes and alumni and discouraging disruptive types, college gym games are consistently high-level affairs.

Open gym at high schools often means that someone has a key and a select group gathers to play. It's harder to find these games if you're not a member of the community.

The Home Gym
If you've got one of these, you don't need this book. In fact, you probably don't *need* anything; it's all just wants at this point.

"I Got Next": How to Get into a Game

Once you've made it to a court, your next challenge is to get into a game. For many beginning players (and veterans as well), the most unsavory element of a trip to a new court is finding a way to get on it. Every court has its own peculiar rules and hierarchy, and as an outsider you are at a distinct disadvantage—ignorant of the rules and at the bottom of the pecking order.

Don't let this discourage you, though; it just takes a little strategy. If there are players waiting, the first step is to find out how the games are lined up. The most common systems are free throws, lists (known as "downs lists"), and captains.

Free Throws
When a group of more than ten players is assembled, often the first ten to hit from the charity stripe will play the first game. This method

of choosing a team reserves a place for the otherwise extinct free throw in the world of pickup basketball. Free throws are also often used to determine which players will play next if there are more than five people waiting for the next game.

Downs Lists

Downs lists are sign-up sheets that make playing hassle-free; you just put your name on the list and wait. After each game, the winners will stay on and the next five guys from the list will go on the court. Generally, lists are used when games are played under supervision and indoors. The downside to using a list system is that if the Three Stooges walk into the gym right after you, you're stuck playing with them.

Captains

When players are left to their own devices, the less democratic system of captains predominates. The first ten guys at the court will play ball, and the next player to show up will call the next game (usually barking out, "I got next," "I got winners," or "I got game") and then "pick up" four other players of his or her choosing. Like any general manager, a captain wants a stacked squad, so they will often disdain picking up newcomers and instead wait and nab good players off the losing team. If a local stud pulls up to a court in his car, it's not uncommon for him to be picked up before he has fully exited the vehicle, even if there are twenty other players waiting. This phenomenon has two consequences: it keeps the locals and good players on the court, and it keeps "unknown" and lesser-skilled players off the court.

TACTICS

So if you fit into that second category, how do you get into a game? First off, always be assertive right away; if you just hang out at the park like a wallflower at a junior high dance, waiting for someone to ask you if you're going to play, you'll never get into a game. Find out who has the next game and if they already have five, go down the list until you get picked up or get the last game. When calling next game,

shout it out so nobody disputes it later. If you get picked up by someone and you're unknown, it's best to stay near that player until game
time to make sure they don't "trade" you, either on purpose or because
they forgot they picked you up.

One way to enhance your chances of getting on a team is to look
like a good player. For this reason, it's never a bad idea to show off a
bit when shooting around; casually knocking down twenty-five-
footers can do wonders for your playing time. In that same vein,
while dunking does not always equate with talent, it sure looks good,
and a few nonchalant reverse slams can take a little man from obscu-
rity to lottery pick awfully quick. Of course, if you're 6′ 10″, there's no
need for you to be doing anything. Big men are a rare species on the
playground, so if you just stand around looking suitably tall, you'll be
approached right away, whether or not you can play. Note: Throwing
up half-court sky hooks, jumping up and touching the bottom of the
backboard, and working out the kinks in your underhand Rick Barry
free throw are *not* going to impress anyone.

Another practical tactic for getting into a game is to scout the
court ahead of time (you've already done this to an extent by pur-
chasing this book). What is the level of competition, what are the
best days, when do they start playing, who are the good players?
This way you can get to a court early, warm up, and get in the first
game. Even if you lose, if you showed some skills, someone waiting
might pick you up. Arriving early is a fail-safe method because the
first ten guys at a court usually start the first game. If you find yourself frozen out even then (i.e., they wait for eleven so they don't have
to play with you), you might want to consider taking up badminton
or chess.

A last piece of advice when heading to new courts: if you can, bring
your own five. Heading into uncharted waters is a lot easier if you
show up as a squad, and it eliminates the Stooge factor (having to play
with very bad players). If you can't rally a quintet, try to bring at least
three. This way, your trio will comprise the majority of one squad.
Even showing with one buddy helps because then at least one of your
teammates will pass you the ball. If you're a little man, bring along a
big fella. This gives you rebounding help, and the two of you might get
picked up together because of the big guy.

SCORING THE GAME

If you're in charge of the game you can play to whatever you want—first to seven or first to seven hundred if you've got the energy—but most pickup games are played to a set score, and each court usually has a customary scoring system. The most common way to score games, in the interest of keeping things simple, is to play with each basket worth one point. This means you can hit a full court shot and it's worth exactly the same as a layup. It also means there won't be any free throws coming your way. Games will usually be played to a low score such as eleven or fifteen points, with close games either decided "win by two" or "straight up."

Variations on this format include scoring shots from behind the three-point arc as worth two points and all others worth one, a setup that rewards long-distance bombers. Still other mathematically inclined players run games by twos and threes to higher scores (to 35 points, for example). It's all a matter of preference, though be aware that most players have a hard time keeping track of a 5-3 score, so playing to 60 points could lead to a lot of confusion.

The Organized Game:
Leagues, Tourneys, and Instruction

If venturing out and finding a game isn't your style, fear not; there are plenty of other options available.

LEAGUES

Leagues offer a more organized game and, most of the time, better competition than pickup play. They also fulfill the egotistical urge in all of us to have someone keep track of how many points we score. In major cities, there are leagues for every level of player. Generally, top players (pros, semipros, and top college players) will run in invitation leagues and city pro-ams. For the recreational player, many gyms offer men's leagues and youth leagues. With a little searching, it's not hard to find women's leagues and senior leagues, often broken into categories such as thirty-five-and-over, forty-and-over, and fifty-and-over.

The majority of leagues are played indoors, though some summer loops are run on the blacktop. For your entry fee you will usually receive the benefits of refs and a scoreboard, two additions which minimize the arguing and fighting that often slow down playground games.

TOURNAMENTS

For many weekend warriors, three-on-three basketball tournaments are their only chance to play ball competitively. For other players, they are eagerly anticipated events prepared for over a period of weeks. Either way, tourneys provide players with the chance for instant gratification. In contrast to leagues, they are completed in a matter of days and are usually held over the course of a single weekend.

Larger competitions often attract crowds and have a festive atmosphere; dunk contests, music, and excitable p.a. announcers can lend a "one big party" feeling to the proceedings. While individual organizations and gyms often sponsor 5-on-5 or 3-on-3 competitions, the majority of tournament events are run by national companies with 3-on-3 "tours." The three largest are Hoop-It-Up, Triple Crown, and Gus Macker.

The oldest of the three, the Gus Macker Tournament, started in the driveway of brothers Scott and Mitch McNeal in Lowell, Michigan, in 1974. Their creation, named after the fictional Gus Macker, steadily grew into a major event. The success of Macker led Texas entrepreneur Terry Murphy to start a similar tournament called Hoop-It-Up. (For the full story on Murphy and the roots of Hoop-It-Up, see page 122.) Hoop-It-Up has been even more successful than Macker and is now worldwide, with close to 500,000 participants in 26 countries in 1997. To give you an idea of the global market, consider that out of the six largest Hoop-It-Up events in the world, three—Tel Aviv, Athens, and Madrid—are on foreign soil.

Hoop-It-Up, Macker, and Triple Crown are primarily summer competitions. Between the three of them, they blanket the country every year, with events in every major U.S. city. For more information or

3-on-3 tourneys like Hoop-It-Up cater to weekend warriors

event dates you can contact Hoop-It-Up at (972) 392-5700, Macker at 1-800-875-HOOP, and Triple Crown at (303) 989-4084.

BASKETBALL INSTRUCTION

Youth basketball camps are so popular that any twelve-year-old with a pair of Air Jordans can spend a whole summer going to different camps to work on his or her game. But what if you're in your thirties and never learned how to run the weave or make a backdoor cut?

Your options for schooling, while not as numerous as those for youngsters, have grown in recent years. Twenty years ago, the only way for older players to learn the game was by mimicking other players in hopes of picking up moves. These days, however, many athletic clubs offer individualized instruction, and there is even a national outfit called Never Too Late Basketball that runs a series of clinics designed to allow adults to learn the game along with others at their own skill (or non-skill) level. Begun as a series of weekend camps in 1991 by former Harvard assistant coach Steve Bzomowski, the NTL has now expanded to include twelve-week co-ed programs in major cities around the country (including Boston, New York, Washington, D.C., Minneapolis, Orlando, San Francisco, and Chicago). For more information or to sign yourself up, call 1-888-NTL-HOOPS.

The Women's Game

Women are developing the same type of basketball devotion as their male counterparts; young girls are picking up the rock early these days and learning to box out and throw elbows before they learn to apply mascara. Countless women are involved in leagues and on school teams, but only limited numbers play in unorganized pickup games. The reason for this might be a chicken-and-egg situation; because not

More and more, ladies are mixing it up with the fellas

many women play pickup, other women are discouraged from heading out to play. As a result, women who do play usually have to compete with nine guys, an experience that can be mentally as well as physically intimidating.

In an encouraging sign, more rec centers and gyms are setting aside "ladies' nights" once a week for women players. Especially for beginners, it's more fun to play against other women than to get knocked around by a bunch of sweaty, overly intense guys. For women who are confident in their abilities, the best thing to do is go to any of the courts mentioned in this book and test yourself against the male competition. As Olympian Dawn Staley, who grew up smokin' the fellas at Hank Gathers Rec in Philly, told me, "Go where the guys are . . . they're the best teachers I know."

Older Players

It is impossible to find a more devoted group of players than men in their forties and fifties. Their lunchtime games are so reliable you can set your watch to them, and they will play through any injury or pressing engagement. If a bunch of older guys were tied 10–10 in their daily noon run and World War III were to break out, I'm positive that they would not hesitate to finish their game. And it would be win by two, of course.

For an in-depth look at this subject, see "Playing Past Forty: The Tricks of 'Old Guy Basketball' " (page 278).

Coping with the Game:
Inevitable Injuries

Basketball is the cause of more emergency-room visits each year than any other sport, so the chances are that at some point in your playing career you're going to hit the deck and be slow getting up. "Unfortunately, there is a tendency among athletes to dismiss sports injuries as 'just part of the game,' " writes Dr. Lyle J. Micheli, former president of the American College of Sports Medicine, in the imposingly titled

Neither a bad back, stiff knees, or hard concrete can keep
old guys from their appointed rounds

Sports Medicine Bible. "What distinguishes responsible athletes is
how they respond to injuries."

To make your time on the injured reserve as short as possible, there
are some simple injury-prevention and -treatment methods you can
follow.

Basketball injuries can be divided into two major categories, acute
injuries and overuse injuries.

Acute injuries often precipitate a fit of cursing and an impromptu
huddle on the court as players peer down at their fallen comrade.
Examples include bone breaks, muscle strains, tearing/stretching of
ligaments (including the dreaded ACL knee injury), cuts, and bruises.

Overuse (or chronic) Injuries, as you might infer, result from the tendency of hoops junkies to play "one more game" even when their bodies are pleading for a rest. Chronic injuries usually result in delayed cursing fits that are precipitated by an attempt to bend over and untie your shoes after the game. Included in the overuse injury category is the whole "-itis" family. Favorites include tendinitis (inflammation of a tendon), bursitis (inflammation of protective sacs between muscle and bone), and neuritis (an irritation of a nerve).

PREVENTING INJURIES

There are a number of simple steps that can be followed to prevent both acute and chronic injuries.

Stretch

Your grade-school P.E. teacher had the right idea: The more you stretch, the less likely you are to strain a muscle or sprain a ligament. The most important areas for basketball players to stretch are shoulders, back, hips, thighs, groin, calves, and the Achilles tendon.

Wear Protective Gear

From mouth guards to jock straps to sports bras, outfitting yourself with some protective gear prior to playing can prevent numerous injuries. Sure, too much gear can be expensive and cumbersome, but it is a good idea to guard against the basic injuries, especially ankle sprains, the most common injury in athletics. Wrapping up your ankles in some manner, whether it be a lace-up brace, air or gel cast, or the old-fashioned tape job, can keep your crossover lightning quick. It's also a good idea to keep your feet happy by wearing shoes with well-padded insoles and sturdy ankle support. To reduce leg shock even more, you can purchase insole inserts.

Strength Training

Yes, you with the toothpick legs, that means entering the weight room. If done correctly, weight work can help prevent injuries by giving extra protection and range of motion to joints. People might even stop calling you Slim.

Be Light on Your Feet

Easier said than done, but with every jackhammer impact you impose on your legs when hopping around the court you increase the chance of joint problems. How do you learn to be catlike on your feet? One simple way is to use a jump rope on a regular basis and get used to landing on the balls of your feet. Another is to wear high heels—if you're a guy, please do it in the privacy of your own bedroom.

Know the Game

If you're injury-prone, stay away from outdoor courts with steep dropoffs, uneven surfaces, or overly physical players. Playing inside cuts down on the amount of on-court obstacles and is easier on the knees.

INJURY TREATMENT

So you didn't follow the prevention advice and got yourself hurt. Now what? First off, if you have sustained a head injury, see a doctor immediately. If your injury is of the minor, nagging variety, the following may help:

RICE

RICE is the all-encompassing sports-injury-treatment acronym. It stands for the following:

Rest—Obvious.
Ice—Icing down in the first seventy-two hours after an injury is crucial. Icing decreases swelling, bleeding, and pain.
Compression—Reduces swelling and is best done with an elastic bandage.
Elevation—Of the injured part of your anatomy. This helps keep fluid and debris from accumulating in the injured area (now isn't that a pleasant image?).

If started within the first fifteen to twenty minutes after an injury occurs, RICE can make a difference of days or weeks in the time it takes for you to return to action.

Anti-inflammatory Drugs

Drugs such as ibuprofen and aspirin help alleviate pain and subdue inflammation. Many players claim marijuana does as well, but you didn't hear it from me.

The Sports Doctor

If you're still hurting, don't waste your time suing me for bad advice. Go see a sports doctor, who can recommend recovery exercises.

Regal Runs

THE FIVE BEST PICKUP BASKETBALL COURTS IN THE U.S.A.

Here they are, the five best courts in the country. The courts you should drive out of your way to play at, the courts you could *vacation* at. They are located all over the country and include both sun-baked asphalt blacktops and glossy-floored hardwood gyms. On the right day, you can walk up to any of these five courts and witness NBA players shooting it out, but all of them also provide plenty of time for the basketball proletariat—kids, hackers, and beginners. Run at all five and you will experience the joys of pickup ball in all its incarnations, from free-wheeling city streetball to pick-and-roll team play.

The criteria? Here they are: quality of the court, quality of the competition, consistency of the competition, availability of the court, atmosphere, location, safety of surroundings, extracurricular events (leagues, tourneys, etc.), reputation, and the ease of getting into a game.

Got a problem? Wondering where *your* fave is, left off the list like Mo Cheeks from the NBA's 50 greatest players list? Well, first check to see if it's present in the expanded top thirty rankings on page 339. Second, if you're voting for Rucker Park (number 12) in New York City or St. Cecilia's (number 17) in Detroit, they didn't make the top five because both are almost solely league-oriented, and, unlike West Fourth Street or Venice Beach, there isn't much in the way of pickup play. As for colleges, their exclusivity—you usually have to be a student to play—kept them from being considered for this list.

1. West Fourth Street, New York City

The cracked, cramped patch of asphalt that rests at the corner of West Fourth Street and Sixth Avenue in Manhattan is not much to look at when empty—just another basketball court in a city infested with basketball courts—but then again, West Fourth, the basketball hub of New York City, is rarely empty.

Within its caged confines amidst the bohemian community of Greenwich Village in Lower Manhattan can be found the essence of street basketball: all the grit, showmanship, competition, and spectacle that make the game great. New York City is the nation's capital of pickup ball, and many of the city's greatest players, playground giants like Lew Alcindor (better known as Kareem Abdul-Jabbar) and Joe "The Destroyer" Hammond, have done battle at West Fourth. But so have many of New York's worst players. This is the beauty of the court—it is an equal-opportunity forum; one day you'll see NBA players out there, the next you'll see a short local guy named Benny decked out in paint-smattered jeans and work boots.

Of course, Benny wouldn't find his way into the high-level games or the West Fourth League (along with the Entertainers League in Harlem, one of the country's top two outdoor leagues, routinely drawing college and pro scouts). But there would still be ten to fifteen people, probably an assortment of bums and camera-toting tourists, watching as he tossed up his running hook shot. This is the draw of West Fourth—it is the greatest street basketball stage in the world. The court's location, only a stone's throw from Washington Square and directly in the path of countless tourists and New Yorkers, means that in the course of any summer Sunday, several thousand people will pass by. Some stop and watch, others just peer in on the action. The court provides a free show for all, the ultimate off-Broadway production.

"It's the guys that come to West Fourth Street that become legends," says Ken Graham, the long-time commissioner of the West Fourth League. "People come down here to watch guys play, and they

walk away saying 'Oh that guy's unbelievable.' Whereas in the neighborhood, they'll just be a legend in the neighborhood. At West Fourth
Street, they'll be a legend citywide."

Not only do they become legends, some of them become highly paid
NBA stars. In the last ten years, Mario Elie, Anthony Mason, and
Lloyd Daniels have all made the jump to the pros in part because of
their success at West Fourth. Playing the physical brand of ball that
predominates on the short court (the fence is there for a reason—so
that no one goes flying onto the sidewalk) against top players with
hundreds watching prepared these guys for the big time.

"West Fourth taught you how to be physical, it taught you how to
fight," Mason says, laughing. "It let you know that nothing was gonna
be handed to you, 'cause when they come out there, they come out to
play. Nobody comes out there to impress the crowd—you want the
crowd to ooh and ahh, but you also want to win."

The subway—travelers surface a mere ten feet from the court—provides easy access for players from the entire metro area, and all five
boroughs are often represented either on the court or on the sidelines.
On Sundays a downs list is often used, and starting around 1 p.m. when
things heat up, the crowd packs in up to four deep around the fence.

Taking it strong at West Fourth Street

The allure of West Fourth is such that even rain can't stop the players. After a deluge, the stalwarts just head to the McDonald's across the street for a broom to sweep off the puddles; after all, at West Fourth Street the show must go on.

2. Fondé Recreation Center, Houston, Texas

The scorching summer heat in Houston can fry the brain a bit, so you can be forgiven if, upon seeking refuge in the gym at the Fondé Recreation Center, you have a hard time believing your eyes. But what you see is no mirage: On the gleaming hardwood floor not only are NBA players running in the games but there is also an NBA player running the games.

The NBA player in question is Major Jones, who played center and forward for the Detroit Pistons and the Houston Rockets in the early 1980s. Now, instead of pulling down rebounds with his 6′ 9″ frame and long arms, Jones presides over a downs list at Fondé (pronounced Fon-dee) that often has names like Olajuwon and Drexler scribbled on it. In addition to having an ex-pro gym director and pro players, Fondé has, simply put, the best talent in Texas playing year-round at the top recreation center in the country.

"Summertime it's nothing but players, all day long," said James Herbert, who runs the Houston Pro-Am. "A guy can walk in and watch the caliber of play, and he knows if he can play at Fondé or not. Most guys won't even attempt to play."

If this sounds like idle boasting, consider this: when he was coach of the San Antonio Spurs John Lucas took the whole team up to Houston to play at Fondé so they could get some competition. How'd they do? "David held his own," is Major's less-than-glowing assessment of the play of 1995 league MVP David Robinson against the Fondé competition.

That's not to say you need to have made the big league to play on the NBA-quality court at Fondé. You just need to play big-league ball. "You get some local guys who've played together a lot—they might come in and end up winning all day, pro or no pros," Jones says. In fact, the best player at the gym on many days in the last ten years has been a six-foot dynamo named Dwayne Rogers, who has no NBA pedigree whatsoever. "In his prime," Jones says, shaking his head and smiling ever so slightly, "nobody could guard Dwayne. Period."

Rogers, a notorious talker, is a Houston legend—even Rudy T comes out to watch him in the games—who has always had a little too much street in his game to rise to the next level. "If they can't guard him," Jones says charitably, "Dwayne's going to be the first to let a guy know."

If you make the trip to Fondé, don't worry; you most likely won't get the opportunity to have Dwayne tell you how bad you are. Staff members control the games to keep the pros and top college players (University of Houston, mainly) on the main court. First-timers should

Ex-Rocket Major Jones, open gym supervisor at Fondé Rec

come by in the evening and play in some of the less intense games. Then, if your rep grows, you can think about running with the big boys.

3. Venice Beach Courts, Venice, California

Strolling down the boardwalk at Venice Beach in L.A. is like visiting a human zoo. Magicians, dancers, and artists have set up booths alongside the concrete pathway, and hippies, yuppies, junkies, and tourists all walk by, stopping to check out hemp activists, sand-sculpture artists, a man offering "Free Advice," and the self-proclaimed "World's Greatest Wino."

As impressive as this spectacle is, it pales in comparison to what awaits at the end of the boardwalk, sandwiched between a row of shops and a white sand beach that borders the Pacific Ocean. There, basking in the warm California sun, sit six baskets on a celebrated slab of asphalt that has become the most famous outdoor basketball court in the world. Immortalized in Ron Shelton's 1992 film *White Men Can't Jump*, which was filmed on location, the Venice game is a unique blend of talent, theatrics, and California panache.

Bleachers line the main court, and thousands wander by to watch full-court games populated with everything from college studs to beach bums. To the west sit four half-courts that host nonstop three-on-three matchups, and to the south is Muscle Beach, an outdoor gym where pumped-up bodybuilders bench-press with their shirts off. Mixed in are hordes of Rollerbladers who flit around the courts, stopping to watch the action and yell out encouragement before skating off down the beach.

If you head to Venice, you'll have plenty of chances to soak up the fabled atmosphere; the wait for a game can be extremely long, especially if you don't arrive early. For actual play, the half-courts offer more action; the players on the main court often spend more time arguing and grandstanding than playing. That's not to say there isn't arguing on the half-courts; there are just fewer people to do it. At Venice, debating skills are just as important as playing skills, regardless of which court you're on.

Showboating surfside at Venice Beach

For watching games, you can come down any warm day or weekend and catch all types of action. But the annual highlight is the National Outdoor Basketball Championship, run by Kenn Hicks every Labor Day weekend since 1981. Local studs compete against pro players such as Chris Childs and Kobe Bryant in a tourney with a distinctive West Coast flavor. Rap acts perform at halftime, celebrities turn out in the stands, and in the past, male and female swimsuit competitions have entertained in between the basketball. As for the games, they are high-scoring affairs where players can shoot anything from a three-pointer (NBA distance) to a six-pointer (from half-court) to a seven-pointer (from behind the opposite NBA line).

4. Run N' Shoot Athletic Center, Atlanta

It's four in the morning, it's pouring rain, and you want to play ball.

For most people, the only solution to this problem would be to suppress the urge and go back to sleep. For players in Atlanta who live near the Run N' Shoot, a converted warehouse gym with seven full courts that's open twenty-four hours a day, inclement weather conditions and regular waking hours have no effect on whether or not they play.

"That place is incredible," says Terrance Ramsey, who runs the Atlanta Metro Pro-Am. "You get guys who don't even arrive until eleven o'clock at night. I'm not even sure if they close on Christmas." They don't. The Run N' Shoot, like your neighborhood 7-Eleven, is open twenty-four hours a day, 365 days a year, and it has everything but a slurpee machine; in addition to the courts, the complex boasts a giant weight room, a running track, exercise machines, and a big-screen TV for that postgame *Sportscenter* fix. And, oh yeah, the competition—which has included players like Rumeal Robinson, Travis Best, Nick Van Exel, and Terry Cummings—isn't too shabby either.

Jerry Stackhouse, whose brother lives in Atlanta, is another guy who stops by when he's in town. "It's nice," says Stackhouse, his eyes lighting up. "I really like that concept of being able to go in any time of the night." Stack likes it so much, in fact, that he's thinking of opening up a similar gym himself.

Basketball bliss awaits inside the 24-hour Run N' Shoot

He's not alone. Ever since the first such basketball facility, Detroit's Basketball City, opened in 1991 to long lines, entrepreneurs across the country have been rushing to fill market demand. "A lot of people come in and see it and want to do it," says Greg Hall, operations manager for Run N' Shoot, which opened in 1993. "It's not as easy as it looks, though."

Opening up another gym might not be easy, but getting into a game at this one is. All you have to do is sign up on the game list, kept on a computer system, and wait until your name is called over the loudspeaker. Games are quick and relatively hassle-free—to 15 points or fifteen minutes, by twos and threes.

Beware, though—like the all-you-can-eat pizza buffet or an open cocktail bar, the Run N' Shoot can lead to overindulgence. If you find yourself debating whether work and sleep are really more important than another game at 3 a.m., well, then it's time for a friend to drive you home. Remember, when it comes time to leave the gym, friends don't let friends stay to drive and dunk.

For more on the Run N' Shoot, check out the "Tales from the Road," page 195. It chronicles our full day (twenty-four hours in a row) at the gym.

5. Rocky River Courts, Rocky River, Ohio

Walk by the two courts in Rocky River, a well-to-do suburb northwest of Cleveland, and you will hear the familiar sounds of outdoor ball: basketballs on blacktop, music from a courtside box filtering through the calls of "Screen," "Oh no!" and "Got ya," and the chatter of spectators critiquing the play. It may sound and look like the same game of streetball played at parks everywhere. When examined a little closer, it is anything but.

First off, there are two courts and people are playing on both of them. More important, good players are playing on both. The common phenomenon of all the good players waiting seven teams deep for the better court is not evident here. Why? There's a list and a rotating competition system, which means no captains, no picking up the same seven-footer every game, and no yelling about who's got next. Second, the games are quick. First to nine points, using ones and twos. The average game is about ten minutes. No hour-long contests where every point is debated as if it were a matter of national import.

It's not uncommon to find this type of game in a health club, where a court monitor can keep track of this stuff. But on an outdoor court? Unheard of. I mean, come on, who's going to sit around and keep track of this stuff?

Mike McLaren, that's who.

McLaren is the living, breathing definition of a hoops junkie. Twenty years ago, when he worked nights as a bartender, he would pick up his friends when they returned home from work in the afternoons and shuttle them to a local park in Kensington (down the road from Rocky River) for games of three-on-three. They would play every day, and though the teams might differ from day to day, you could always count on Mike being there. Word spread and soon there was a core group of ten, fifteen, twenty, and eventually thirty guys who were coming out to play ball. With the aid of Barry Clemens, a ten-year NBA veteran and regular at the park, McLaren devised the democratic list system (winner stays on the A court, playing the winners from the B court) and christened his creation the Kensington Basketball Association.

To accommodate the increase in players, in 1990 the KBA moved to the two full courts at a public park in Rocky River and renamed themselves the RBA (River Basketball Association, or "real bad athletes," as Mike jokes). Word of mouth began attracting new players up toward Lake Erie every week.

Today, McLaren, forty-eight years old, oversees an average of 100 players that show up on any given day, driving from all over the city to play at Rocky River. During the summers, Cleveland Cavaliers have stopped by to play (Danny Ferry and John Amaechi have both played), and the daily run usually includes a number of college players. Not bad for a guy who just wanted a place to find a reliable game.

"We draw athletes from all over the city," McLaren says. "We'll have seventy guys waiting on the weekends sometimes. It can get pretty intense at times like that, because if you lose, you've got a bit of a wait."

Why are the courts so popular? "People like to come to a place where there's no arguing and the games are fair," McLaren explains. "Guys like to play organized ball and do it outdoors."

With his blond, stringy hair and goatee, McLaren doesn't look much like a basketball player. On the contrary, his wiry body, tattoos, and deep tan suggest a surfer or maybe a triathlete. Growing up in Lakewood, Ohio, he pursued his high school passion, football; he didn't even play on the basketball team. He spent time in the marines before starting work as a commercial artist.

"I'm a starving one," McLaren says of his line of work. "I spend all my time here." He's not exaggerating, either; Mike has been at the court every day they've played for the last twenty years, from when the games start, around 5 p.m., to when the darkness forces play to stop, and from 8:30 a.m. to 2 p.m. on weekends. Mike, who derives no income from the RBA, provides all the balls (he has gone through over forty of them) and brings the radio, which he locks down and sets to a local rock station, and the all-important list. "Mike's the guy who gets it organized," says Dennis Kelly, a regular who's still playing at fifty-four. "He's put his life into this."

Rocky River has no set season. If there's no snow on the ground, they're probably playing, the hard-core regulars trudging out loyally whenever the weather allows. "We'll start in January if it's forty degrees and sunny," Dennis Kelly says. "The guys waiting for games on the sideline will be wearing gloves. When your game comes up, the gloves come off."

If this sounds like the type of consistent game you wish you had in your neighborhood, try telling that to the city of Rocky River, which doesn't enjoy the basketball players in their central park. It's a bit hard for McLaren and company to be inconspicuous—the courts are sandwiched in between city hall and the police department—and though there have been only a couple skirmishes over the years, the city doesn't like its peaceful atmosphere disturbed by visiting players. "This thing got so big," McLaren says. "I don't think they expected it or like it now that we're here."

In November 1996, the city voted on whether or not to tear down the courts and in their stead erect a new city hall, a back-handed attempt to get rid of the RBA. Fortunately for the players, the bill was

Mike McLaren presiding over the runs at Rocky River

rejected by the voters, who unknowingly preserved what is, for the basketball community, a national treasure. If the city makes a second attempt to halt the games and succeeds, don't worry about Mike. It takes more than that to stop a true junkie. "If they kick us out, we'll just find a new court," he says. "Heck, I wouldn't know what to do with myself without basketball every day."

Amen to that, Mike.

4
Court Criteria

EXPLAINING THE COURT RATINGS

The following chapters list close to 700 of the best pickup basketball courts in the United States. Of course, not every good park and gym in the country is included here—that would take five or six books—but you will find courts listed in every major city. I've tried to provide a diverse mix by focusing on putting in both suburban and urban courts, indoor and outdoor games, and courts with top-level as well as novice-level competition. I've shied away from putting too much emphasis on college rec centers because everyone knows they have good games and they generally don't admit non-students.

The chapters are divided into geographic regions. Some regions encompass six or seven states but two chapters are devoted to a single state each, New York and California. Within each region the states are listed alphabetically, and within each state, cities are generally listed by size. Major U.S. cities receive most of the attention; in each city area a few select courts, generally the top spots or the most interesting courts, are featured while other worthwhile runs are listed in a text format in the "Also in . . ." sections. Selected other cities are listed in the "Elsewhere in . . ." section for each state.

Sprinkled throughout the regions are "Tales from the Road." These are stories from the seven-month trip that myself and three "research associates" took to gather the info for this book. They range in subject matter from pickup legends to game stories to vignettes from our daily life on the road. Also mixed into the regions are short feature stories on interesting basketball-related people and places, including a story on Cal Ripken's regular pickup game at his home gym (in "The Middle Atlantic Region") and a story on streetball legend Earl "The Goat" Manigault in "The New York Region."

There are also four "Flavor of the Game" chapters, which cover the culture of pickup ball and the finer points of the game. The four chapters are: "The Cast of Characters"; "Making the Highlight Reel"; "Talking the Talk"; and "Playing Past 40: Tricks of Old Guy Basketball." These chapters highlight the lighter side of pickup basketball and are illustrated with cartoons by Bob Porter.

A number of icons are used in the region chapters to describe each court. Here's how they break down:

Hoops/full courts. You see, for example, 4/2. The first number tells you how many buckets are standing; the second tells you how many full courts there are. So, 4/2 means that there are a total of four hoops on two full courts.

Indoor/outdoor. You see or . Indicates whether the court is roofed or outdoors.

Level of competition. You see one to five . This rating gives an idea of the type of play to expect, with five the highest. Of course, depending on who shows up on any given day, almost any court can be a hacker's haven or a NBA hangout, but most courts have a reputation for attracting a certain type of player. The levels of play are approximately as follows:

: Retired and current pros play and the majority of games feature top college-level competition.

: Average college and topflight high school players, with the occasional big name.

: Average high school level of competition and occasional college level.

: Recreational adults and low-level high school. For those who are interested in a spirited run but who want to be called "big man" if six feet tall.

: Hackers and couch potatoes. If you're new to the sport of basketball these are good starter courts.

Quality. You see: one to five . This rating provides an assessment of the quality of the court, with five the best. Indoor and outdoor courts are ranked only against other indoor or outdoor courts—a five-backboard outdoor court is probably nowhere near as high quality as a three-board indoor court. The ratings are based on factors such as surface (well paved? wood floor?), hoops (are the backboards metal, fiberglass, wood?), rims (double, bent, breakaway?), size of court (is it regulation? cramped?), general scenery (beach courts are always nicer to play at), and other individual factors.

Location. You see , , , , meaning suburban, urban, rural, and beach, respectively. These indicate the area and environment of the court.

Outdoor lights. You see if there is court illumination.

Rough play. The symbol warns that there may be some sharp elbows and trash-talking going on, so taking charges isn't recommended. The symbol can also mean that the court is not for the meek or faint of heart.

Dangerous Area: The symbol is intended as a warning sign; be careful in this neighborhood, especially if you're from out of town. Generally, only courts with exceptional competition are included when they are in a dangerous area. The symbol appears only rarely in the book.

Female players. The symbol indicates places where women play often. Where there are women's leagues, the court description mentions them.

Pay to play: The **$** symbol indicates it costs money to play, or it's a gym where you need a membership.

League play: The ⟨◎⟩ symbol means that the court hosts leagues or frequent tournaments.

5
The Golden State

CALIFORNIA

From the surfside parks of Southern California to the inner-city slabs of Oakland to the high-Richter runs in San Francisco, streetball tremors can be felt throughout earthquake-prone California. These shake-and-bake West Coast games don't have the same culture and tradition as their East Coast counterparts, but they make up for it through sheer numbers of players. For these hoopsters, it's never hard to find a game; you don't have to worry about shoveling snow off the perennially sunny beach courts of San Diego, and open gyms are a lot easier to locate in the sprawling terrain of Los Angeles than in the claustrophobic confines of Manhattan.

During our travels in the Golden State we discovered that, like the state's population, California pickup ball is richly diverse. We ran into a remarkable variety of people who love the game—from Berkeley hippies to Compton street kids to Santa Barbara surfers.

SOUTHERN CALIFORNIA

LOS ANGELES AREA

Los Angeles is not really a city but more of an amoebalike entity that expands outward from the coast in every direction. The sprawling landscape and warm climate mean that, unlike New York City, where the schoolyards host the best games, the best ball in Los Angeles can be found either in summer league gyms or seaside at the innumerable beach parks that come equipped with rack and twine.

The Circuit

For indoor hoops in central Los Angeles County, there's a quartet of excellent rec centers where L.A.'s finest play. The same core group of collegians and pros will often rotate among the centers, lighting up different gyms on different days. All are in safe areas and are relatively hacker-free.

TALES FROM THE ROAD:
Raymond Who?

We could spend months exploring all of the nooks and crannies of the Los Angeles area, but since we only have weeks, we proceed on an abbreviated tour. We move up and down the coast, head to the rough streets of central L.A., travel out east through suburban communities like Diamond Bar, and then cruise north through "the Valley."

To get a feel for the city, we spend a morning making phone calls to rec center directors, coaches, and sportswriters. In most big cities, there are a number of NBA players whose names dominate the talk of "the greatest to come out of the city." When we ask about L.A. legends, though, one name, unfamiliar to us, crops up again and again: Raymond Lewis. A typical conversation would go like this:

ME: So, who do you think are the best players to come out of L.A.?

COACH: Well, there was Marques Johnson . . . Paul Westphal was pretty good . . . John Williams was dominant in high school . . . but the best ever? Without question that would be Raymond Lewis.

ME: Raymond Lewis?

COACH (*sounding like he's close to hanging up*): You do know who Raymond Lewis is, don't you?

ME (*lying through my teeth*): Oh yeah, of course, *that* Raymond Lewis.

COACH: Yeah, well, he was the best . . . man, nobody could stop him when he was on. He'd shoot from thirty feet out, score forty a night without even trying.

After hearing repeated testimony to the greatness of this Lewis guy, we start to feel pretty ignorant; everyone except for us seems to know exactly who he is. I pull out the *NBA Encyclopedia* to see if it provides any insight. Under "Lewis," it skips right from Ralph to Reggie, no Raymond.

Finally, after talking with a sympathetic sportswriter, I am able to piece together the story of Raymond Lewis. It turns out that he was a skinny 6' 1" guard who led Verbum Dei High School to three straight state championships from 1969 to '71, twice being named California Interscholastic Federation player of the year in the process. From Verbum Dei he went to Cal State–Los Angeles, where he was the nation's leading freshman scorer. His sophomore year, he averaged over 30 ppg and finished second in the nation to another playground legend, Fly Williams of Austin Peay State. Lewis, once described by Jerry Tarkanian as having "tremendous shooting ability and total control over the basketball," then left school early and was drafted by the 76ers. Depending on what version you want to believe, he consequently either caused his own demise or, owing to contract disputes, was blackballed out of the NBA. Either way, the result was that Lewis never played a minute of pro ball.

Armed with this knowledge, we quickly become Raymond Lewis name-droppers, acting as if we'd seen him play in all those summer league games over the years. What is amazing is that, twenty years later, people still remember and revere Lewis, a testament to the enduring recognition accorded to playground legends.

Rogers Park
Beach Avenue and Eucalyptus Avenue
Inglewood

2/1,

The play at Rogers peaks in the summer, when local heroes come back to reestablish their reps. Over the years, Inglewood natives like Byron Scott, Harold Miner, and Reggie Theus have held court. Games are fast and furious, with no shortage of backboard-swaying dunks (due in part to the slightly low rims). To make sure you get in the morning or evening full-court runs, arrive early and put your name down on the chalkboard that sits courtside. Once games start, whoever has next is entrusted with the piece of chalk and the duty of keeping score.

For some pregame nutrition, hit up Randy's Donuts on Manchester and La Cienega. It's hard to miss; there's a forty-foot donut on top of the building. It's open twenty-four hours a day and serves the best donuts in Los Angeles.

Westwood Recreation Center
1350 Sepulveda Boulevard
Westwood

12/4,

At the Westwood Recreation Center, the nicest of the four circuit gyms, you can check out the parking lot to determine who's in for the day—often it's Benzes and Beamers as far as the eye can see. The reason for all the German engineering is the center's location near Hollywood and its safe, professional atmosphere. Comedians, actors, and assorted entertainment types come in to play against the first-rate competition, which often includes UCLA players and pros like Chris Mills.

The center has two gyms, but the action takes place almost exclusively in the North Gym. Be there by 9 a.m. during the week to ensure getting in a game.

Del Aire Community Center
Isis Avenue and 127th Place
El Segundo

6/2,

Del Aire, or Isis Park, as it's often called, heats up on Tuesdays and Saturdays, when the older guys take over the hardwood and charge $3 to weed out the hackers. The hoops troops on hand answer to director

Phillip Cooley, a.k.a. Sarge, a onetime star at Auburn who keeps all the games orderly and makes sure no one goes AWOL with any of the center's basketballs. The ladies (including former USC and UCLA talent) storm the gym on Thursday nights.

Memorial Recreation Center
1401 Olympic Boulevard
Santa Monica

6/2,

Talk about a run—Memorial even has its own information line you can call to find out when they're playing. Just dial (310) 450-1121 and then plan accordingly. Generally, the top runs are on the weekends from 3 to 7 p.m. when Clippers, local collegians, and visiting pro players are often in the house—(Barkley and Olajuwon, to name two). After the game, you can head out to the Santa Monica beach and cool down by swimming out past the breakers.

The Beach Courts

Laguna Beach
Broadway and Pacific Coast Highway (PCH 1)
Laguna Beach

2/0,

You can't beat Laguna for location. At a site in a valley bordered by craggy hills, two half-courts look out on a Fantasy Island white beach and, beyond that, the Pacific Ocean. Of the two courts, the one closer to the water harbors the better games—pro and college talent sweat it out here on weekends—while the second court is for the hackers. Games are played four-on-four to 11 points and start up in the early afternoon during the week. For the day-long weekend action, ballers arrive early with their folding beach chairs and take up position courtside on the grass. Joining them on the sidelines are casual onlookers, waiting players, and bikini-clad spectators.

Given this visual distraction, a "win-by-two" rule, and incessant arguing, games can last up to an hour and a half. Once on the court players are understandably reluctant to leave, but it's tough when guys like Scott Brooks (Rockets, Mavericks), a local legend named Marcellus (who is said to stand 7′ 1″ and bears the nickname Baby Shaq), and NBA journeyman Sean Rooks show up. One of the beach mainstays, a tall guy with a blond ponytail, relates a story about his showdown with Rooks. "Rooks showed up one day at the beach, and of course I have to guard him," the big guy says. "Well, at the start of the game he's not trying very hard and I manage to get a couple putbacks over him.

"Now he gets a little pissed off, being an NBA player and all. So, when they get the ball back"—surfer dude pauses dramatically—"he dropsteps and dunks all over me. And I mean right in my mug. Then

The sublime slabs of Laguna Beach

when he comes down from the rim, he turns to me, smiles, pats me on the butt, and says, 'I got nothing but love for you, baby.' "

" 'Nothing but love for you, baby!' " one of his buddies echoes, laughing raucously.

Bayshore Park
54th Place and Ocean Boulevard
Long Beach

4/2,

For summer hoops highlights in Long Beach, Los Alamitos Bay provides the breeze, the tan beachgoers provide the audience, and the sunstroked asphalt basketball court at Bayshore Park provides the arena. Down at "the Bay," weekends bring out lots of Long Beach State alums, including NBA studs like Lucious Harris and Bryon Russell, to play in the three-on-three games. According to court lore, another Long Beach State alum, Rudy Harvey, provided the court's most scintillating highlight when he pulled off the world's first 540-degree dunk, helicoptering around one and a half times before throwing it down.

Venice Beach Courts
Venice Boulevard and Pacific Avenue (off the boardwalk)
Venice

6/3,

Out on the California coastline there is a famous basketball court where the black men yell a lot and the *White Men Can't Jump*. Venice is an institution with its own unique character and core group of regulars. For the whole scoop, check out this court's entry in Chapter 3 as one of the country's top five courts.

Also in Los Angeles Area

Interested in stargazing? Hit the **Hollywood YMCA, 1553 North Hudson Avenue** (8/3, 🀫 🀫=4 ◉=3 ⛰ $♀), where Tinseltown hoops junkies like Denzel Washington and George Clooney work on their

WHITE MEN CAN'T JUMP:
Venice Beach Factoids

Did you know?

- According to Billy Hanley (not Billy Hoyle, mind you), the rec assistant in the Venice recreation office, the movie wasn't filmed on the Venice courts. Director Ron Shelton wanted a more laid-back scene, so they set up courts and filmed a few blocks down by the Rose Avenue parking lot. That's why, in the movie, you can see the pagodas in the background.

Frank Wallace: The real Sidney Deane?

- The model for Woody Harrelson's chumpy-looking white ringer character in the movie was former Orlando Magic point guard Scott Skiles.
- According to Venice regular Frank Wallace, the model for Wesley Snipes's fast-talking, fancy-passing character in the movie was . . . Frank Wallace. "Tell Wesley Snipes that I'm the real thing," boasts the loquacious Wallace, a pro-am player who does look like Snipes. On the other hand, Hanley says of Wallace, "I wouldn't believe a thing that guy says."

---

moves off the set. Wednesday and Friday nights are reserved for aspiring starlets. Another Hollywood option is the **Poinsettia Recreation Center, Poinsettia Place and Willoughby Avenue** (2/1, [icons] ⌐=3 ●=3 ⛰ ☞ ⚲)), where John Belushi once threw his considerable girth around on the court.

Want more beach? Good, sometimes rough, games can be found a block from the surf at the **Newport Beach Courts, 38th Street and Balboa Boulevard** (3/1, [icons] ⌐=4 ●=4 ⛰ 🌴 ⚲)). In Manhattan Beach, **Live Oak Park, 18th Street and Valley Drive** (5/2, [icons] ⌐=3 ●=3 🌴 ☼), has great Saturday runs and a solid rep, not to mention a sign that says "Please watch your language." Ignore at your peril; the city once took down the racks because of excessive trash-talk. In Playa del Rey, hackers can be located at the **del Rey courts, Con Roy and Pacific** (3/1, [icons] ⌐=3 ●=2 🌴). In Santa Monica **Lincoln Park, California Avenue and Lincoln Boulevard** (4/2, [icons] ⌐=3 ●=2 🌴), attracts an eclectic crowd, including some Russian immigrants learning the world game.

In Compton, if you're looking for talent and are confident of your game, head to **Wilson Park, 123 North Rose Avenue** (2/1, [icons] ⌐=3 ●=4 ⛰ ☞ ⚲ ✈)), or to the city's other rec center, **"Pop" Leuders Park, Rosecans Avenue and Bullis Road** (2/1,

Only in L.A. do hoopers shoot their jumpers avec shades

Catch the Beach Basketball frenzy while you still can!

=4 =3). Marvin Hunt at Wilson runs the Stats League, where they keep track of individual players' points, rebounds, blocked shots, free throw percentage, and three-pointers made. One glaring omission: assists. "There's no reason to keep assist stats," shrugs Hunt. "No one passes the ball."

In Gardena, to the west of Compton, more city ball runs out of **Rowley Park, 1670 West 162nd Street** (6/2, =2 =4). In the Lakewood area of Long Beach, the collegiate women play in leagues at **Pan American Park, 5157 Centralia Street** (2/1, =3 =4). The fellas, including overseas players, heat up the floor of the cramped gym for midday summer runs.

At UCLA in Westwood, you have three options, depending on your ability to get into games. **The Men's Gym** (6/3, =4 =3) is no problem; it's open to students and nonstudents alike. Depending on the day you show, it can be hackers or college players.

The **John Wooden Gym** is for students only, so sneaking in requires duping the card readers. During the summers **Pauley Pavilion** is rented out by Magic Johnson, who invites some of his Laker buddies to play against his traveling team. If you can find your way into this game, you deserve the Pickup Ballers' Purple Heart for Bravery and Trickery.

In El Segundo, Magic and Shaq Diesel both play at the ritzy **Spectrum Club—Manhattan Beach, 2250 Park Place** (4/1, 🖼 🗔=4 ◐=4 🏠 $ ☞ ♀). Unfortunately, the majority of the pickup is unleaded. In Irvine, **The Sporting Club at Lakeshore Towers, 18008 Von Karman Avenue** (5/2, 🖼 🗔=4 ◐=3 🏠 $ ☞) doesn't have any NBA stars, but it does have beach basketball, "the world's fastest-growing beach sport," according to a promotional flyer. The object of the sport, played using a funky mutant basketball, is to score on a single backboardless rim placed in the center of a sand pit.

Out east in Claremont, L.A. residents can escape the thick smog of the Inland Valley by heading to the San Gabriel Mountains, where a heavenly schoolyard, the **Higher Court, Mt. Baldy Road** (2/1, 🖼 🗔=4 ◐=1 ➡), sits halfway to the summit of Mt. Baldy in the Angeles National Forest. Fir trees and a gurgling stream surround an exceptional court decked out with breakaway rims and a three-point arc. To reach the court, just "drive" Base Line Road through Claremont until you hit Mt. Baldy Road. Take a left and follow it up through the forest for about fifteen minutes until you see the court next to the road on your right. Mt. Baldy Lodge is close by for postgame refreshments.

In nearby Diamond Bar, the talent converges on the suburban blacktop of **Ronald Reagan Park, 2201 Peaceful Hills Road** (2/1, 🖼 🗔=4 ◐=4 🏠 ⚡ ☼). Don't expect any trickle-down rebounds though; most wayward boards are snagged by the likes of Keith Van Horn, one of a number of top players who spent their early years at Reagan.

SAN DIEGO AREA

Pacific Beach Recreation Center
1405 Diamond and Gresham Streets
San Diego

6/2,

"PB" has it all: good outdoor games, good indoor games, and the best leagues in the city. Weekends, it's an all-day run on the two outdoor courts, one of which has slightly low rims. Indoors, the days to show are Mondays and Fridays 2–6, when the crowd can include local surf boy Jud Buechler or the King of Clang, Chris Dudley.

If you don't mind a little arguing (or a lot), come by for the indoor half-court games on Saturday mornings. The gym opens at 9 a.m., but since the first to show get dibs, many players roll up around eight. On the court, it's so physical it often looks more like football than hoops— which is only fitting, considering that a number of the regulars are San Diego Chargers.

Tierrasanta Recreation Center
Clairemont Mesa and La Cuenta
San Diego

4/2,

Like the Pacific Beach Recreation Center, both the gym and outdoor racks get serious use at Tierrasanta, the gym where UCLA star Jelani McCoy grew up blocking shots off the top of the backboard. The location, in northeast San Diego, is suburban, but the center draws the city's best, especially on weekends, when the wait can be three deep both inside and on the two courts outside. There are also first-rate leagues, including a women's circuit run by University of California–San Diego coach Judy Malone.

Also in San Diego Area

At Mission Bay, see if you can throw it in the ocean at the **Mission Bay courts, E. Mission Bay and Clairemont** (4/2, ▦ ▫=4 ◕=2🌴),

30 yards from the sparkling blue water. The play at Mission leans toward hackers, and the same goes for **Robb Field, West Point Loma Boulevard and Bacon Street** (4/2, 🏠 ▣=4 ◕=2 🌴 ☼), where the "dude" crowd runs.

Down in quirky, bohemian Ocean Beach, at the **Ocean Beach Recreation Center, Santa Monica Avenue and Sunset Cliffs Boulevard** (4/2, 🏠 ▣=2 ◕=3 🌴), you can go four-on-four in the tiny gym, where the wall is the out of bounds. If you'd rather work on your tan, you can play out on the adjoining blacktop courts.

The **University of San Diego** has the best lunchtime game in town.

Male and female players are migrating to a rough part of town for the games at the new **Mid-City Gymnasium, 4302 Landis Street at Fairmont Street** (6/2, 🏠 ▣=4 ◕=3 🏙 ☞ ♀ 🤾). No need to worry about safety, though; the gym is on the same property as the police precinct. While this proximity to the San Diego Police Department should make some feel safe, "Some of the good players might *not* come because of the police station, if you know what I mean," one local said.

There isn't a police station on premises (but maybe there should be) at the **South Bay Recreation Center, 1885 Coronado Avenue** (6/2, 🏠 ▣=3 ◕=4 🏙 ☞ ♀ 🤾), where the motto—as Olivia Newton-John would say—is "Let's get physical."

Thirty miles north of San Diego in the residential hills of Carlsbad they play surprisingly good ball at the **Calavera Community Center, Glasgow and Middleton Drives** (4/1, 🏠 ▣=3 ◕=3 🏋). If you play so well that you just have to celebrate, head down to the beach and get lit at the Coyote Bar and Grill on Grand Avenue, where they have over fifty types of tequila.

In La Jolla, the **La Jolla YMCA, 8355 Cliffridge Avenue** (6/2, 🏠 ▣=4 ◕=3 🏋 $ ☞ ♀) has a good rep; the **Sporting Club at Aventine, 8930 University Center Lane** (6/2, 🏠 ▣=5 ◕=2 🏋 $ ☞), caters to the wealthy set. Students at UC–San Diego, when not playing at the **Triton Gym** on campus (no ID required), head to **Doyle Park, Nobel Drive and Regents Road** (6/2, 🏠 ▣=3 ◕=3 🏙 ♀ 🚲). The San Diego skyline shimmers in the background during early-afternoon runs on the outdoor courts. A strong noon and late-afternoon crowd plays indoors.

TALES FROM THE ROAD:
Million-Dollar Basketbrawl at a Health Club

In the afternoon we stop by La Jolla's Sporting Club at Aventine, a relentlessly posh health club with a suspended wood floor. We get into a sloppy full-court four-on-four run with a group of guys in their late thirties and early forties who take the game very seriously, arguing on just about every play. In our third game, a brown-haired guy on our team takes an inadvertent elbow to the jaw while going up for a rebound ("up" here means an altitude of about 10 inches off the floor). He holds his jaw, winces, and then starts complaining.

"All right, who hit me in the jaw?" he asks, trying to look tough but having a hard time in his orange tank top.

"Nobody hit you, Fred," responds the guy guarding him.

"Well, I felt you hit me in the jaw, Jim. It f——king hurt," Fred counters, glaring at Jim.

All diplomacy, Jim answers, "Hey, I'm sorry your jaw hurts, but f——k you, Fred."

At this point one of the other stockbrokers on the floor breaks up the discussion and play resumes with the two still crying like a couple of forty-year-old, Porsche-driving babies. The next trip down the floor, Fred heads into the lane as if to take up inside position, but instead of doing so, he barrels right into Jim, knocking him with his forearm. Jim wastes no time in cold-cocking Fred, socking him in his already tender jaw. Fred fires right back, and the two start swinging wildly at each other like a couple of drunks. Fred then launches himself at Jim's midsection and the two go down in a heap on the gym floor. After some wrestling, Jim manages to get Fred into a head lock, whereupon he starts grabbing at the top of Fred's head. During this scuffle, a couple of us make halfhearted attempts to break up the fight, but it's tough when it's so entertaining.

Jim's head-grabbing technique finally pays off as he rips Fred's toupee loose. This is the end for Fred, and he lies there on his stomach clutching his hairpiece to his forehead and looking very much like a sheepdog. Jim gets up and walks away, spewing profanities all the way. Fred continues to lie there prone, calling Jim a pussy. Everyone else in the gym mills around as if they've seen something they weren't supposed to see. The three of us on The Hoops Nation Team don't know how to react, so we just stare intently in the opposite direction. Eventually, Fabulous Fred gets up and heads to the bathroom while Jim sits on the sideline nursing a scratch mark. "If you ever touch me again, I'll kill you," Jim shouts out at the retreating Fred.

After two months on the road in some of the worst neighborhoods in America, playing on courts with gang members and physical players, it is ironic that the first fight we witness on the trip is between two rich guys at a $120-a-month health club in the suburbs. So much for stereotypes.

ELSEWHERE IN SOUTHERN CALIFORNIA

Bakersfield

Local collegians and Bakersfield's baddest clog up the gym at **Martin Luther King Park, Owens Street and California Avenue** (6/2, 🏠 🚪=3 ☀=4 ⛰ ☞ ♀ 🐾), on Monday and Wednesday afternoons and early Sunday mornings. Sign up on the list as you come in and make the most of your game; it's so competitive that if you lose you might not get back on the rest of the day. Thursday nights are for the ladies, and the hackers toss them up year-round on the rec center's four outdoor courts.

Palm Springs

In this desert oasis swarming with old people, palm trees, decadent golf courses, and inebriated college students, there is a little place carved out for roundball at **Ruth Hardy Park, 700 Tamarisk** (4/1, 🏠 🚪=3 ☀=3 🛗 ☀). The games, predominantly half-court, are surprisingly competitive, owing to local high school players and a few nongolfing regulars.

Santa Barbara

North of the city on the campus of UC–Santa Barbara, the **Recreation Center** (8/3, 🏀 🔲=4 ◉=3 🎋 ♀) has daily pickup. If you'd rather enjoy the beautiful weather, head across the soccer field to the five outdoor courts. After playing ball, make sure to stop at Freebird's for a burrito—they make the second best in the country (see page 75 for number one).

NORTHERN CALIFORNIA

BERKELEY

People's Park
Haste Street (one block off Telegraph Avenue)
Berkeley

3/1,

In the sixties and seventies People's Park served as a gathering place for activists in the counterculture revolution, creating enough of a commotion that then governor Ronald "No Jumper" Reagan sent in troops, resulting in the death of one Berkeley student.

Two decades later, in 1993, amidst much outcry from activists, the city bulldozed the park and installed a sand volleyball court and the basketball court. Despite the renovations, the flavor of the park remains, as evidenced by a wall mural that depicts sixties history and benches adorned with slogans such as "Be Free" and "Truth Is a Virus to Power." The crowd reflects the Berkeley lifestyle as well; dreadlocked Rastafarians play alongside burned-out hippies, ponytailed wannabe-hippies, Asian students, intellectual coffee-shop guys, and scruffy dudes with goatees.

In addition to the diverse assortment of players, you'll often find an interesting mix of spectators on the park lawn watching the game and

WHATEVER HAPPENED TO . . .
Balboa Park Muni Gym?

As recently as 1994, the municipal gym at Balboa Park was *the* place to play in San Diego. All-day free play on the three courts brought the best competition in San Diego. In Alex Wolff and Chuck Wielgus's *The Back-in-Your-Face Guide to Pick-up Basketball* it got the top competition rating, and Wolff and Wielgus wrote: "Local TV stations make occasional forays here to get a word with the regulars. (It ought to be like a ski report: 'Conditions good to excellent, runnin' 6' 6" to 6' 8".')."

We arrive only to find that the projectiles of choice at Balboa these days are birdies, not basketballs. That's right, badminton. The city has renovated the gym to make it a training facility for badminton, table tennis, and volleyball. A posted notice claims that a new Balboa Park Activity Center, with facilities to handle these three crucial sports, "is expected to be open to the public in the fall of 1998," at which time basketball will move back into muni gym.

That's if they finish on time. I called up the city office and spoke to Joyce Euper, who's involved with the project. Will it be open by 1998? "I wouldn't bank on it," Euper said. She estimated it could take up to two years longer than that. If, as Euper estimates, it does take an extra two years for the gym to reopen, then San Diego players will have to wait until the next millennium to reclaim their game at Balboa.

Pushing the rock at People's Park

exercising their right to peaceful assembly. Included in the human omelette are the homeless, students, fans, and tourists.

Also in Berkeley

In the off-season, Warriors and Golden Bears claw it out on campus at **UC–Berkeley's** seven full indoor courts. It'll cost nonstudents $10 to play, though according to one local, the gym can be accessed gratis through the back locker-room door.

One regular called the action at **Live Oak Park, Shattuck and Berryman** (4/2, 🏀 ⌨=2 ☯=3 🏠 ⛰ 🚗), "street theater at its best" in reference to the spirited discussions that accompany the topflight games. Adding to the dramatic atmosphere, the court slants down considerably from sideline to sideline, meaning you have to improv when shooting from the baseline.

OAKLAND

Flea Taylor—Oaktown Historian

Every city has a street historian, a guy who's been wired in for years, knows all the players, and can recite playground lore for hours. In Oakland, the capital of Northern California street ball, that man is Lee "Flea" Taylor, rec director at the **Tassafaronga Recreation Center.** Flea has coached or supervised virtually all of Oakland's top players over the years, including Gary Payton, Cliff Robinson, and Jason Kidd. But to hear him tell it, the real stars from Oaktown aren't the ones who went NBA, they're the ones who had all the skills but didn't have their heads on straight.

Take Donnie Martin, for example. Donnie was a skinny 6′ 2″ guard who played one year of college before dropping out. "Donnie Martin was the best point guard to ever play in Oakland," Flea says without hesitation.

Better than Kidd or Payton? "Oh, yeah, ask Gary or Jason about him, Flea says. "This is the guy they grew up wanting to be like."

Then there was Michael Taylor, a 6′ 1″ pickup legend from the late seventies. "They called him Black Jesus," Flea recounts. "He would shoot it from half-court and people in the stands would yell "Layup." As soon as he would cross half-court, it was—pow!—money in the bank."

Ever heard of Lathan Wilson? "Until I saw Magic as an eleventh-grader, I'd never seen anyone like Lathan," Taylor says, shaking his head. "He could do it all, whatever was needed. Rebounds, scoring, assists; he would do it. He never grew past six-four, though, and grades killed him."

Before *White Men Can't Jump*, Flea explains, there was the tandem of Snake and Love, who would work Mosswood Park and Live Oak Park back in the late seventies, playing guys for money. They would pick up a third—usually Love's little brother, who would be sitting in the crowd—and play guys three-on-three. "They were strictly street rats," Flea says. "Snake was a skinny six-eight guy from New York who loved to dribble behind his back, and Love was a five-six guard from Chicago. People would say, 'Man, we can beat that skinny Snake and that little Love,' but those two would beat everybody and earn about two hundred dollars a day doing it."

Flea Taylor with future street legends at Tassafaronga Rec in Oakland

Another Oakland legend was Demetrius "Hook" Mitchell, a 5′ 11″ skywalker with a 48-inch vertical leap who has reputedly never lost a dunk contest in his life. "The only guy I ever saw who was a better jumper than Hook was Arthur Williams," Flea says. "Arthur once jumped up, reached into the rim, and took the ball out on a free throw. He could touch the top of the square on the backboard with his head. Now the poor guy walks around the park mumbling to himself."

So why do all these players live on only in the memory of guys like Flea, while some "untalented" Oakland players like Lester Conner make the NBA? "It was the guys who listened who made it," Flea says. "Jason and Gary were cocky, but they listened and worked to get better. The guys who don't listen don't go anywhere."

Take ex-Warrior Conner, whom Flea coached for a while. "Lester wasn't very good, but he listened," Flea says. "He was like the sixth best guy on the team, but he made it because he worked on his game."

Mosswood Park
Broadway Street and West MacArthur Boulevard
Oakland

4/2,

This is Oakland's legends park, where Kidd dished and Payton swiped when they were just young ratballers. The courts are situated in the corner of a nice family park, though there is nothing familial about the conversations that occur on the court—some of these guys make Payton seem polite. Best runs are from 3 to 7 p.m. in the spring and summer.

The annual summer three-on-three tournament draws the Bay's best. Winning the tourney means playing big-league ball; one former champion team included both Brian Shaw and Antonio Davis.

Also in Oakland

If Mosswood doesn't float your boat, and **Tassafaronga, 85th Avenue and E Street** (6/2, 🏠 🔲=4 ⬤=3 🏙 ☞ 🚫), is too hard to pronounce, other Oaktown courts can feed your need. **Bushrod Recreation Center, 59th Street and Telegraph,** used to be the best in town when Kurt Rambis and Cliff "Treetop" Robinson would play. It's currently being redone from the ground up. **Brookfield Recreation Center, Edes and Jones Avenues** (4/1, 🏠 🔲=4 ⬤=4 🏙 🚫), is next to the BART (Bay Area Rapid Transit) station and has a nice gym.

Verdese Carter Park, 96th and Sunnyside Streets (4/2, 🏠 🔲=3 ⬤=3 🏙 🚫) provides a good outdoor run. The women play Wednesday mornings and "Hook" Mitchell plays weekly at **Club One, 12th and Clay Streets** (2/1, 🏠 🔲=4 ⬤=3 🏙 $ ☞ ♀).

SACRAMENTO

Salvation Army Center
2550 Alhambra Boulevard
Sacramento

6/2,

Five days a week during the brutal Sacramento summers, Guss Armstead, the local pro-am director and a player agent, runs organized pickup games for pro and college players in the air-conditioned confines of the Salvation Army. The majority of the players are overseas guys and borderline NBAers, but Mitch Richmond is a regular, and visiting players like Chris Mullin, Tim Hardaway, and Brent Barry drop in.

"It gets you in shape competing against these guys," said former Laker Frankie King in between games, sweat rolling down his shaved head. "You get a lot of college guys who want to go at the pro guys, and

An NBA-hopeful finishes the break in style at the Salvation Army

pro guys who don't want to get shown up by the college guys, so they play a little harder."

The games are by invitation only, so those of us without big-name status are relegated to the pickup play for normal humans, which runs summer afternoons and winter evenings. You can still enjoy the gym, though; it has all the three-point arcs, glass backboards, and a squeaky clean wood floor.

Also in Sacramento

Roosevelt Park, Ninth and P Streets (4/2, 🏢 🔲=3 ⚫=3 �️ �️), smack in the middle of downtown Sacto, has good runs from 12 to 3 daily. The competition includes "the best never to make it," as a local domino player describes them. On the weekends, the crowd moves to scenic **McKinley Park, Alhambra and F Streets** (2/1, 🏢 🔲=4 ⚫=3 �️), where palm trees surround the court. An exquisite playground with wooden turrets and bridges will keep the kids busy all day so you can play ball in peace.

The **Capital Athletic Club, 1515 Eighth Street** (6/1, 🏢 🔲=4 ⚫=3 �️ $ ☞), has good leagues and top pickup on Saturday mornings.

SAN FRANCISCO

Sunset Recreation Center
28th Avenue and Lawton Street
San Francisco

6/2, 🏢 🔲🔲🔲🔲 ⚫⚫⚫⚫ 🏙 ☞ �️

The domed gym at Sunset rocks with inner-city talent from Hunters Point and Oakland on weekends, when the run is the best in the city. Weekday noon games are competitive as well, though be aware that center director Shana McGrew keeps in mind the priorities of the "yutes," as she calls the little ones. If it gets too crowded in the gym she'll halt the full-court games.

If you get chased off the court, you can always try your hand on the two tournament-style table-tennis tables that sit in an alcove off to one side of the gym. Don't expect it to be easy, though; this isn't underhand serve, dink-donk, summer-camp Ping-Pong. This is heavy-spin, sweeping-forehand-slam table tennis, played daily by a group of local Asian Americans who bought the tables to train for tournaments. They prefer playing here, because, according to McGrew, "They think they're too good for Chinatown, they say there aren't any good players down there." And you thought the ex–college guys at the park could be elitist when picking squads.

Also in San Francisco

The venerable **Potrero Hill Recreation Center, 22nd and Arkansas Streets** (6/2, ▦ 回=5 ●=3 ▟ ☞ 🏀), hosts the San Francisco Bay Area Pro-Am, a summer forum for Kidd, Payton, and local college stars (for the women's pro-am, head to Kezar Stadium, Stanyan and Waller Streets, on Saturdays). Other Potrero pluses: daily pickup play and an impressive view from outside the gym of the city skyline and the Bay Bridge.

The old-timers come out around 9 a.m. on Saturdays for three-on-three half-court ball at **Rochambeau Playground, California Street and 25th Avenue** (4/2, ▦ 回=3 ●=2 ▟). Watch out for camp director and hoops historian Cap Lavin; he's deadly with the set shot. At **Funston Playground, Chestnut and Webster Streets** (4/2, ▦ 回=3 ●=3 ▟), a group of friendly regulars play at the court on the west end of the park (the east court is less congenial). Gusts of wind from the Bay, four blocks away, provide plenty of reason to pass on the outside shot and take it to the rack.

Local leapers take advantage of the slightly low rims on the asphalt court at **Moscone Playground, Laguna and Chestnut Streets** (2/1, ▦ 回=2 ●=3 ▟ ☼), in the Marina District, near attractions like Fisherman's Wharf and Pier 39. Across the park is a small indoor gym for when the fog gets too heavy. **Julius Kahn Playground, Maple Street and West Pacific Avenue** (2/1, ▦ 回=3 ●=3 ▟) in the Presidio has good, clean games in a caged court.

If you tour the gardens of Golden Gate Park, stop by the **Panhandle courts, Clayton and Oak Streets** (4/1, ▦ 回=3 ●=3 ▟ ⌖), so named because they are located in the skinny part of the park shaped like, yep, the handle of a pan. The competition can vary greatly, but you'll always experience some culture. Expect to share the park with bums, crack dealers, hippies, and intellectuals parked on benches reading Tolstoy.

The **Embarcadero YMCA, 169 Steuart Street** (2/1, 🖼 ▣=3 ◉=3 ⛰ $♀), has the strongest Y games in the area. The **Olympic Club, 524 Post Street,** caters to the urban professional set.

North of San Francisco—Marin County

In Marin County, a wealthy area where "the hood" refers to part of your Lexus, well-heeled talent plays at **Drake High School, Sir Francis Drake Boulevard and Aspen Court** (8/4, 🖼 ▣=2 ◉=4 🏠), home to the best ball north of the Golden Gate Bridge. The high school team won a state championship in the early eighties and the tradition is carried on at the dirty, dusty outdoor courts adjacent to the school. After you're finished playing, head down the road to High-Tech Burrito, where they serve up the best burritos in the country.

Out at the **Stinson Beach courts, Highway 1 and the Beach** (2/1, 🖼 ▣=3 ◉=3 🏄), a renovated outdoor slab rests right off one of

Stopping and popping can be a risky endeavor on the gravelly courts of Drake High in San Anselmo

the West Coast's most beautiful, and least commercial, beaches. The water is good for body surfing, and a hippie atmosphere prevails in this funky little town. Come the weekend you'll find some of Marin and SF's competitive players coming out for a day of sun and roundball. The Parkside Cafe, across the parking lot, has tasty burgers and soft ice cream.

SAN JOSE

The place to play in San Jose is **Cherry Park, Cherry and Hillsdale Avenues** (4/2, ▦ ▣=3 ◉=4 ⛰ ⚷), officially known as Paul Moore Park, in the south part of town. "On Saturdays and Sundays the bad players show up at ten-thirty in the morning to make sure they get a run," said one veteran. "The good players will arrive around noon, when the games get serious, because they know they'll get picked up."

The low rims at **Lowell Elementary School, East Reed and South Seventh Streets,** provide an outlet for the monster dunker trapped within all of us. If you want to feel like the man, and I mean The Man, play in the leagues at **San Jose Athletic Club, North Third Street** (2/1, ▣=3 ◉=1 ⛰ $ ☞).

ELSEWHERE IN NORTHERN CALIFORNIA

Fresno

Outdoors, the courts are always packed at **Dickey Playground, Blackstone and Calaveras** (8/4, ▦ ▣=4 ◉=3 ⛰ ⚷ ☀). Indoors, both a midnight league and pickup run out of **Frank H. Ball Recreation Center, A and Inyo** (6/2, ▦ ▣=4 ◉=3 ⛰ ⚷).

Santa Clara

The best games at **Carmichael Park, 3445 Benton Street** (4/2, ▦ ▣=3 ◉=4 ⛰), are Saturday mornings when the "breakfast club" runs. Fortunately for the level of competition, the talent is closer to Anthony Mason than Anthony Michael Hall.

FLAVOR OF THE GAME:
The Cast of Characters

Pickup Personalities and Court Fashion

Everybody's Got a Role:
Pickup Personalities

Play in enough pickup games and you'll notice that certain types of players seem to turn up wherever you go; every court has its resident hot shot, big man, and at least one limb-flailing hack. Of course, not all these players are fun to play with, but part of the challenge of winning is doing so even though one of your teammates shoots every time he touches the ball and another one just learned to play basketball last Tuesday.

The courts are filled with these characters, and they're not gender-specific, either. Maybe you've run into a few of the following:

The Big Man

"Go down in the paint where you belong, Big Man." "Hey Big Man, stop shooting that—you don't see Shaquille O'Neal shooting three-pointers, do you?"

If you're over 6′ 4″, you have heard these admonitions before and are resigned to the fact that you will be called Big Man wherever you go. It sounds good, but what it really means is that you are expected to crash the boards, clog up the middle, and play defense while your teammates cherrypick—though it's true that if you're a 5′ 10″ guy playing at the Y, few things are more gratifying than being called Big Man.

As a result of these expectations, every Big Man secretly wants to be a guard, and most won't hesitate to bring the ball up the court or start launching threes if the opportunity presents itself. The key to preventing your Big Man from taking off on wild ball-handling binges is to keep him happy by feeding him the ball in the post on a regular basis.

The Three Guard

The Three Guard is a hybrid of the point guard (often known as the "One") and the shooting guard (often known as the "Two Guard"). The Three Guard's name derives from the fact that he not only brings the ball upcourt, the traditional duty of the one, but he also shoots it just about every time, shooting as much as the One and Two Guard combined. $(1 + 2 = 3$, after 3, after 3). This type of guard is crucial, nay indispensable, to any team that wants to make sure there isn't an overabundance of passing, chemistry, or team play on their squad.

Note: The Three Guard is thought to be the reason why Big Men often try to bring the ball upcourt themselves. The theory being that if the Big Man has the ball, the Three Guard can't shoot it from 25 feet.

The Unselfish Defender

This player concentrates on defense, rebounding, passing, and setting screens. Unselfish Defenders always block out on rebounds and make the extra pass. They take only the good shot and play excellent help-side defense. Sounds great, right? Well, there's only one problem: The Unselfish Defender does not exist on the playground.

You see, if you play defense on the playground, you won't have the energy to shoot the ball, and if you don't shoot the ball, you won't get picked up for the next game. This "truism" provided the inspiration for one notorious Philly nondefender who said, "It's the first to twelve points, not the first to twelve steals." He promptly lost the next game when his man torched him.

Self-Designated Team Coach

The Self-Designated Team Coach considers the afternoon YMCA game to be the equivalent of an NBA Finals game, only vitally more important. The Self-Designated Team Coach feels that his vast storehouse of coaching knowledge, culled from hours of listening to Dick Vitale, is essential to every pickup game, and he spends the majority of the game chastising teammates and yelling out advice. If you let him, he will diagram inbounds plays, set up a completely ineffective offensive strategy, and take you aside for a private discussion about your role on the team.

The Self-Designated Team Coach

Mr. Hot Potato Hands

This player is afraid of the ball and gets that deer-in-the-headlights look whenever you pass it to him. His first reaction is usually to do one of two things: a) travel b) pass it to the other team. You can even pass him the ball underneath the basket for a wide-open layup and he will quickly pass it right back to you. Can be useful to have on your team because it means, yep, more shots for you.

The Bomber

In the Bomber's world, shots from outside 25 feet are worth 10 points, 25 percent is an exemplary shooting percentage, and mid-range jumpers are for wussies. Unfortunately for their teammates, in the real world, where the rest of us reside, twenty-five footers are usually worth the same in a pickup game (one point) as shots taken from five feet.

The Hack

The sole purpose of the Hack is to foul. Hacks spend years in apprenticeship at parks watching their elders maul offensive players.

The Hack: No Easy Buckets Allowed

They then go through arduous training to perfect such strong fouls as the Clothesline, the Submarine (coming under a player when he elevates toward the basket), the Gouge, the Forearm Karate Chop, and the ever-useful Shot-Attempt Bear Hug (when a good player goes for a post move, the Hack will grab him and pin his arms to his body).

While Hacks are frustrating to have as opponents, they make for great teammates. Since you can't foul out in a pickup game, the Hack can often amass upward of forty-five solid fouls in one game. This means (1) the other team has a hard time scoring, and (2) the Hack will probably get punched out. Figure that until he gets KO'd, it is better to have him on your team than on the other squad.

The Ground Jordan

Michael Jordan's entrance onto the national basketball scene in the 1980s not only propelled the popularity of the game to new heights, it created a new brand of playground player dedicated to trying to play like M.J.—the Ground Jordan. Tongue hanging out, these marvelously untalented teenagers barrel toward the basket, leap into the air, and then attempt to spin and throw the shot in by launching it over their head. These "shots" often hit nothing but the backboard, though if the Ground Jordan's game is really on they may nick the rim.

The general concept that eludes these players is that Michael is able to make these spectacular midair moves because (1) he can jump like crazy, (2) he has incredible coordination, (3) he practices these things, and (4) he is not human. Since none of these apply to playground Jordans, they usually succeed in resembling Mike in only one way: They are wearing a no. 23 jersey that says "Bulls" on it.

Captain Oblivious

Hello, we're playing basketball here? Nope, this seems to have no effect on this guy, who will seize the ball and dribble in circles with his head down. He does not play defense, will shoot the ball over the backboard if he gets his hands on it within 30 feet of the basket, and dribbles out of bounds at every opportunity. The rules of the game escape him completely, but he has no urge to learn them. Of course, he will insist on playing, and the one aspect of the game he has most definitely learned is how to call "Next." Do not, I repeat, *do not* allow him to join your team; avoid this player like the plague.

Looking the Part: Court Fashion

When the good Dr. Naismith first sent his charges into the gym to play ball, their athletic gear consisted of knickers and button-down shirts. If you were to show up at the court wearing such an outfit today, you'd be laughed right off the court and back to your peach-basket.

These days, every player has to take court fashion into consideration; often first impressions are generated by your clothes and accessories. The latest styles set apart the chumps from the, well, the well-dressed chumps. Over the years, hoops fashion has changed with the times. Knee-high socks went from in to out to sort-of in (witness the Kerry Kittles one-sock-up-one-sock-down look). Shorts went from I-didn't-need-to-see-that embarrassingly short to dribble-impeding calf-length long. The afro went from in (Dr. J), to out, to the anti-fro shaved-head look. On the Caucasian hair front, you don't see many sporting the Larry Bird–Bill Walton 1979 hair mushroom anymore—though it's hard to argue that Rik Smits's Partridge boy haircut is much of an improvement.

Of course, everyone's got a different idea of what constitutes good fashion sense, which is why on-court fashion varies so greatly. Head out to the playground and you might catch some of these popular fashion statements.

MALES

24-Karat-Suave Look
The goal here is to wear more gold than all three members of Run-D.M.C. combined. Gold earrings, a gold tooth, big gaudy gold rings, and, of course, enough gold chains to make Mr. T look like a lightweight.

I-Just-Got-Back-from-Foot-Locker Look
Outfitted with all the latest gear, including special-order NBA socks, a Reggie Miller finger band, and the latest trash-talk T-shirt underneath a Shawn Kemp jersey. Guaranteed to suck.

Want to Know Where I Play My Ball?
Like I couldn't guess from the matching shirt, warm-up jacket, shorts, and socks?

Want to Know Where I Pretend I Play Ball?
The shirt, shorts, warm-up jacket, and socks all say UNC, but the jumper says CYO.

24-Karat-Suave Look

Just Got Back from Foot Locker: Now if only he could buy some skills

I-Won't-Wear-It-If-It-Doesn't-Say-MJ Look

The all-Mike outfit: no. 23 shorts, limited edition no. 45 comeback jersey, UNC undershorts, and Birmingham Barons baseball hat. Always wears at least three layers for maximum Mike exposure.

Straight-Outta-the-Burbs Look

Pulling up in the Honda Accord, blasting rap music ("I'm down with all that, really I am"), it's . . . Suburb Boy! Note the shirt with basketball camp insignia ("This proves that I can play"), the new high-tops, and the resemblance to that squeaky-voiced punk from Beverly Hills 90210.

Rastaman Look

Irie from the top of the key. Has been known to block a shot with his dreadlocks. As for goaltending, ask this bro and he'll tell you they should "legalize it."

Preppie Boy Look

The brand-new cross-trainers match the polo shirt and fashionable shorts, while the polo socks add just the right hint of color (namely, lime green) to the outfit. Continually looking over to the parking lot to see if BMW is safe.

College Alcoholic Look

He shows up smelling of booze and wearing a dirty shirt with beer stains, his roommate's shorts, the girl he slept with last night's underwear, and a baseball hat worn backward to contain the uncombed do. Bleary eyed and carrying a large jug of Gatorade, the majority of which is consumed *before* the game. Not guaranteed to get back on defense.

Superhick Look

Cutoff jeans shorts, a plain-colored cotton tank top, and 1986 Air Jordans, with a thick mustache optional. Will pull up in his

College Alcoholic Look

Surfer Look: Ready to rip it up   Bong Boy: Hey, is anybody hungry?

pickup truck blasting Megadeath, and always carries a bottle to spit his chew into.

Surfer Look

The waves must be on strike today because, with Billabong shorts, a killer tan, a blond ponytail, unpredictable footwear, and a vocabulary full of phrases like "no worries, brah," this guy looks like he came straight from the beach.

Took-a-Bong-Hit-This-Morning Look

Air Jesus Birkenstocks; nappy beard; T-shirt with a Phish emblem, those damn dancing bears, or JERRY LIVES on it. Cutoff jeans and a bead necklace complete the ensemble. Thinks everything is very, very funny.

Still-Got-My-Chuck-Taylors-Double-Knee-Brace Geezer Look

Outfitted with goggles, comb-over, headband, short tennis shorts, maroon T-shirt, a whole roll of athletic tape wrapped around various appendages, and sixteen different neoprene braces. Likes to crack jokes regarding age ("I served the food at the Last Supper"), and favorite saying is "When I was your age . . ." followed by superhuman feat such as "I could touch the top of the backboard with my head."

FEMALES

Came-to-Play Look

Wearing all the serious gear, including Dawn Staley U.S.A. Olympic jersey, no-nonsense sneaks, baggy shorts, and hair scrunchie or Rebecca Lobo cornrows. Motto is "Makeup is for sissies."

Please-Notice-That-I'm-a-Girl Look

Hard not to in that Lycra top with the midriff showing, eyeliner, short shorts, and lipstick. Banks on the fact that guys will fall over themselves not to block her shot. Gets lots of uncontested layups.

Guess-the-Chromosome Look

The baggy sweatshirt, buzz haircut, and hairy pits say male, the voice says female.

Female Fashion: distraction or destruction

6

The Pacific Northwest, Alaska, and Hawaii

OREGON, WASHINGTON, ALASKA, HAWAII

In the Pacific Northwest, weather often determines where you're going to find a game. The seemingly unending rainy season in Oregon and Washington has spurred the evolution of numerous covered outdoor courts like Irving Park in Portland and the under-the-freeway courts in Eugene. Up in Alaska, it's not so much the weather as the season: The midnight sun in the summer means you can play outdoors all day and night; then, dark, icy winters send players scurrying inside.

Hawaii, which obviously isn't in the Pacific Northwest at all but got stuck in this chapter anyway, is the opposite case: The weather's so nice you can play at just about any time of the year, but it's hard to concentrate on the game when white sand beaches beckon.

WASHINGTON

SEATTLE AREA

Green Lake Park
7201 East Green Lake Drive N.
Seattle

2/1, [icons]

If you're from L.A. and miss the atmosphere of Venice Beach, Green Lake is the closest you'll come in the Northwest. There aren't quite as many interesting people (a.k.a. freaks) at Green Lake, but on a sunny weekend you'll find plenty of ballplayers and a diverse assortment of spectators out to catch some sun. There's also the allure of the lake, which actually does have a green hue, possibly due in part to the great number of toddlers splashing around in the water (remember, yellow and blue make green!).

If you plan to play on the weekend, make sure to get there early and be prepared to fight for your game—many a soft-spoken soul has lost his "nexts" for lack of lung power. The quality of competition can go as high as the Rain Man and Gary Payton, though most of the time it's

TALES FROM THE ROAD:
Every (Old) Dog Has His Day

On a warm summer Sunday, the whole population of Seattle appears to have headed to Green Lake Park in central Seattle. The park's grassy expanse is home to a chaotic mix of activity; volleyball, soccer, and Frisbee enthusiasts coexist with numerous Rollerbladers, dog walkers, people watchers, pasty-white sunbathers, and, of course, basketball players. Green Lake's outdoor court is where the city's best play in the summer, with top talent arguing and hacking to the delight of the spectators. Today is no exception, with ten people on the court and another thirty would-be players sitting in the bleachers or on the grass.

Looking out on the scene is one waiting player, with his hands on hips and a black Sonics hat on backward, who stands out in sharp contrast to the young, muscular men on the court. Hopper (I have dubbed him this because of his resemblance to the actor Dennis Hopper) is an older white guy who looks to be about sixty. He is wearing a dark-green long-sleeved shirt, black shorts, and black basketball shoes without socks. When we arrive, Hopper has called the second game, and he waits patiently for the first two contests to end, which takes close to two hours.

When his game comes up, Hopper heads out to center court, now with his shirt off, displaying his pale old-man body, stick arms jutting out of a pear-shaped hairless torso. There is some argument as to whether he has next game, with the players referring to him as "the old man" and telling him to get off the court.

Having witnessed the situation unfold, we know that it is indeed Hopper's game, and if this were the local Y, he wouldn't have any problem. But he is trying to play with a group of college-level players at the top court in the city on a summer weekend. And, to make matters worse, he is short, white, and old.

Not easily dissuaded, Hopper starts vocalizing his claim to the game, walking around yelling out "Thank you! My game!" The courtside crowd is now caught up in the whole drama, watching as a group of twenty guys argue at midcourt and Hopper circles them like a valence electron, declaring "My game!"; "Thank you, Dr. Naismith!"; and "Thank you, God!"

The delay lasts about half an hour; it is finally decided, after much discussion, that it isn't the old man's game but that he will be allowed to have the next game. Hopper is not happy about this, but has little choice, so he heads to the sideline, where the spectators stare at him like he's crazy. Hopper takes it all in stride, drinking some water out of a squeeze bottle and chatting it up with the waiting players. To prepare for his upcoming game, he starts doing wind sprints up and down the sideline. Shuffling along with his arms pumping comically, he seems very serious about his warm-up program, and I can tell that though the spectators think he is nuts, they are also a bit in awe of this guy. An old white guy getting a game on a Saturday at Green Lake, you must understand, is about as likely as Shaquille O'Neal winning an Oscar for his role in *Kazaam.*

The game ends, and once again the prevailing opinion among the players is to pass over Hopper. In an impressive display of court honesty, the player who initially had the game after Hopper argues that it is the Old Man's Game, goddammit, and because of his efforts and the continued declarative chirping from Hopper, the old guy finally gets on.

Picking up four good players, Hopper takes the court all business. He is forced into guarding a 6′ 6″ black guy with goggles and muscles bigger than Hopper's head. From the sidelines there are hoots of "Clear it out on him" and "Go right at the old man."

On offense Hopper runs around setting screens, exhorting his teammates to "come on, use it!" On defense he puts his stubby little body into the big guy and yells out "Help! Help!" whenever the ball swings to his side. Strangely enough, whether it be out of scorn, stupidity, or a strange sense of respect, the opposing team never really goes at Hopper, and when they do, his teammates quickly double-team.

Thanks mainly to a slick shooting forward, Hopper's team stays in it, each successful shot by his teammates followed by an exultation of "Thank you!" from Hopper. He does not shoot and touches the ball only a few times, but he hustles like a madman and uses his greatest asset, his vocal chords, to maximum capacity.

To the delight of the spectators, and to the head-shaking amazement of the waiting players, Hopper's team gets to game point. They bring the ball down and get it to the shooting forward, who knocks down a jumper to win the game. Hopper turns, smiles, thrusts his bony arms in the air and declares, "How sweet it f——k-ing IS!"

Hopper tells it like it is at Green Lake

more at the college level. Beware though: One local warned about Green Lake, "It's got good competition, but it's one of the worst places to go if you want to *play* basketball."

Indoors, the Green Lake Rec Center, which has one full court and good noon games, attracts similar competition and has less argumentative games (probably due to the absence of spectators).

A rare moment of actual game play at Green Lake

Miller Community Center
19th Avenue E. and East Thomas Street
Seattle

16/5,

Joyce Walker, or "Jazzy J" as she was known when she played with the Harlem Globetrotters, grew up honing her formidable skills at Miller. She still plays with the guys in the daily pickup games, which are run using a clock to keep things moving. From 2 to 4 p.m. the white-collar crowd comes in. From 4 to 6 p.m. it's kid time, and from 7 p.m. on it's a blue-collar crowd. The talent level in the top games is pretty tough—"Pac-10 dropouts" is how one regular described it.

Pro Sports Club
4455 148th Avenue N.E.
Bellevue

6/2,

Off-season pros who want a workout in Seattle steer their Beamers to Bellevue's luxurious Pro Sports Club, which advertises itself, with no snottiness whatsoever, as "simply the finest and largest club in the Northwest if not the entire country."

If the club is not the country's finest, it's pretty close. All the usual amenities (pool, weight room, etc.) complement two full-length bas-

Vincent Askew cleans the glass at the Pro Club

ketball courts, one of which boasts the floor used for the 1989 NCAA Final Four. Every day during the summer, Sonics conditioning coach and club employee Steve Gordon, his unruly black hair barely contained by a baseball cap, runs afternoon sessions for Supersonics and visiting players like Shawn Bradley, Michael Dickerson, Doug Christie, Steve Kerr, and Rik Smits.

While Gordon is running the Dutchman into the ground on one court, some distinctly shorter and less-talented club members play pickup on the other court. The competition consists mainly of local businessmen, with a healthy dose of Microsoft employees from up the road. Word is Bill Gates has got mad rise.

Also in Seattle Area

There aren't too many sunny days in Seattle, so if one does come around, get your fat ass off the couch and head to an outdoor court. In the city, they run at **Denny Park, West Lake and Denny Way** (2/1, 🏀 🖼=3 ☀=3 🏙), a popular spot that sits on an island amidst traffic in downtown Seattle. *Sports Illustrated* did a story that described Shawn Kemp playing with the bums at **Regrade Park, Third and Bell Streets** (1/0, 🏀 🖼=2 ☀=2 🏙 ☼ 🏀), a half-court nestled amongst the downtown buildings. We can attest to the fact that there are lots of bums—didn't see Kemp, though.

In the northern burbs, short tilted courts don't prevent locals from showing up at **Grass Lawn Park, Old Red Road and 148th Avenue N.E.** (6/3, 🏀 🖼=1 ☀=3 🏠), in Redmond. They play four-on-four at the Lawn as well as at nearby **Peter Kirk Park, 202 Third Street at Kirkland Avenue** (2/1, 🏀 🖼=3 ☀=3 🏠), in Kirkland. To the south in Renton, University of Washington players occasionally show at the court at **Liberty Park, Garden Avenue and Bronson Way N.** (3/1, 🏀 🖼=3 ☀=3 🏠 ☼), which is visible from Interstate 405.

Back to reality: It's raining. Grab your stuff and motor to the indoor gym at Green Lake or Miller, or check out the Monday-night short-court games at **Ravenna Community Center, N.E. 65th and 22nd Avenue** (6/2, 🏀 🖼=2 ☀=3 🏠). Other options include the **Ballard Community Center, 6020 28th Avenue N.W.** (6/2, 🏀 🖼=3 ☀=2 🏠), in Ballard, the **Northshore YMCA, 1181 N.E. 195th Street,** and Bellevue's **Eastside YMCA, 14230 Bel-Red Road.** For some serious

Expect some matador defense at Liberty Park

leagues taken very seriously (see box), head to the **Washington Athletic Club, 1325 Sixth Avenue** (2/1, 🏠 💷=4 ●=4 ⛰ $ ☞ ♀), in downtown Seattle.

The best indoor ball in Seattle can be found at the colleges. The Intramural Athletics building (IMA) at the **University of Washington** is constantly packed, and **Seattle University,** Elgin Baylor's alma mater, and **Seattle Pacific University** both host good runs.

ATHLETIC CLUB DREAMERS

Competitive pipe dreams die hard; every thirty-five-year-old who played high school ball still wishes he or she had one more shot at national glory, one more chance to steal the spotlight.

For members of the Washington Athletic Club and over a dozen other affiliated health clubs around the country, the annual National Association of Club Athletic Directors (NACAD) basketball championships provide a chance to reclaim that glory. Begun in 1988 by four athletic clubs in the Midwest, the championships now include fourteen clubs from all over the country who have banded together under the NACAD banner to hold a spring tourney. Players from the individual clubs competing in four divisions—Open, A, Masters (forty-years-old and over), and Golden Masters (fifty and over)—meet in a different city every year to battle for the national title.

"These aren't your recreational players either," says Nathan Hoerschelmann, the league coordinator at Washington Athletic Club, which has won twelve combined division titles since 1989. "We have some big players, guys who played at UCLA, we're talking our center is 6'8" and can play."

At the WAC, Hoerschelmann chooses an all-star team every year from the club's 340 league players (the WAC has the largest athletic club league program in the country). This squad receives jerseys, a coach, and even travel funding—all the better to bring home more titles. With all this preparation, it's no surprise that some players think people take the championships a bit too seriously. "You'll see a guy taking the ball out of bounds and he'll call out 'three' and hold up his fingers," says Mike Hackman, who plays for the Indianapolis Athletic Club squad in Indiana. "It makes us laugh because not only do they have an out-of-bounds play, but they have three of them."

Still, with each passing year, more and better players are showing up, which gets the competitive juices flowing among the athletic directors. There are some rules—players have to be out of the NBA for at least ten years and must be regular club members—but this doesn't stop enterprising athletic directors. Jim McQueeny, the athletic director at the Indianapolis Athletic Club and one of the NACAD founders, knows what it takes to stay competitive. "We'll be scouting Butler [University] guys right after they graduate," he says, only half-joking.

ELSEWHERE IN WASHINGTON

Spokane

A rough crowd congregates at East Central Community Center, 500 Stone Street, in the city, while a more suburban group runs at **Valley Mission Park, Woodward and Mission Avenue (2/1,**

⌨=3 ◉=2 🏠), where the courts get so much use that they have to change the nets every month. Better yet, make the half-hour drive east to Coeur d' Alene, Idaho, and visit the Slab (see page 269).

Tacoma

A magnificent view of Mt. Rainier serves as the backdrop at the four outdoor courts behind the **Sprinker Recreation Center, Old Military Road and South C Street** (8/4, 🏢 ⌨=4 ◉=2 🏠). Indoors, check out the morning run three times a week at the **Lakewood Community Center, 9112 Lakewood Drive S.W.** (6/2, 🏢 ⌨=3 ◉=2 🏠 $).

OREGON

I'll have two Jumpers, a Monster Swat, and Three Layups with Extra Spin, Please: Fast-Food Basketball at the Hoop.

Sometimes the love shows up in the most unlikely places. Like Salem, Oregon, for example. No, this isn't the Salem where all that witch-burning stuff went down; this is the Salem where the Hoop, the West Coast's first basketball gym franchise, went up.

Despite its small size, Salem is a big basketball town teeming with hoops junkies. Foremost among the local hoopheads is Barry Adams, coach of the 1996 state champion South Salem High basketball team. Adams, along with a group of local investors, came up with the idea of building a facility designed expressly, to quote the Hoop's motto, "For the game and its players." The result is the Hoop, a giant gym that houses six full courts. Adams and company built the Hoop on the outskirts of Salem rather than moving to a bigger city. If you're going to fail, they reasoned, it's better to fail small than fail big.

But failure was not in the cards. When the Hoop, with its state-of-the-art floor, backboards, and equipment, opened in 1994, the gym attracted four full courts of pickup nightly. Leagues and camps followed, and in 1995 the Hoop opened a second facility just west of Portland in Beaverton, Oregon.

The Beaverton Hoop was an immediate success, and its membership outpaced the Salem branch within the first six months. Like any good fast-food franchisers, the braintrust moved forward, hitting Van-

Even the finger rolls seem sweeter inside The Hoop

couver, Washington next. Possible future target cities include Phoenix, Spokane, and maybe even Los Angeles. If you aren't near any of these cities, don't fret, for at the rate they're expanding, in a few years there will be one right down your street, next to the Subway and McDonald's.

PORTLAND AREA

Wallace Park
N.W. 25th Avenue and Raleigh Street
Portland

4/2,

The atmosphere at Wallace is similar to that of Green Lake Park in Seattle: Sunbathers and spectators watch the action from the grass while players showboat and yap it up on the two full courts. Weekends bring out college players, and the city's best summer run, which used

When it's not raining, Portland's finest converge on Wallace Park

to be at Irving Park, can now be found here. One warning: When running the break, be cognizant of your neighboring hoopers or you could get an inadvertent pick set on you; the courts are so skinny that their out-of-bounds lines overlap, meaning that part of each court is in bounds for the other court.

The Hoop
9685 S.W. Harvest Court
Beaverton

16/6,

If you're looking for no-nonsense games in a top-of-the-line facility, look no further than the Beaverton Hoop, a mammoth gym outfitted with six basketball courts, a grove of aerobic exercise equipment, and racks of free weights. During prime pickup hours (when games are to eight minutes or 15 points by twos and threes) a court monitor holds the sign-up list and keeps score on the electronic scoreboard. The Hoop's code of conduct—no trash-talking, no hats, and no verbal or physical intimidation—keeps extraneous stuff from interfering with ballplaying.

As for competition, it can be good, though because of the membership fee, the talent pool is limited. (They used to have a day use system, but that was phased out in early 1997.) Women play often, and local Olympian Katy Steding holds her basketball academy at the Hoop. The gym also has a popular weekly schedule set up, with times reserved for different groups (women, older guys, college level, etc.).

Also in Portland Area

Terrell Brandon grew up competing in the top-notch summer five-on-five tournament held at all-weather **Irving Park, N.E. Seventh Avenue and Fremont Street** (14/5, ▨ ▣=5 ◉=3 ⛰ ☞ ♨ ☼). The park boasts four courts under the sun and one lit sheltered court for rainy days.

Laurelhurst Park, S.E. Stark Road and S.E. 39th (4/1, ▨ ▣=2 ◉=3 ⛰ ♨), has consistent outdoor games. Indoors, good collegiate runs can be found at **Portland State** and **Clark College,** where local boys Damon Stoudamire and Brandon often run in the off-season.

ELSEWHERE IN OREGON

Ashland

If you find yourself in Ashland, a peaceful hippie town just north of California (and home to the annual outdoor Shakespeare Festival), you can take your act indoors at Southern Oregon State or rehearse your J at the **Briscoe School, High and Laurel Streets** (2/1, ▨ ▣=2 ◉=0 ▣), which boasts a multicolor map of the entire United States painted at center court.

Eugene

Under the Bridge
Jefferson and First
Eugene

6/2,

The city of Eugene's basketball solution to the constant precipitation in the Northwest was to put two full courts underneath Interstate 105. Now the only thing getting wet at this court is the net as players rain jumpers from the extradeep three-point line (about 27 feet at the top of the key, though it tapers to a mere drizzle-inducing 17 feet at the baseline). You'll find a number of Ducks out of water coming down from nearby U of Oregon, and the inimitable Danny Ainge grew up sliding around on the court's slick concrete.

Salem

Basketball nirvana awaits you inside the spacious confines of the **Salem Hoop, 3575 Fairview Industrial Road** (18/6, 🏀 ▦=5 ◉=3 💪 $ 🎾 ♀).

ALASKA

Alaska is by far the largest of the fifty states, with one fifth of the land mass of the United States and 33,000 miles of coastline (that's eleven times the distance from New York to California). Despite its enormous size, Alaska is sparsely populated—only Wyoming has fewer residents—which can make finding a game harder than pronouncing the name of the Alaska town Kwigillingok.

ANCHORAGE

The Parkstrip
Tenth Avenue and E Street
Anchorage

4/2,

Good shooters can light up the summer sky with their own personal aurora borealis at the Parkstrip, the best run in Anchorage. The full-size courts reside in the middle of a skinny park and former firebreak that spans eight blocks of downtown. There are no lights, but for a very good reason: With the nineteen hours of daylight they get in the summer up here, wimpy fluorescent illumination is irrelevant. As a result of the long days, regulars often continue to play until after midnight. The court is laid out within a hockey rink, so when the brutal Alaska winter hits, the city can pour ice on the court and create a haven for young Gretzkys.

Also in Anchorage

The best leagues and indoor pickup are at the **University of Alaska–Anchorage** gym complex. Alaskan native son Trajan Langdon used to run here while attending East Anchorage High.

At **Fairview Recreation Center, 1121 E. Tenth Avenue** (6/2, 🏚 🖫=2 ◕=2 🏔 ☞ ♀ 🐾), the women run Sunday mornings, a regular crowd runs at noon, and the top players show on Monday and Saturday nights. If Fairview's booked up, head to **Spenard Recreation Center,** Anchorage's other city center.

ELSEWHERE IN ALASKA

Cordova

The youngsters in this coastal city gather at the Cordova High Gym on Fishermen Street. The gym is on your left when you enter town from the airport.

Juneau

When the blacktop isn't iced over, locals play at **Adair Kennedy Park, Mendenhall Road** (4/2, 🏚 🖫=2 ◕=2 🚩), or across the street at Floyd-Dryden Middle School. During the winter, the city runs a league from November to mid-February out of three local middle schools, all of which are occasionally open for drop-in play as well. Contact Juneau Parks and Recreation (586-5226) for open gym information.

HOOPING IN NOME:
Win one for Rover

The remote Alaskan outpost of Nome, an icy city accessible only by airplane, is probably the last place any sane tournament organizer would consider as the site for a basketball tournament. With a population of 4,500 and only one rec center, the city isn't exactly a bustling hoops hotbed. Still, Lonnie O'Connor, a Nome native, decided in the late seventies that his hometown would be the perfect place to hold a basketball tourney.

Call him crazy, but twenty years later the Lonnie O'Connor Basketball Classic tournament has done the impossible and become the largest double elimination five-on-five basketball tournament in the United States. O'Connor, who passed away in 1992, wanted to provide an event that would coincide with the annual Iditarod dog-sled race, which runs from Anchorage to Nome. He figured that a tournament would entertain people while they were waiting for the dogs to come in.

The first few years only a handful of teams entered, but these days the event draws an average of 65 teams a year who make the journey from all over Alaska (and even Seattle) to play in the weeklong hoopfest, which kicks off the second week of March and has both men's and women's divisions. With only two courts at their disposal—the Nome Rec Center and the nearby National Guard Armory—tourney organizers have to run games from 8 a.m. to 1:30 a.m. for six days. This doesn't bother any of the participants though; for many of them, this is the only time of the year they'll see one another. "Everybody knows each other up here, but because the villages are so widespread and the country is so big, this is really the year's only big get-together," says

Kavik Hahn, one of the tournament organizers. "So everybody catches up on the last year's activity and gets to see their friends. Not to mention there's a little tipping of the beer."

In between tipping the beer, talking dogs, and fighting the elements—tourney time weather has varied from 40 above to 30 below over the years—the teams knock each other out until the final games are played on championship Sunday. With the end of the tourney, and the Iditarod, the players say their good-byes and head back into the Alaskan wilderness, disappearing until the following March, when they will return from all reaches of the frozen tundra for another round of ice buckets.

Nome

A core group of regulars plays daily at the **Nome Recreation Center, 425 Sixth Avenue E.** (6/2, 🏠 🚪=3 ●=2 📣 ☞ ♀).

HAWAII

HONOLULU

Paki Park
3503 Leahi Avenue
Honolulu

2/1, 🏠 🚪🚪🚪🚪 ●●● 🏙️ 🐢 💡

Dunkers can grab the rim and engage in a different sort of "hang ten" at Paki Park, the best run in Hawaii. The court, which is located next to the Kapahulu Fire Station and only a few blocks from Waikiki beach, was renovated in 1996 and sits adjacent to two volleyball courts. A lot of trash-talking goes on, but if you come on the right day, the games are top-notch. Noted beach bum Magic Johnson even played here once.

Atkinson YMCA
401 Atkinson Drive
Honolulu

6/2, ⬜ ⬜⬜⬜⬜ ●●● 🏙 $

A less mouthy, more consistent game than at Paki can be found at the Atkinson Y. The best games are Saturday mornings and weekday afternoons 5–7 p.m. The stalwart seniors even run at the ungodly hour of 6:30 on weekday mornings. If someone gives you a sweet pass, impress them by saying "Mahalo nui loa," Hawaiian for "Thank you very much."

Also in Honolulu
Crane Community Park, next to Kaimuki High School, hosts a mid-level outdoor run.

Both **Klum Gym** and **Gym 2** at the **University of Hawaii** are worthy indoor spots. Best games are Monday through Thursday 6–9 p.m. in Gym 2. If you can get on, the competition is good at the various island military bases.

ELSEWHERE IN HAWAII

Kailau
Kailua Recreation Center
21 South Kainalu
Kailua

6/2, ⬜ ⬜⬜⬜⬜ ●●● 🌴 ♀

On the windward side of Oahu, near the famous surfing waves of the North Shore, islanders take a break from the Big Kahuna to play at Kailua. The top-notch gym, which is funded by town taxes, heats up with good games on Monday and Wednesday evenings. If you'd rather play under the island sun, there are also two outdoor courts, one of which has nine-foot rims.

7

Texas and the Southwest Region

ARIZONA, NEVADA, NEW MEXICO, TEXAS, UTAH

Summertime in the Sun Belt means either you play at night or you play indoors. If you have the gall to play outdoors during the heat of the day, do so in December and with a wet towel wrapped around your head. While the heat can be tough, the flip side is that every season is basketball season; no snow to shovel, no frozen fingers smacking against the ball.

Because of the scalding temperatures, indoor runs are a must and air-conditioning often becomes a major factor in any decision on where to play ball. With chilled-out gym options like Houston's Fondé and Dallas's Fretz Center, ballers should be able to keep cool.

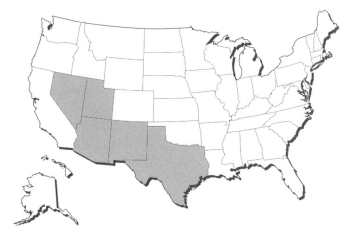

ARIZONA

PHOENIX-SCOTTSDALE AREA

Kiwanis Park
All-America Way and Guadalupe Road
Scottsdale

Kiwanis Park heats up on Thursday nights and Sunday mornings, when a gym supervisor runs an electronic scoreboard to keep things moving. The indoor run (there's also one lit outdoor court) was deemed "Best pickup basketball game" by the *New Times*, a free weekly, for their 1994 "Best of Phoenix" issue. On peak days, when Dan Majerle and members of the Arizona Cardinals have been known to drop by, this might be true, but the competition, like Majerle's game, can be inconsistent.

Also in Phoenix-Scottsdale Area

White man's paradise might just be found at **Whittier Elementary School, Longmore and West Seventh Place,** (14/5, 🏢 🏠=3 ●=2 🏠 💡), in Mesa. Choose from one of ten low rims, varying in

height from 9 to 9½ feet. Games run full court the short way and consist mainly of high school and junior high dreamers.

The **Village Racquet and Fitness Club, 4444 East Camelback,**
(6/2, 🏠 ⬜=4 ◕=3 🔒 $ ☞ ♀), advertises itself as "Phoenix's most
exclusive athletic club," so you can probably guess what type of people
belong—yep, big bucks and no hops. The doctor-lawyer factor
notwithstanding, the games are pretty good.

A well-deserved five backboards in the quality department, the
outdoor court at **Indian School Park, Hayden and Camelback**
(4/2, 🟨 ⬜=5 ◕=3 🔒 ☼), in Scottsdale features shaded barbecue
areas, sand volleyball courts, the majestic Phoenix Mountains to the
west, and the spring training facility for the San Francisco Giants.

A young sun rat practices at Indian School Park

When it's too hot outside, which is most of the time in Arizona, the park has one indoor full court where they run noons and evenings.

In Phoenix, two good outdoor spots are **Encanto Park, Seventh Avenue and Encanto Boulevard** (6/3, 🏀 📺=3 ●=3 ⛰ 🏕 🔆), the closest court to downtown, and **Hermoso Park, 20th and Southern** (4/2, 🏀 📺=3 ●=3 ⛰ 🏕 🔆), in the southern part of the city.

ELSEWHERE IN ARIZONA

Holbrook

For years, the Budenholzer family has been the unofficial caretaker of **Hunt Park,** the only outdoor court in this tiny northern Arizona town. If players forget their ball, they stop by across the street and pick one up from "the Buds," a basketball family. Dad coached his son Mike, now an assistant coach with the San Antonio Spurs, at Holbrook High. When the day's action is done, last one to leave returns the ball.

Tucson

Udall Recreation Center
7200 East Tanque Verde
Tucson

6/2, 🏀 📺 📺 📺 📺 ● ● ● 🏫 $ 🐚 ♀

To reach Udall, you have to drive down what locals refer to as Fast Food Row, a five-mile strip that harbors at least three of each major fast-food restaurant. If you aren't able to run the gauntlet without a stop for a sweet (deep) dish at Pizza Hut or an Ultimate Cheeseburger (1,060 calories) at Jack in the Box, don't worry because you can burn off those calories in the fast-paced, competitive full-court runs at Udall. The best games are weekends from 12 to 3:30.

The rest of the time it's primarily high school kids, though skilled ones. A word of advice: To win, just hustle and rebound; you may not look as good, but you'll stay on for next game.

If you've still got a hoops hunger, the **University of Arizona Rec Center, 6th Street and Highland,** is only a couple of miles away and is one of the best campus runs in the country. Stray Wildcats often mix it up with the students.

NEVADA

LAS VEGAS

The slogan of the Las Vegas Parks and Recreation Department is "Beyond the neon," and that is where Hoops Nation will take you. The city is renowned the world over for one reason: gambling. Mix in extravagant casinos, over-the-top shows, and over-the-hill musical acts and you've got the tourist attraction that is Vegas. But what of the people who actually live in L.V., NV? We went out searching for a different type of 21 and were pleasantly surprised to find some stellar options.

Sunset Park
Sunset Road and Eastern Avenue
Las Vegas

16/8,

Sunset is the premier place to play outdoor ball once you've made your donations to the casinos on the strip. The eight full courts are filled with players year round, except for when the temperature soars over 110 degrees. UNLV players past and present, including Anderson Hunt (the 1990 NCAA Tournament MVP), play here, though with eight courts there's a game for all skill levels. When you're done sweating it out on the court, a minimart across the street can take care of your postgame rehydration needs.

Also in Las Vegas

The best run in Vegas (besides the on-campus games at **UNLV**) is at **Doolittle Recreation Center, West Lake Mead Boulevard and J Street** (6/2, =4 =4), where one-time Running Rebel and local boy Greg Anthony came up playing his ball. In addition

TALES FROM THE ROAD:
Rolling the Dice at the Sporting House

The closest we come to the glitz of the strip while in Vegas is the Las Vegas Sporting House, an athletic club a block away from the heart of the casinos. The club is a magnet for local celebrities; regulars include Mike Tyson, Randall Cunningham, pretty-boy magicians Siegfried and Roy, and a whole gaggle of Elvis impersonators.

We swing by at noon on a Saturday hoping to get in a game, but the basketball has been canceled for the day because of an exercise-bike demonstration taking place on the court. The receptionist we talk to gives us the lowdown on the leagues and pickup, but we don't get a chance to play and leave a little disappointed. The next day I go online with my laptop computer and receive the following e-mail from a kindred soul who noticed our website address painted on the Hoops Nation van:

> I saw your van today in the parking lot of the Sporting House. You can imagine my embarrassment when our gym was closed so some AEROBICS INSTRUCTORS COULD LEARN HOW TO WORK SOME STUPID Reebok exercise bike. I really wanted to play some ball today, too.
> Sincerely,
> The Lonnie Shelton of the
> Sporting House Advanced Basketball League

It's good to see others out there have similar priorities. (Lonnie Shelton, for those who aren't familiar, was a 6'8" forward with the Knicks, Sonics, and Cavs in the early eighties.)

to pickup, Doolittle hosts a competitive midnight basketball league. Crosstown, **Dula Gym, Bonanza Road and Las Vegas Boulevard** (2/1, 🏠 ▣=5 ●=3 🏔 ☞ 🚻), has lower-caliber games than Doolittle but a better facility. The gym is also home to the local bocce ball league (if you don't know what bocce ball is, think old Italian guys tossing metal balls).

You can also get a game at the **Chuck Minker Sports Complex, Stewart Avenue and North Mojave Road** (6/2, 🏠 ▣=3 ●=3 🏔 ☞ 🚻); just beware of the dead spots on the gym floor. When the exercise bikes haven't monopolized the gym, Vegas's upper crust play ball at the **Las Vegas Sporting House, 3025 Industrial Road** (2/1, 🏠 ▣=2 ●=3 🏔 $ ☞). Outdoors, **Lorenzi Park, West Washington Avenue and Twin Lakes Drive** (4/2, 🏠 ▣=2 ●=2 🏢 🚻), offers a view of the Stratosphere from its two outdoor courts.

RENO AREA

Alf Sorensen Community Center
1400 Baring Boulevard
Sparks

6/2, 🏠 ▣ ▣ ▣ ▣ ●● 🏘 $ ☞ ♀

As Nevada's second city of gambling, Reno attracts droves of tourists and gamblers to its mountain locale. The city also attracts all types of people to work at the casinos. As a result, the friendly games at Sorensen often look like something out of a liberal arts college brochure; every imaginable ethnic group is represented in what may be the most culturally diverse game in the country.

Also in Reno Area

They run mainly half court at **Riverside Park, Island and Arlington Avenues** (2/1, 🏠 ▣=2 ●=3 🏔 🚻), the best outdoor game in town. The Lombardy Rec Center at the **University of Nevada, Reno** is the local campus run.

NEW MEXICO

SANTA FE

Ft. Marcy/Mager's Complex
490 Washington Avenue and Artist Road
Santa Fe

6/2,

The sun shines 300 days a year in Santa Fe, a quirky town nestled in the foothills of the Sangre de Cristo Mountains. To escape the heat, the local players head to the adobe confines of Ft. Marcy. The competition is hit or miss (Saturday afternoons are best) and the wood gym floor seems to have been moved from Boston—there are strategically placed dead spots in the key under each hoop—but they play a refreshing brand of team ball up here. Don't be surprised to see three or more passes before a shot goes up.

For nighttime entertainment, head to the Blue Corn Bar, where the same altitude that had you huffing and puffing on the court will have you dancing on the table after three beers; up here in the mountains, one beer has the same effect as three at sea level.

ALBUQUERQUE

The **Johnson Gym, University of New Mexico** has the city's best game. If you can't find your way in to play with the Lobos, head to **Wells Park, 5100 Mountain Northwest Road** (2/1, 🏀 ▣=3 ●=3 ⛰ ☞ ⚷), which has indoor and outdoor courts. The center also has a senior 50-plus hoops program for both men and women and a great wall mural in the gym, which translates as "long live the council." Show up on a Tuesday or Thursday at 6 P.M. for the best games. The **Westside Community Center, 1221 Arenal Road** (2/1, 🏀 ▣=3 ●=2 ⛰ ☞ ♀) has more genteel, less competitive games than does Wells.

Look to the wall for inspiration at Wells Park Rec

ELSEWHERE IN NEW MEXICO

Alamogordo

Alamogordo Family Recreation Center
Oregon and 10th Streets
Alamogordo

6/2, 🏟 🔲 🔲 🔲 🔲 ⚫⚫ 🏚 $ ♀

If you travel to see the White Sands National Monument, a mind-blowing expanse of white gypsum dunes in southern New Mexico, you'll most likely be staying in the nearby town of Alamogordo. The only game in town is at the Alamogordo Family Recreation Center, a nice facility kept so in part by the rule that you hand-carry your street shoes into the gym so as not to scratch the gym floor. Outside, you'll find two full courts, a scenic view of the San Andres Mountains, and the longest necks on a basketball hoop you'll ever see.

If you can't drive the baseline at Alamogordo Rec, you can't go baseline *anywhere*

TEXAS

HOUSTON

Fondé Recreation Center
Sabine Street and Memorial Drive
Houston

6/2,

Fondé is not only the best rec center in Houston, it's the best in the country. Summers find U of Houston Cougars mixing it up with Houston Rockets and local playground legends. The games are so good that when he was growing up in San Antonio, Shaq would drive the three hours to Fondé just to play pickup.

The best games are from 1 to 5 p.m during the summer and 10 a.m to 1 p.m. in the winter. The play is strictly weekday—the gym is usually rented out on weekends. For more on Fondé, check out its entry in the Top 5 on page 37.

TALES FROM THE ROAD:
Whiskey and Sky Hooks at MacGregor

Saturday morning we head out in the a.m. and find a game at Mac-Gregor Park, an outdoor court in south Houston with a pavilion roof that provides welcome shade from the blistering summer heat.

Players begin arriving in the midmorning and play three-on-three exclusively on the far basket. A beat-up radio pumps out some R&B tunes, and those not playing watch lazily from the white concrete benches on the sideline. While members of the older crowd may have lost some of their athletic ability, they certainly haven't lost their voices. Arguments spring up about everything, though they contain none of the violent edge we've seen at some courts—it's basically a bunch of forty-year-old black guys whooping it up for the fun of it. I ask one of the younger guys present about the court. "The players here are the older guys in town," he tells me. "To give you an idea, I'm twenty-four and they call me 'the kid' around here."

We sit back and watch the action while waiting for our game. One of the teams playing is spearheaded by a character named Red. Red, who true to his name has a red afro, is in his mid-thirties and is the proud owner of a baby beer gut that pokes out above his athletic shorts. He spends the majority of the game yelling and dramatically questioning the other team's calls, even falling to the ground in mock disbelief on one traveling call. Every two points or so he goes to the sideline to puff on his cigarette or take a swig of whiskey, all the while warning his defender that he's about to be embarrassed. At game point he calls for the ball and fires an ugly jumper from the top of the key. The shot banks in to win the game, and a vindicated Red screams and informs the other team, in colorful language, of exactly what he thinks of them.

We've got next game, so once Red is done with his smoking break, we step onto the court and promptly sweep Red off it, despite his attempts to change the score every time it's called out. He is not happy about this, but seems too winded from playing successive games to put up much of a fight. Our next game is against three guys who are older than dirt but appear to have written the book *Skyhooks and other Tricks of Basketball*. Their best player, who must be close to fifty, looks like Sammy Davis, Jr., and speeds around as if stuck on fast forward. He starts hitting hooks left and right, one from the three-point line, and I realize we've come up against one of the most dangerous opponents in basketball: the pet-shot old guy. These are the guys who have worked on a particular shot for forty years and can hit it drunk with their eyes closed.

Sammy Davis and his slow-moving teammates beat us when Sammy nails a running hook on game point. We head to the sideline, humbled by the thorough schooling in all the tricks of the trade—shirt grabbing, arm hooking, over-the-head fade-aways, and so on. I make a mental note to put them into practice once I have kids.

As we're leaving, Red is on his way out as well, presumably headed to refill the old whiskey bottle. He sees the van and asks what we're doing. I tell him about our trip and ask his opinion on the best courts in Houston.

"The best courts in Houston?" Red replies. "There's only one,"—he pauses dramatically—"Mack-Gregor!"

Game action at "Mack-Gregor"

Moody Park Recreation Center
Fulton and Averill Streets
Houston

4/1,

Come to Moody Park for a Saturday-morning run and you'll experience a singular phenomenon: pickup games with referees. That's right, zebras call fouls, toss up jump balls, and allot free throws. However much they pay these guys, it's not enough; the refs take constant abuse from agitated players who scream, yell, and hurl the ball at them. Ironically enough, this was the only pickup game we saw on the trip with refs, yet it was also one of the most argumentative (and that's no small feat).

Also in Houston

The same crowd that balls at Fondé will often head to **Judson-Robinson Gym, Almeda Road and Hermann Drive (2/1,**  **=5**

The unique refereed pickup games at Moody Park start with a jump ball

=4), an impressive court located in the middle of Hermann Park. After playing, enjoy the park; Shakespeare's stuff gets its due at Miller Theatre in the summer and the Houston Museum of Natural Science showcases over 2,000 varieties of butterflies.

If monarchs aren't your thing but leagues are, your best bets are the **Downtown YMCA, 1600 Louisiana Street,** and **Chancellor's Racquet and Fitness Center, 6535 Dumfries** (2/1, 🏛 ☐=4 ●=2 🏢 **$** 🐦). The better players are at the Y.

MacGregor Park, Calhoun and MacGregor South (2/1, 🏀 ☐=4 ●=3 🏙 🕯 ☼), hosts the weekend old-timers run.

DALLAS AREA

Walnut Hill Recreation Center
Walnut Hill and Midway
Dallas

8/3,

Walnut Hill is one of those gyms where, if you're good, you gotta have a smooth nickname. You can't come in with a name like Bill if you're going up against a big man like "St. Louis," a local bus driver in his forties who once played college ball; his nemesis, "Big Freak," also an ex-collegian; or "Chicago," a toothless younger guy ("his front grille is out," is how one local described him) with some sweet moves.

Director Art McGee runs the show, bringing out the clock if there's too much arguing during the afternoon pickup. Games are sort of rough, so if you show and play poorly you might as well just wear a name tag that says "Chump."

Beckley-Saner Recreation Center
114 West Hobson
Dallas

16/6,

A good gym in a bad area. Six gleaming full courts greet you inside Beckley-Saner, home of the Dallas Pro-Am. The play is physical and the arguments frequent, but the talent can be extraordinary. Heed the sign that warns "Keep an eye on your keys at all times" or you may find yourself jogging home.

Fretz Park Center
Beltline Road and Hillcrest
Dallas

8/1,

Fretz has good pickup games and is in a safer area than Beckley, but it's the leagues that make playing here really worthwhile. Big names like Spud Webb, Deion Sanders (are there any sports this guy doesn't play?), running back Rodney Hampton (reportedly showcasing crazy 30-foot range), and Steeltown legend Rod Woodson all have played. They also have leagues for the over-thirty set and other nonsuperstars.

Also in Dallas Area

Hometown hero Larry Johnson grew up playing ball all over the city's rough south side. In addition to playing at Beckley-Saner, he dunked on fools at the **Kiest Recreation Center, 3080 South Hampton Road** (8/3, 🏠 ⬜=3 ⚫=4 ⛰ ☞ ♀ ⚡), where the best games are weekday afternoons, and haunted the gym—and has recently run his summer leagues—at **Thurgood Marshall Recreation Center, 5150 Mark Trail Way** (6/2, 🏠 ⬜=4 ⚫=4 ⛰ ☞ ⚡).

These days you're more likely to find Johnson hitting the weights at the **Premier Club, 5910 North Central Expressway** (6/1, 🏠 ⬜=4 ⚫=3 ⛰ $ ☞ ♀), a posh health club in north Dallas. LJ doesn't play in the pickup games, but some local college players do. If you aren't a member at the Premier Club and Fretz is dead, a third north Dallas option is **Lake Highlands North Recreation Center, 9940 White Rock Trail,** where the games are run four-on-four on a short court.

For health club play farther north in Carrolton, hit up **World Gym Fitness, 2625 Old Denton Road** (2/1,⊡=3 ◉=2 🏠 $), where a basketball court sits like an oasis in a large room amidst exercise equipment. If you're staying at the Best Western, you can get in free if you show your room key.

SAN ANTONIO

SGM Physical Fitness Center
Fort Sam Houston
San Antonio

8/3, 🏢 ⊡ ⊡ ⊡ ⊡ ◉◉◉ 🏙️ $ ♀ 🚗

Shaquille O'Neal grew up shaking the backboards on this base while attending Cole High. He doesn't come around much anymore, but the troops still play hard in the afternoons and at lunchtime, when the self-proclaimed NBA (Noon Basketball Association) takes the floor.

Sam Houston veterans who balled with the young Shaquille are less than starstruck. "Well, I retired his dad," one older base member said, "so I've seen plenty of that kid. He's just a local guy."

Yeah, a local guy who just happens to be 7' 1", 300 pounds, and an NBA All-Star.

Also in San Antonio

In a city where over 50 percent of the population is of Mexican descent, the hombres who play do so on the Southwest Side at **Cuellar Community Center, Old Highway 90W and 36th Street** (2/1, 🏢 ⊡=2 ◉=2 ⛏️). Winners of the center three-on-three tourney take home—don't get too excited here—a twelve-pack of soda. In the mainly white northern part of the city, the games are at **Hamilton Community Center,** Lady Bird Johnson Park. In the predominantly

THE MAN BEHIND HOOP-IT-UP

When he was in college at San Jose State, Terry Murphy, the man behind the Hoop-It-Up 3-on-3 basketball tournament, was just another scrawny white guy trying out for the basketball team. In fact, he was one of the least talented scrawny white guys trying out. "I played under Stu Inman and my first year on varsity I scored four points the whole year," Murphy, now in his fifties, says from Hoop-It-Up headquarters in Dallas. "The next year, Stu took me aside and said, "You're one of the worst players I've ever coached. I'm never gonna cut you, you're enthusiastic and you play hard and you're a good guy, but I don't even know if you're going to make the road trip. Why don't you go play volleyball?" So I did, and I never looked back on basketball until 1985 when I read that story."

"That story" was a *Sports Illustrated* article on the popularity of the Gus Macker 3-on-3 basketball tournament. Reading it in his Dallas office, Murphy, who, it must be noted, went on to make the U.S. National volleyball squad after quitting hoops, decided that it was time to get back to the game he had loved as a gym rat growing up in Manhattan Beach, California. If two Michigan schoolteachers could organize a hoops tournament, he figured, so could he.

He began his effort by putting up fliers and spreading the word around the blacktops of Dallas about his creation, a three-on-three tourney he called Hoop D Do. The initial reaction was lukewarm at best; with only a week before his inaugural tournament, Murphy had a total of forty teams entered. "I remember thinking to myself, 'Doggone it, another Murphy idea that sucks,' " Murphy remembers. "Here we were, a week before the thing was scheduled, and I had no one to play in it."

Fortunately for him, and for hoopsters everywhere, Dallas' faithful came out en masse during that last week as an astounding 450 teams entered the tourney. Murphy even attracted some local pro players. "The first year in Dallas, Karl Malone, Spud Webb, and two of Spud's friends entered a team," Murphy says. "Not a single time did Karl go inside twenty-five feet—all he did was stay outside and shoot jump shots. He didn't know what was inside and he didn't want to find out. They went two and out, but it was great for the tournament to have them out there."

With the tournament's first-year success, Murphy decided to make Hoop D Do an annual event, and by 1988 the hoopfest was attracting over 2,000 teams. The next step, he figured, was to go national, so Terry promptly quit his job and started making plans for a countrywide tournament. He visited Macker tourneys trying to get a feel for what they were doing, and what they were doing wrong. "I saw how they were putting together their setup not from a player's perspective, but from an organizer's perspective," Murphy says. "It was totally different for me."

Renaming his competition Hoop-It-Up, Murphy expanded, and by 1997 he had seen his small-time tourney transformed into a global phenomenon. Hoop-It-Up now has events in 70 cities worldwide, and in 1996 over 500,000 people participated. With tie-ins to NBC, the NBA, Nike, and numerous smaller sponsors, it's almost impossible to avoid Hoop-It-Up these days. As for Murphy, he continually sees bigger things on the horizon. His business, Streetball Partners, has branched out into tournaments in football (Air-It-Out), volleyball (Spike-It-Up), hockey (NHL Break Out), soccer, and even golf. Ironically, the man who was cut from his college basketball team is now one of the most powerful men in basketball, not to mention the patron saint of weekend warriors everywhere. How does it feel? "I'm loving every minute of it," Murphy says, "I even get out there and play every once in a while."

Spoken like a true hoops junkie.

black southeast the best games are at **Sam Houston High School, East Houston Street.** Half a mile south, **Copernicus Park, Lord and Sellinger** (2/1, 🏠 ▣=2 ◉=2 ⛰ 🎫), is a run-of-the-mill indoor/outdoor rec center.

The Spurs do their weight lifting at the **Concord Athletic Club, Jones-Maltsburger and Oblate** (6/2, 🏠 ▣=4 ◉=3 🚉 $ ☞ ♀), and both George Gervin and his son can be found icing the competition in the short-court pickup games with the doctor-lawyer crowd. "When Gervin plays he'll just jack it up from half-court," says Crane Canavan, ex–Alamo Heights High star and club member. "He's still money from anywhere."

ELSEWHERE IN TEXAS

Austin

Clark Field at the **University of Texas** is the place to play in the Lone Star State's capital. The four outdoor courts, across from Memorial Stadium on the southern part of campus, fill up daily with students and off-campus ballers alike who slide around on the concrete. The games on Court One are some of the best in the country; Texas team players and visiting college studs rule the roost and you need to know somebody just to get on. The top flight play draws college scouts, who often hang out by the green fences just to check out the action.

If you're not a Longhorn fan but want an outdoor game in Austin, you can head to **Givens Park, corner of Springdale and East 12th,** or **Westenfield Park, Enfield Road off Mo-Pac Boulevard.**

College Station

The Student Recreation Center, just north of the Olsen Baseball Field on the campus of **Texas A & M University,** has both indoor and outdoor courts that are bustling with students and locals. Professors, faculty, and graybeards run indoors from 11:30 to 1:30 during the week.

El Paso

The **El Paso Central Branch YMCA, 701 Montana Avenue** (8/3, 🏠 🖼=4 ◉=3 ⛰ $ ☞ ♀), takes into consideration both the short in stature and the long in tooth; the gym has leagues for those who are thirty-five and over as well as those who are 6′2″ and under.

Washington Park, Paisana Drive and Washington (2/1, 🏠 🖼=2 ◉=2 ⛰ 🎾), is a couple blocks away from the U.S. Customs and Port of Entry from Mexico and is a largely bilingual game. After late-night games, head across the street to Chico's Tacos, which is open until the a.m. for all your grubbing needs. For better outdoor competition, visit **Cielo Vista Park, Cosmos Drive,** near the airport.

Ft. Stockton

Summer pickup runs from 3 to 6 p.m. at **Ft. Stockton High School, 1200 West 17th Street** (6/2, 🏠 🖼=2 ◉=2 🥤). Be careful when changing directions, the floor is slippery enough to play sock hockey on. A huge weight room is adjacent to the gym, so the next time a big guy grabs your rebound and tells you to "hit the weights," you can do so in between games.

Ft. Worth–Arlington

During the summer, players from the local colleges converge on **"The Sweatbox,"** the student gym at the University of Texas–Arlington. UTA players will open the gym up for weekday afternoon runs and on Saturday mornings.

The **Ft. Worth Downtown YMCA, 512 Lamar Street** (8/3, 🏠 🖼=4 ◉=3 ⛰ $ ☞) has strong adult leagues and good pickup on Tuesdays and Thursdays.

Texarkana

Monday nights are ladies' night at the **South-West Center, 3222 West Highway 67** (2/1, 🏠 🖼=3 ◉=2 🥤 ☞ ♀ 🎾). Fellas play all day on weekends and evenings during the week.

UTAH

SALT LAKE CITY

Liberty Park
500 East and 1100 South
Salt Lake City

4/2,

Frequented by a mixture of college players and hacks, Liberty is the saltiest run in the Lake City. The best games are on the weekends, especially Sunday afternoons "after work," as one player put it. Driving to the courts can be tricky—the one-way loop at Liberty Park is confusing—so enter from the north side for easiest access to the hoops, which are on the west side of the park.

Also in Salt Lake City

The city's best games used to be at Deseret Gym, an indoor complex run by the Church of Latter Day Saints (Mormons, for those of you not

Stormin Mormons at Liberty Park

familiar with the official name) that reverberated with thunderous dunks on weekend mornings. In 1997 the church tore down the gym to make way for a parking lot, which they deemed more lucrative. Priorities, priorities.

The demise of Deseret means that the games at the **University of Utah,** already stellar, have gone up a notch. In the off-season, Utes players will show and nonstudents can join the fray for a couple bucks.

Sugarhouse Park, 2100 South Street and 13th E. (2/1, 🏛 🖵=3 ◑=2 ⛰ 🐾), once the best outdoor run in S.L.C., now plays second fiddle to Liberty Park. The scenery's still more appealing down at the 'House though; the views of both nearby Wasatch Forest Mountains and occasional female spectators are easy on the eyes.

OGDEN

Marshall White Community Center
28th Street and Lincoln Avenue
Ogden

6/2, 🏛 🖵🖵🖵🖵 ◑◑◑◑ 🏙 **$** 🖐 🐾

During the winter months, the best competition in the Salt Lake City area is at Marshall White Community Center, where it costs a whopping fifty cents to play in the daily noon run with a bunch of highfliers. The adjacent outdoor court was donated by former regular Tom "Head At The Rim Dunk" Chambers, a local.

Also in Ogden

Health club action revolves around the **Ogden Athletic Club, 1212 East 5800 Street** (5/1, 🏛 🖵=4 ◑=3 🏋 **$**), which has a great floor for dunking, and the **Total Fitness Center, 550 25th Street** (8/2, 🏛 🖵=3 ◑=2 🏋 **$** ♀), where a group of true believers run at 6 a.m. every morning.

ELSEWHERE IN UTAH

Orem

Come cut the rug at the **Orem Fitness Center, 580 West 165 S.** (7/2, 🏢 🖵=3 ⬤=3 🏠 $), where only the truly competitive dive for loose balls on the center's carpeted floor. In the summers the noon run (12–2p.m.) attracts the older guys, whereas the afternoon games are for the Clearasil crowd. They play with an interesting rule: The losing team gets the ball first in the next game.

FLAVOR OF THE GAME:
Talking the Talk

Arguing like a Playground Pro
and Hoops Lingo

Blacktop Bickering: How to Argue like a Playground Pro

Youngsters who learn the game at the organized level are taught to play a certain way: don't argue with the ref, respect the call, and so on. Players who grow up on the playground often learn to play a different type of game entirely. Out on the blacktop, it's not the actual rule involved in a play that matters, but rather how you interpret that rule and how well you can argue your case. As a result, asphalt attorneys everywhere have decided that their mouth, not their jumpshot, is often their most effective weapon on the pickup court; since their games can't do the talking, they have chosen to just do the talking. For these players, the following three rules might be considered the holy trinity:

Rule 1. "I have never committed a foul."

Good pickup players need to be good defenders, and the best of them have such quick hands, such incredible anticipation, that they literally never foul offensive players. Don't take my word, just ask one.

With this mantra in mind, feel free to debate any foul called by the man you're guarding. Practice phrases like "C'mon man, you were already bleeding," "FOUL?!?!" (say this as if you have been accused of assassinating the president; continue to shake your head incredulously as play resumes), and "Hey man, nose is part of the ball."

The key component of many phrases is "ticky-tack." For a macho male basketball player, being accused of calling a "ticky-tack foul" is the equivalent of being accused of enjoying Barbra Streisand movies. Use the term liberally.

Rule 2. "The only reason why a great shooter like me ever misses a shot is because I was flagrantly fouled."

Good pickup players have honed their games to the point where they do not miss shots anymore. Intense hours spent practicing, diligently watching TV, and playing video games have developed their skills to the point where they are like computers, calculating shooting angles in midair and releasing

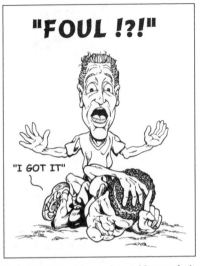

"FOUL !?!"

"I GOT IT"

Rule #1 of the pick-up player: Never admit the foul

soft jumpers with just the right amount of spin on them. The only thing that can stop these playground deities from knocking down J after J is if they are blatantly, rudely fouled.

Therefore, if you find yourself in the unlikely and unfortunate position of having launched a shot skyward that may not go in, waste no time in hollering out "Foul," "I got it," or "And one," even if no one is within 10 feet of you. Remember to act as if the offending player, players, or even entire team practically decapitated you, those brutes.

Another thing: You don't have to be on offense to call a foul. Feel free to call offensive charges, traveling, carrying, and anything else you can think of. Opposing players will always honor these calls. If they debate them, refer them to the NBA rule book. This will quiet them down and play will resume. (If you believe this, I have some "valuable" Chris Washburn rookie cards I want to sell you).

Rule 3. The game score is always negotiable.

Most pickup games are played without a scoreboard or designated scorekeeper. This means it is up to the players to keep track of the game score, a reality that leads to the increased importance of a type of player known as the Loud Guy. For example, in a game to eleven points in which Team A scores fourteen baskets and Team B (with a Loud Guy) scores nine baskets, Team B *can win the game!*

You see, on the playground it is not how many points your team scores but how many points you can convince the opposition that your team has scored. And if your team has one or more Loud Guys, you are at an advantage, because everyone knows that, on the asphalt, Loud Guys are more valuable than good shooters.

The key to aiding your team through creative scorekeeping is to pretend you're a magician. When magicians pull off a sleight-of-hand trick, they divert your eyes from the real trick (the card going up the sleeve, the rabbit exiting the hat, your wallet going in their pocket) by distracting you with something else. On the court, you need to employ your other arguing skills to divert their attention. Here's an example:

Your team is up 5–4 and the point guard from the other team drives and calls a foul when you throw him to the floor.

YOU: (*practicing Rule 1*): FOUL?!??
OPPOSING POINT GUARD: You almost broke my back!
YOU (*Rule 1, Subsection B*): Broke your back? I hardly touched you! I see we're calling ticky-tack fouls now.
OPPOSING POINT GUARD (*who hates* Prince of Tides): Oh, come on man! You call that ticky-tack? I'm surprised I can still walk.
YOU (*shaking your head disapprovingly*): Okay, we'll give you this one.
OPPOSING POINT GUARD (*feeling good about winning argument*): You ain't giving me anything, let's play.
YOU: All right, check ball, six-three us.

In all the arguing, the score has been forgotten, so now an argument will ensue about the score. The key to this argument is to make the other team feel as if they win it (a scientific psychological technique known as "bullshitting"). By saying the score is 6–3, you can then relent during the argument and "give them a point," to put the score at 6–4 and resume play.

Final outcome: Twenty minutes after the original foul, you have gained a point without even shooting the ball (let's see the Good Shooters do that!) and are now leading 6–4 instead of 5–4. Of course, you haven't actually played any basketball either, but this doesn't seem to bother the playground pro.

Dialect to Dunk By: Hoops Lingo

If you think "grabbing some boards" requires heading to the local hardware store and "cleaning the glass" involves a bottle of Windex, then this section is for you.

Like any culture, basketball has its own unique language, full of descriptive terms, derogatory phrases, and esoteric allusions. If you want to succeed on the court, you need to be hip to the dialect of the game; playing ball without a grasp of the game's vocabulary can be a confusing endeavor.

Many of the basic terms used on the basketball court aren't too hard to figure out. For example, "comp" is short for "competition," "rep" is short for "reputation," "props" means respect, and "run" is an all-purpose term for playing ball, as in "Who's running today?" or "They have good runs at the park."

Other terms aren't as easily deciphered; for example, "cleaning the glass" and "grabbing a board" both refer to rebounding. So, for those in need of a little basketball speech therapy, here is a glossary of some common hoops lingo. Included are some useful game phrases, complete with examples of correct—and incorrect—usage.

The wrong way to "clean the glass"

GLOSSARY

around the world: a game played by taking shots from around an arc. Players move from spot to spot until they miss a shot. You try to get "around the world"—that is from the first spot to the last—before your opponent does.

blocks/down low/the weight room/the paint: the area close to the basket in and around the key.

bounds: short for rebounds.

box out: to gain position for a rebound by throwing your ass into your opponent's thighs.

brick: an ugly shot with no chance of going in. In some parts, people will say, "that shot is broke."

bring it up: to advance the ball up court.

burn (n): playing time. **(v)**: to get beaten badly on a move by an opponent.

butcher: one who fouls often and with great authority.

butter: good, talented, smooth. Pronounced "buttah."

by two: a style of play where the victorious team needs to win by two points.

cash: a good shot or a good shooter. Also: **money.**

change/courtesy: the practice while warming up of passing the ball back to shooters after made baskets.

check ball: for one team to start possession with the ball at the top of the key (known as "up top").

cherry picking: the practice of a player trying to score easy points by staying under the opponent's basket while his teammates retreat on defense.

clank: a big guy with limited offensive skills.

coast-to-coast: to dribble the ball from one basket to the other and score.

cup: the basket. Also: **bucket, rack, hole, hoop.**

D: short for defense. Rarely seen on pickup courts.

dish: an assist, a good pass. A superlative pass is classified as a "sweet dish." Also: **look, dime.**

do or die: the practice at the start of a game of one player shooting the ball from the top of the key to determine who gets possession.

downtown: deep territory, beyond the three-point arc.

drain: to swish a shot.

drop: to score points, as in, "Joe dropped thirty on us last week."

en fuego: hitting all of one's shots, literally "on fire." Also, **in the zone.**

fan gui: "foul" in Chinese. Impress your friends with this one.

fat lip: a bent rim. In reference to the basket looking like someone is sticking out their lower lip.

firsts: possession of a jump ball. During a tie up, the player to call "firsts" gains possession.

flush: to dunk. Also: **throw down, jam, slam, bang, yack, cram, hawk, punch.**

garbage: 1) easy offensive putbacks, or 2) derisive term for bad players.

hacker: an unskilled player prone to committing fouls and throwing up airballs.

handicapped line: the free throw line, as in "why you shooting from the handicapped line instead of the three-point line?" Also: **the charity stripe.**

hops: jumping ability. Also: **rise, ups, leaps, springs.**

H-O-R-S-E: a game where players match each other's shots. Every time you miss a shot your opponent hit, you get one letter. Once you spell H-O-R-S-E, you're done.

hung: to attempt a dunk and have it stick against the front of the rim.

hustle: a southern term for the game of **21**. A group of players plays one-against the rest on a half court. The first player to score twenty-one points wins.

Iced it: finger-rolled it, in honor of George Gervin.

J: Jump shot. It's handy to have one of these.

jomama: your mother.

josister: your sister.

jocarjustgotrippedoff: your car just got ripped off.

juke: to fake out.

knee condom: a neoprene knee brace.

knockout: A game where players follow each other shooting from the free throw line. If you miss your free throw and the player behind you hits his before you corral your rebound and put it back in, you are "knocked out" of the game.

loser's outs: a style of play wherein after each made basket, possession rotates to the other team.

nice stick: complimentary phrase used to describe a made jump shot or a defensive stop.

outtahere: wherever you're playing defense when you block a shot, as in "get that shit outtahere!"

rejection/swat/Mutombo: a blocked shot.

the rock/the orange/the pill/the melon: the ball.

run the point: to take control of the ball and play point guard.

send it: to emphatically block a shot.

shirts n' skins: to play with teams divided into the clothed and the bare-bellied.

shoot for it: the practice of one player shooting from the top of the key to determine possession during a dispute.

shooting blanks: throwing up bricks, missing outside shots.

sick: very impressive.

steps: traveling with the ball.

stop-n-pop: to pull up on a fast break and shoot a jump shot.

straight (up): first team to a certain number of points wins. Compare to **by two**.

strip/pick/swipe: to steal the ball.

stroke: to shoot well.

strong take: an authoritative, successful move to the basket.

talk to God: to jump particularly high.

take to school / school is in session: to humiliate an opponent by "schooling" him in your personal repertoire of offensive moves.

that check bounced: when a shot hits nothing but the backboard.

the bomb: awesome. Often used in conjunction with "da," as in "that move was da bomb!"

trash talk/shit-talk/smack-talk/: Verbal byplay, often derogatory, that accompanies the game. Subjects often invoked include your mother, your lack of game, and your imminent demise.

tri-fecta: a three-pointer. Also a "trey."

up top: the top of the key. See "check ball."

wack: depending on the local dialect, this can mean very good or very bad.

weak: unimpressive.

wedgie: when the ball gets stuck between the rim and the backboard.

White Man's Disease: a lack of jumping ability, often localized in the calves of Caucasians.

window: the backboard (also "the glass").

winners (or winner's outs): the team that makes a basket retains possession. Also known as "make it, take it."

USEFUL GAME PHRASES

"And one": used to call a foul on a shot attempt. Also: "I got it"; "Stay here"; "Got one"; or "Foul, goddammit!"
Correct usage: Drive hard to the basket and as you shoot the ball, defender draped over you, say, "And one!"
Incorrect usage: "And one! more thing, Tyrone, I love what you've done with your hair."

"Ass!": phrase used to declare superiority, an update of "face" or "in-your-face." After a player hits a shot, he turns and derides his defender by saying "Ass!" To teach someone a lesson is to "tap that ass."
Correct usage: Blowing by someone, scoring, and saying "Ass!"
Incorrect usage: Turning to the large man guarding you, smiling, and saying, "Nice ass."

"Bank's open": an utterance used to denote use of the backboard on a shot. Comes from "to bank it in."
Correct usage: Shooting one off the board and declaring "Bank's open, baby!"
Incorrect usage: Shooting one that hits nothing but the backboard and declaring "Bank's open, baby!"

"Boo-yah!": exclamatory term used after an impressive play, deriving from the Latin phrase "boolis ad yahseum," meaning "damn that was nasty." Can be replaced with Craig Kilborn's *Sportscenter* creation, "Ju-manji!"

Correct usage: Your teammate dunks and you yell, "Boo-yah!"
Incorrect usage: Your teammate head butts the basket support and you yell "Boo-yah!"

"Breaking Ankles": to fake out a defender using a crossover dribble. Often known as a "killer crossover." Also: "dropping him off"; "losing him in the sauce."
Correct usage: "Marbury was breaking ankles out there today."
Incorrect usage: "That dude with the sledgehammer was breaking ankles out there today."

"I got next": to reserve the next game. This can be done by "calling next" or saying "I got game." The player who has the next game is said to be "down" or have "winners."
Correct usage: Walking up to a court and loudly declaring, "I got next."
Incorrect usage: Walking over to two players who are fighting and loudly declaring, "I got next."

Superquick guards are said to "break ankles" with their crossover dribble

"Keep it!": used to punctuate a blocked shot.
Correct usage: Blocking a shot to half court and emphatically yelling "Keep it!"
Incorrect usage: Saying to the guy shooting around with your ball, "Hey, you with my ball—Keep it!"

"Lighting it up": dominating the game.
Correct usage: "Damn, Bill's lighting it up—he must have scored twenty in the first half alone."
Incorrect usage: "Damn, Bill's lighting it up—he must have smoked three joints in the first half alone."

"Mad handles": exceptional dribbling ability.

Correct usage: "Tim Hardaway has got mad handles."
Incorrect usage: "Tim Hardaway has got mad love handles."

"Raining": to drop in long-distance jump shots.
Correct usage: "Oh man, he was raining threes on us!"
Incorrect usage: "Oh man, he was raining layups on us."

"run it back": to play another game with the same squads.
Correct usage: "Hey you guys want to run it back?"
Incorrect usage: "If you guys kick it off to us, we'll run it back."

"Your world": phrase used to tell a teammate that he can take his man. Also: **"All day."**
Correct usage: Clearing out a side of the court for a teammate and saying, "You got him Tony. Your world, baby."
Incorrect usage: "Tony, this world is your world, this world is my world . . ."

8

New York

NEW YORK CITY AND NEW YORK STATE

Pickup basketball is now played nationwide, on blacktops in cities from Phoenix to Fargo, but the game came of age on the streets of New York City. In the fifties, sixties, and seventies, playground legends challenged NBA players for New York supremacy, facing off in epic battles in the Rucker Tournament and on schoolyards citywide.

Today the five boroughs still echo with the sound of bouncing basketballs and thumping bodies. The city's finest spend their summers matching dunk for dunk on playgrounds with netless rims and metal cheese-grater backboards. In areas like Harlem, the courts are never empty; whether it's five-on-five, three-on-three, 21, or just halfhearted one-on-one, there's always a game in progress. Every year, droves of prep stars come out of New York, though for every Stephon Marbury or Kenny Anderson who makes it, there are hundreds of Fly Williamses and Earl Manigaults who don't.

Once a predominantly inner-city-playground pastime, the New York City game has now expanded to rented school gyms and health clubs, where lawyers and bankers play with a fanaticism only neurotic New Yorkers can muster. Loops like the Urban Professionals League and the Lawyers League are immensely popular, and the winter demand has spurred the creation of indoor pay-for-play facilities like Chelsea Piers.

NEW YORK CITY AREA

Playing the N.Y.C. Game

Once asked why he loved New York, the ever eloquent Charles Barkley replied, "I own a gun."

Ah yes, the tranquil streets of the Big Apple, where everyone's a stranger and no one's your friend. If you're not familiar with the city, or are a beginning basketball player, New York can be an initiation to the game, a Street Basketball 101 of sorts. When playing, expect to get banged around, talk some junk, and receive zero respect for any weak foul calls (N.Y.C. playground motto: "No autopsy, no foul").

On the courts, constant usage means New York baskets are a unique breed: the orange color of the rims has faded to silver everywhere but at the heel, and very few hoops have nets. This isn't a surprise if you're from the Big Apple; you could probably spend your entire life playing streetball in N.Y.C. and never catch a glimpse of a net—they are as hard to find as a friendly driver in New York.

If you aren't from the city, don't let the lack of nets faze you, just adjust your game accordingly, with more drives to the basket and fewer outside jumpers. Even a sweet shooter like Chris Mullin, who grew up playing outdoor ball in New York, adjusted his game. "I used

As much of a net as you're likely to find in New York City

to drive more," said Mullin in an if-you-can-believe-that tone of voice. "When I'd play outdoors in the summer, if you really needed a basket, you were going to drive the ball. And then [when you're playing] inside in the winter you could work on your skills all over the place."

MANHATTAN

Holcombe Rucker Park
West 155th Street and Eighth Avenue
Harlem

In 1946, a motivated young teacher named Holcombe Rucker started the Rucker Tournament (originally held at 130th Street and Seventh Avenue), a league intended to keep kids off the street and provide an organized forum for pickup ball. From these humble beginnings, "the Rucker" grew into the biggest street sports spectacle in New York. Thousands of spectators would line the streets and climb the trees that surrounded the court to watch street legends like Connie Hawkins and Earl "The Goat" Manigault face off against pros like Wilt Chamberlain and Julius Erving. Hawkins was so revered that he once failed to show for any of the league games but was still named the MVP.

The play of these legends inspired countless young players to dream of playing at Rucker. "Growing up I got to see the Earl Manigaults, the Pee Wee Kirklands," says "Master Rob" Hokett, a Rucker legend himself in the late eighties. "Those were the best guys I ever got to see for free. Guys like Joe Hammond, they called him the Destroyer. He could come out drunk and hit twenty jump shots off the backboard."

The Rucker Tournament of old is now defunct, but a new incarnation, the Entertainers Basketball Classic, still runs here in north Harlem, across from the towering Polo Grounds projects, and occasionally indoors at **Dunlevy Milbank Center at West 118th Street and Fifth Avenue** (6/2, 🏠 🖥=4 ◉=4 ⛰ ☞ 🐕)). Teams with names like Dogs of War and Flavor Unit face off as rap music blasts, the p.a. provides commentary, and college coaches like Jerry Tarkanian sit conspicuously in the bleachers. The best street players, now sporting nicknames like "Black Widow," "The Undertaker," and "Predator," still play, as do college stars and even future pros. Recently, Joe Smith, Allen Iverson, and Kevin Garnett all stopped by before taking their games to the NBA (as Jamal Mashburn, Mark Jackson, and Chris Mullin did before them in the eighties). How did they fare?

"Kevin Garnett looked like he'd been in New York his whole life," Hokett said. "He got on the court, and he smiled and was, like, 'Yo, this is my park. I been hearing about this park since I was young.' He was throwing guys' shots out of the park, dunking on people backward. Joe Smith loved it and Allen Iverson was throwing the ball between people's legs, throwing behind his back. It just amazes me when I see guys that are about to get all this money, and they don't really have to be here. But they came out and, by showing up, they made the park better."

Such is the pull of Rucker that even money and contracts can't keep players from balling. And although there isn't much in the way of pickup play—it's primarily league action at the park—summer games at Rucker are still one of the best free shows in New York.

Riverside Park
West 76th Street and Riverside Drive
Upper West Side

6/2,

Riverside is the Grant Hill of basketball courts: talented and multi-faceted but not overly intimidating. The busy courts attract a good mix of players and all levels of talent to their sunken location, two flights of stone stairs below the honking and screeching of Manhattan traffic. Joggers and Rollerbladers cruise by the action on a tree-lined walkway that runs parallel to the court, and dog walkers will stop and watch the games from shaded benches. On the blacktop, the older guys run some impassioned half-court games on weekend mornings while the young guys leg it out on the full court all day long.

Riverside Park

West Fourth Street Courts
West Fourth Street and Avenue of the Americas (Sixth Avenue)
Greenwich Village

3/1,

Streetball at its finest, amid the multi-culti splendor of Greenwich Village and right next to the subway. During the summer, the West Fourth League, which has a star-filled history almost as impressive as the Rucker's, rages while spectators pack in around the tiny court to get a better view of cats like Anthony Mason, Jayson Williams, and Lloyd Daniels. For the whole scoop on West Fourth, check out the entry on page 35 as the best court in the country.

Riverbank State Park
West 138th Street and Riverside Drive
Upper Manhattan

6/3,

Amidst the poverty of Upper Manhattan, Riverbank Park sticks out like a shiny new Ferrari in a used-car lot. A $130 million complex built in 1993, the park sits high above the Hudson River and encompasses twenty-eight acres of baseball diamonds, football fields, running tracks, swimming pools, and, most important, both indoor and outdoor basketball courts.

With this much on offer, the city goes to great lengths to protect its investment and ensure the safety of those using the facility. To reach the park, one must cross a large concrete bridge with barbed wire on the top, making sure not to get run over by any of the numerous bike cops that patrol the premises with sixteen-shot, 9-mm Glocks on their hips (the police headquarters are located at the park as well).

As for the hoops, there is year-round pickup play indoors, where games are to 12 points or twelve minutes and a downs list is used for teams. To discourage arguing and stalling, gym rules state that if the game is tied at 12 when time runs out, both teams go off and two new ones come on. In addition to the regular pickup, there is a ladies' night on Wednesdays and the New York Pro-Am is held here in the summer. Outdoors, four well-kept full courts are busy whenever the New York weather allows.

So why did a traditionally neglected area receive an incredible park like Riverbank? The answer is under your feet at the park, where a massive sewage plant, built in exchange for state funding of the complex, processes Manhattan's waste. Regardless, the park smells like roses to the youth of Harlem, who have free access to the nicest city facility in the country.

Asphalt Green Center
East 91st Street and York Avenue
East Side

It sounds like a hybrid of golf and hoops, but the Asphalt Green is actually just a basketball court (though it does attract golfers who like to play hoops). The pleasant location next to the East River and FDR Drive draws a talented yuppie crowd to these two well-paved outdoor courts with green basket supports (hence the "green" part of the name). Adjacent to the hardtop courts is a giant hood-shaped rec center that is actually a converted asphalt plant (hence the "asphalt" part of the name). A rubber-floored gym hosts leagues on the fourth floor of the rec center.

Looking for the Goat

There is no showy entrance, nothing about his arrival that would make one think one was in the presence of a legend. The people at the park, an assortment of African Americans, Puerto Ricans, and bums, are used to seeing Earl Manigault. Many nod or smile when he passes them on his ten-speed bike, but there is no rush for autographs, no paparazzi waiting with cameras. Earl slowly parks his bike and gets off, his hooded eyes moving around the park that is named after him.

Two full basketball courts lie off to his left, fenced in along with a handball wall and a large patch of asphalt where a father is playing soccer with his two squealing daughters.

For Earl, who gained the nickname "The Goat" when his last name proved too hard to pronounce, Goat Park is where he made his rep during the seventies, elevating his 6′ 2″ frame up above every big man that got in his way. With every gravity-defying move and stop-the-game-that-was-so-sick dunk that Earl put down, his rep grew and grew. Bring on the seven-footers, the Goat's disciples would say, he'll dunk on them too. And he did.

Take your talent to the pros, they said. You can play with those fools. So Earl did, but his tryout with the Utah Stars was cut short. That drug that is so glamorous these days, heroin, was a ghetto drug back then, and it took its toll on Earl. His arms are now webbed with raised scars, none-too-subtle reminders.

But that is in the past. Now the Goat, still trim, is something of a godfather at his park. His "Goat Tournament" attracts young talent and he likes to spend as much of his time as he can at the park, working with kids. The rest is spent being the Goat.

"The Goat?" a twenty-year-old Hispanic kid in Brooklyn says, "yeah, he had such hops that one time he went up for so long on a drive that they called him for three seconds while he was still in the air."

The stories still circulate around the city. The stories about how he would go up against Wilt and dunk on him. Of how he could do a double dunk. Of how he could grab a dollar off the top of the backboard and make change before coming down. "A lot of that is true," the Goat says when asked about the street lore. "I could grab the dollar, but the part about making change isn't true. The double dunk, I did that. I would put it through with one hand on the way up, grab the rim with the other hand, catch the ball as it came through the net, and swing it around with the free hand. Remember, all this is done while you're coming down."

No one has replaced the pickup legends of the 1960s and '70s, so the kids still talk about the likes of Joe "The Destroyer" Hammond and the Goat. It is the beauty of inner-city New York that its street legends die hard. For here in the concrete jungle, those that can rise above the rest, literally or figuratively, are remembered as deities. The playground legends who didn't make it, like Fly Williams or Pee

Earl "The Goat" Manigault at Goat Park

Wee Kirkland, are afforded the same sort of respect as those who did make it, like Albert King or Stephon Marbury, receive.

The difference is that a reputation can't buy you a nice house in the suburbs, and it can't buy you a life outside the city. The Goat's life, one of *could've*s and *should've*s, has never taken him off the streets, but he has it back on track now, is wiser for his years. And while it can't buy that house, it seems that his rep has brought him a certain acclaim. In 1996 HBO aired a made-for-TV movie, *Rebound*, based on the Goat's life. Originally titled *Angel of Harlem*, the movie portrays Earl's return from the street life that claimed so many of his contemporaries.

Back at the park, Earl, in a black baseball hat and a white T-shirt stamped with his tourney logo, watches over the courts and encourages the local kids. He doesn't play much anymore—"I get out and shoot with the little ones sometimes," he says—but he is still close to the game, and his legend still lives. It is ironic that this once ferociously talented young man idolized citywide is now a different type of role model, living proof that there is more to life than basketball.

Also in Manhattan

Starting in the north and heading south . . .

At the northern tip of Manhattan, just below Ft. Tryon Park, **Jacob Javits Playground, Cabrini Boulevard and Ft. Washington Avenue** (3/1,  ▣=3 ◉=2 ⛰), provides mid-level competition in a scenic location sandwiched between the Harlem River and the Hudson.

In Harlem, every two blocks you'll find a schoolyard or park packed with people playing. **Carmansville Playground a.k.a. the Battlegrounds, West 152nd Street and Amsterdam Avenue** (8/3, ▣=3 ◉=4 ⛰ ⚑), spawned a number of the original Harlem Globetrotters on its three skinny courts. **Samuel Playground, P.S. 139, West 139th Street and Lenox Avenue** (2/1, ▣=4 ◉=4 ⛰ ☞ ⚑), hosts the annual Black Top Basketball Clas-

Samuel Playground

sic, for which the whole community comes out and watches local youth with nicknames like "The Nutty One" and "The Total Package" battle it out. **Abe Lincoln Park, Fifth Avenue and East 135th Street** (2/1, 📷 🔲=4 ●=3 ⛰ 🐕 ☀), hosts lackadaisical runs as well as the Harlem Invitational Chess Tournament. There aren't any aspiring Bobby Fischers, but the runs are a little better across the street at **Bennet Playground.** Indoors, head to the **Bathhouse, 35 West 134th Street** (5/1, 🏠 🔲=3 ●=3 ⛰ $ ☕ 🐕), a converted bathhouse (surprise) that draws an older crowd on Sundays and holds midnight basketball leagues in a tiny gym on its top floor.

Embedded in the bowels of the towering, stately **Riverside Church, West 121st Street and Riverside Drive** (2/1, 🏠 🔲=2 ●=5 ⛰), is a holy court where Ernie Lorch runs his Riverside Hawks, a youth team that battles the Gauchos for city superiority. Guys like Hubert Davis, Stephon Marbury, and Sidney Green spent their youths avoiding the baseline jumpers because of the overhanging balcony in the converted church interior. Over at **Marcus Garvey Park, East 121st Street and Madison Avenue** (4/2, 📷 🔲=3 ●=3 ⛰ 🐕), two courts, one with low rims, are surrounded by a refreshingly nonurban landscape of trees and boulders.

Youngsters emulate the park's namesake by practicing their dunks at **Goat Park, Amsterdam Avenue and West 99th Street** (4/2, 📷 🔲=4 ●=4 ⛰ ☕ 🐕). On 96th Street, the border between the Upper East Side and East Harlem, **Stanley Isaac Park, 96th Street and First Avenue** (4/2, 📷 🔲=3 ●=3 ⛰ ☀), pulls players from both neighborhoods to provide a racially mixed crowd on the court. The Metropolitan Hospital across the street provides lights as well as competition in the form of off-duty interns. College players have been known to show for the late-night games, which sometimes run until 4:30 a.m.

For indoor play farther south, be aware that hoops, like everything else, is more expensive in New York. If you can afford the membership, the **Reebok Sports Club, Columbus Avenue and 67th Street** (4/2, 🏠 🔲=4 ●=3 ⛰ $ ☕ ♀), the **City Athletic Club, 50 West 54th Street** (2/1, 🏠 🔲=2 ●=2 ⛰ $ ☕), and the **Downtown Athletic**

SKATE RATS

At Tompkins Square Park, **East Tenth Street and Avenue A,** (7/2, 🏀 🔲=3 ⚫=3 ⛪ ☞ 🚇) on the Lower East Side of Manhattan, you're likely to see both ballplayers and in-line skaters on the blacktop at the same time. This convergence of enemy factions is the result of the curious sport of rollerbasketball. Played exactly as you would expect, the sport even has a league, the National In-line Basketball League, which was founded by 6'10" Tom LaGarde. LaGarde played at The University of North Carolina, and averaged 14 and 8 for the Dallas Mavericks before his knees forced him to give up conventional basketball.

The sport's top players include LaGarde—who, along with 6'11" NBA center / avid skater Brian Williams, is one of two players who can dunk on skates—and Louie Casillas, a former inline high jump champion who can fly over the hood of a car and complete a 360-degree layup.

All this might sound pretty dangerous, but LaGarde insists otherwise. "We've never had a major injury," he says from his New York office. "Sure, there are a lot of bumps and bruises, but because of the no-checking rule, there isn't much contact."

Brings a whole new meaning to the term "pick and roll," doesn't it?

Club, 19 West Street (2/1, 🏀 🔲=3 ⚫=3 ⛪ **$**), have gyms where visiting celebs get their exercise. Reebok is the best of the three and has women's play on Wednesday and Sunday nights. The **Vanderbilt YMCA, 224 East 47th Street** (2/1, 🔲=3 ⚫=3 ⛪ **$** ☞) has a solid run where a bunch of old Jewish guys go crazy on each other.

The **New York Urban Professionals Basketball League** caters to business types and is a well-run, highly competitive league. Teams play at various Manhattan schools. For more information, call (212)

877-3614. The **Lawyers Basketball League of New York** runs out of private and public school gyms and consists of over 3,000 lawyers, paralegals, investment bankers, and "clients" (a term that refers to the three ringers each team is allowed). For more information, call (212) 777-6901. Farther south, **Chelsea Piers, West 23rd Street and Hudson River** (8/2, 🏀 ▣=4 ●=3 ⛪ $ ☞ ♀), a recently opened sports complex on the water, charges you by the hour to play on the two indoor full courts. In the winter they are jam-packed, with Fridays and Sundays being the busiest times. A women's league rumbles along on Tuesday nights.

In the ethnic jumble of Lower Manhattan, the best game in Chinatown is at **P.S. 1, Madison and Catherine Streets** (4/2, 🏀 ▣=2 ●=2 ⛪), where there is even Chinese graffiti on the walls. On the Lower East Side, at **Hamilton Fish Park, East Houston and Pitt Streets** (4/2, 🏀 ▣=4 ●=3 ⛪ ☞ ♀ 🚭), summer tournaments run during the week and the ladies take the court on Sundays.

BROOKLYN

St. John's Recreation Center
1251 Prospect Place and Schenectady
Brooklyn

6/2, 🏀 ▣ ▣ ▣ ▣ ● ● ● ● ● ⛪ $ ☞ ♀ 🚭

Since the 1950s, St. John's has been a measuring stick for Brooklyn's aspiring ballplayers. The list of guys who have come through the gym reads like a who's who of New York basketball. "Just about every major ballplayer in New York has been through here," says deputy manager Owen Thompson. "Bernard King, Connie Hawkins, Fly Williams—you name 'em, they've played here."

The games aren't quite as high-profile anymore, but you can still find the best indoor run in the five boroughs. The leagues are top-notch, and the outdoor courts are always swamped with kids looking to make a name for themselves. The thirty-five-and-over crowd have their own circuit, and Tuesday nights are reserved for the ladies.

TALES FROM THE ROAD:
Turning the Pages in Brooklyn

During our tour of Brooklyn we head to the Coney Island housing projects where Stephon Marbury grew up. Stephon and his four brothers, Spoon, Jou-Jou, Sky, and Zack, were all basketball prodigies at one time or another in Coney Island. At their respective peaks, each ruled the Garden, an outdoor court next to the towering housing projects. The Garden is a remarkable court to find in such an area; lights illuminate a full court with a clean surface and breakaway rims. Unlike the majority of the project courts we've seen across the country, this one has obviously been lovingly cared for, a reflection of the basketball tradition here in Coney Island.

However, it is an unsettling experience to visit this area of Coney Island after having read about it in *The Last Shot,* Darcy Frey's book chronicling a season in the life of Marbury and his Lincoln High teammates. In Frey's description, the neighborhood is a wasteland of drugs and violence, devoid of shopping markets or even a summer breeze—an isolated pocket of poverty on the tip of Coney Island. His bleak depiction makes us wary when walking around, though the kids are all friendly, if a bit suspicious. What is immediately striking about the area is the number of basketball courts that line the streets; every concrete housing project is accompanied by at least one court, and almost all of them are in use. Basketball appears to be the sole recreational option available to the youths, so they crowd the courts, even in the midday haze. It is unfortunate that, as one of the players in *The Last Shot* laments, the city's only solution to the problems of the projects is to build more basketball courts.

From the streets of Coney Island, we head north through Brooklyn in the early afternoon. With our new direction, we head into *Heaven Is a Playground* territory and Fly Williams country. Fly, a playground legend and national scoring champ at Austin Peay State, was the pseudo-hero of *Heaven,* Rick Telander's classic 1976 book about a summer spent at Foster Park.

We pull up to Foster and walk over to the recently refurbished courts. I try to picture Telander with his tape recorder and ponytail, but all I can see are the scraggly games of 21 being played on three of the six courts. The park has a slightly festive feel—speakers blare music from the small custodial office and kids play in a fountain— but there is still an edge in the air. Walking in and taking pictures, we are immediately scrutinized by all present. "Scout or Cop?" is the unmouthed question. It is an interesting phenomenon that in New

Heaven is a backboard slap at Foster Park in Brooklyn

York, where so much talent emerges from the streets, the kids are accustomed to seeing scouts walking the playgrounds and assume that white outsiders (two of us are white and one black) are either coaches, scouts, or police. Some local teens, convinced that I'm with the force, despite my claims to the contrary and the presence of our gaudy blue van with basketballs painted on the side, follow me around suspiciously for a while.

A pair of middle-aged hoopers, completely unconcerned with whether or not we're NYPD Blue, flag me down and ask if I want some good pictures. They rise from their benched position and start a slow-paced game of one-on-one, a smaller guy versus a stocky woman. They nail mid-range jumpers and jibe back and forth good-naturedly while I snap photos. Their affection for the game is contagious, and soon even the teens are trying to sneak into the background of the pictures. It is reaffirming to find that, even in downtrodden areas of Brooklyn, basketball can still provide a common bond, even if it is a tenuous one.

Also in Brooklyn

The Manhattan Beach courts at the **Parlato Playground, Oriental Boulevard and Irwin Street** (6/3, 🏀 🔲=4 ◑=3🌴), are in a prime location, a bounce pass away from the beach and its numerous bathing beauties, but though they've recently resurfaced the courts, the high-caliber competition of the sixties and seventies has yet to resurface. There is a dependable group that plays half-court weekend mornings, and the full-court runs still occasionally reach cruising altitude in the summer.

Tillary Park, Jay and Tillary Streets (4/2, 🏀 🔲=3 ◑=4 🏙️ 🚊 ☀️), just over the Brooklyn Bridge from Manhattan in Brooklyn Heights, is one of the best runs in the city and hosts a strong summer league. The brothers King, Albert and Bernard, used to hold court here amidst the surrounding traffic. **Kingston Park, a.k.a. St. Andrew's Park, Atlantic Avenue and Kingston Avenue** (7/3, 🏀

Kingston Park

⊡=3 ◉=3 ⛰ 𝕾), is easy enough to reach, with the subway train running overhead. The pavement is packed on weekends for all-day runs, starting with the over-thirty crowd early in the a.m.

In Bedford-Stuyvesant the talent ventures in for the Soul in the Hole tournament. The tourney is held at **the Hole, Monroe Street and Marcus Garvey Boulevard** (2/1, 🚻 ⊡=1 ◉=4 ⛰ ☞ 𝕾), a short court sunk below street level (hence the name) at a Brooklyn schoolyard.

There's year-round Marbury Madness at **the Garden, Mermaid Avenue and West 25th Street** (4/2, 🚻 ⊡=4 ◉=4 ⛰ ☞ 𝕾 ☀), the project court in Coney Island where Stephon Marbury and his brothers honed their games. Up at **Foster Park, Foster Avenue and**

Nostrand (12/6, 🏀 📁=4 ⚫=3 ⛰ 🚲 **)**, the slabs are a central gathering place for ballplayers and hangers-ons.

QUEENS

Lost Battalion Recreation Center
Queens Boulevard and 62nd Avenue
Queens

8/3, 🏀 📁📁📁 ⚫⚫⚫⚫ 🏙 $ ⚲

The Lost Battalion Center—named in honor of the historic 77th Division of World War I fame—hosts some of the best games in all five boroughs at its gym in the Rego Park area of eastern Queens. Strict supervision keeps games enjoyable (fighting gets you kicked out for a year), and winter open gym often attracts up to 100 players, so there's plenty of competition. The championship Knicks teams of the early seventies used to practice here, and a couple of NBA Kennys—Kenny Smith and Kenny Anderson—avoided the between-court wooden poles while playing here in their youth. Anderson would walk over from his nearby housing project, **LeFrak City,** Junction Blvd. at 57th Ave, which he has now endowed with an NBA-quality outdoor court that boasts fiberglass backboards, lights, and bleachers.

Also in Queens

At one time the street's finest, including the Goat, would show for the Elmcor summer league at **Montpelier Playground, 139th Avenue and Springfield Boulevard** (6/3, 🏀 📁=3 ⚫=3 ⛰ 🚲). People couldn't pronounce the French name, so the park became known as Montebello to players. Though the play is less consistent than twenty years ago, there are still pickup games, as well as one nine-foot rim to make us all feel like the Goat for at least a brief moment in time.

He of the chest shimmy, Mark Jackson, perfected his no-look passes at **St. Albans Memorial Park, 172nd Street and Merrick Boulevard** (4/2, 🏀 📁=4 ⚫=4 ⛰ 👁 🚲 💡), a quality outdoor court with the NBA three-point line, lights, bleachers, and a summer league. **Baisley Park, 155th Street and Foch Boulevard** (6/3, 🏀 🖼=4 ◒=3 ⛰ 🌳 ☀) provides three full courts and had leagues until too much drug money was bet on the games and someone shot the ref. "Now we don't have tournaments no more," lamented a local.

I.S. 8, 167th Street (4/2, 🖼=2 ◒=4 ⛰ 🌳), in South Jamaica, where Walter Berry dropped in soft jumpers when young, hosts a summer league and still gets lots of use. At one time **Riis Park, 169th and Rockaway Point Boulevard,** (12/6, 🏀 🖼=4 ◒=3 🌴 ☞ ☀), hosted summer league games featuring the likes of Walt Frazier, Earl Monroe, and Kareem. "There were days when we would literally ride a bike from Brooklyn [to Rockaway] to get out there to see the games," says former Lincoln High player Herb Braithwaite, forty-two, who proudly notes that he was "born, raised, and beat up on the streets of Brooklyn." Now it's strictly summer weekends at Riis. The courts do have great ambience, though; they are right on the beach and the crashing waves provide a soundtrack for weekend battles. Be aware that it'll cost you $1.75 both ways to cross over the Marine Parkway Bridge from Brooklyn.

THE BRONX

Yankee Stadium Courts
East 161st Street and Ruppert Place
The Bronx

4/2, 🏀 🖼 🖼 🖼 🖼 ◒ ◒ ◒ ◒ 🏙 🌳 ☀

"Play ball!" has dual meaning at these two courts, located in the shadow of Yankee Stadium and featuring backboards adorned with the New York Yankees logo. With Manhattanites and Bronx locals battling for hoops supremacy in the afternoons, some days the games outside the stadium are more entertaining than the one inside. If you're more of a sweeper or a striker than a small forward, the field across the street hosts pickup soccer games.

Also in the Bronx

Roberto Clemente State Park, 179th Street off the Deegan Expressway (4/2, 🏢 ☐=3 ◉=3 ⛰ ♀ 🐾), has two courts with plastic backboards. Across the street at **Cedar Playground, off Exit 8 from the expressway,** you'll find another two sets of racks. To the east they play physical ball at **Watson-Gleason Park, Rosedale and Gleason Avenues, off White Plains Road.** The park, also known as Rosedale Park, is where "Master Rob" Hokett of Rucker Tournament fame grew up playing ball. Starting at 7:45 a.m. a friendly over-thirty group crowds the pavement on Sunday mornings at **P.S. 24, 660 W. 236th Street,** (6/2, 🏢 ☐=3 ◉=3 ⛰), in the Riverdale section of the Bronx.

The **Gaucho Gym, 478 Gerard,** (6/2, 🏢 ☐=5 ◉=5 ⛰ 🐚), Lou d'Almeida's top-notch training center for his youth teams, looks conspicuous in the run-down neighborhood just over the bridge from Upper Manhattan. A snorting-bull image stares down from the wall, as college coaches and scouts, often affixed to the bleachers, make subtle eye contact with their recruits. Every fall the Roundball Classic brings the East Coast's best young players to this gym, described by New York basketball guru Tom Konchalski as "an indoor shrine." Take a day off from work and come watch the games at the Gaucho Gym—you may see the next pro superstar out on the floor. If you want to have a little fun, bring a clipboard, put on a suit and tie, and shave real well. This will have all the kids wondering what school you're from, and the other scouts and coaches whispering about "the new guy."

STATEN ISLAND

George Cromwell Recreation Center
Pier 6 (Murry Hulbert Avenue between Victory Boulevard and Hannah Street)
Staten Island

12/6,

Park next to the pier at Cromwell, breathe in the salty smell of the ocean, and look out across the Upper Bay toward Lady Liberty, her arm outstretched to snare a rebound. Then head inside and play with guys from all five boroughs who make the journey to play in this exquisite rec center. Six full courts with glass backboards accommodate heavy winter loads—just look out for the posts in between the narrow courts.

Clove Lake Park, Seneca Avenue and Victory Boulevard (4/2, ▦ ▣=4 ●=2 ▥) has a suburban vibe and is home to the best outdoor games on Staten Island.

ELSEWHERE IN NEW YORK CITY AREA

Greenburgh
Rumbrook Park
560 Dobbs Ferry Road
Greenburgh

6/2,

Rumbrook's lit courts are conveniently located right off the Sprain Brook Parkway in Greenburgh. Local college players drop in for runs and Anthony Mason has banged bodies on the nearly regulation-length court.

LONG ISLAND

As you drive east from Queens out on Long Island, the scenery slowly changes. City turns to suburbs, and soon you feel as if you could be anywhere in America, driving through neighborhoods with identical houses and minimarts on every corner. Then you hit Roosevelt, a lower-income neighborhood that sticks out like a sore thumb. Despite (or maybe because of) the economic situation, some of America's most famous celebrities have emerged from Roosevelt. The members of the eighties rap sensation Public Enemy went to the same high school as Eddie Murphy and Howard Stern. The most famous native son, Julius Erving, after spending his early years in Hempstead, came to prominence playing in Roosevelt.

Julius would face off with the other neighborhood greats back then, though he by no means dominated them. "Dr. J was the best clean player, but there were other guys here in high school who were better," said "Bishop" Frank Stallings, who runs the summer league in Roosevelt. "The other guys got into trouble while Doc had his head on straight. Then he got the break and developed."

A plaque still shines on the fence at **Roosevelt Park, Elmwood Avenue and Lakeside Drive** (8/2, 🏀 🖼️=3 ◉=3 🏠) commemorating Erving's adolescent pickup games, and it reflects the respect for Doc that in over twenty years no one has ever defaced the sign. These days the better competition runs up the road at **Centennial Park, Babylon Turnpike and East Centennial Avenue** (16/4, 🏀 🖼️=4 ◉=4 🏙️ ☞ 🎪 💡), where Stallings's summer tournament draws teams from all over New York City to

Before he was "the Doctor," Erving soared at Roosevelt Park

play on the eight courts. Playing at Centennial is a physical experience—"going to war," as Bishop describes it—so you might want to play in the relatively soft games at Roosevelt Park. If you do play at Centennial, give some respect to hoops-junkie janitors Junior and Lonnie (Lonnie's the one with the sleepy eye).

Prospect Park
Prospect Avenue and Maple Avenue
East Meadow

4/2,

Prospect is an extremely solid run, with a more organized brand of ball and a lower BS factor than you'll find at most outdoor courts (and there are even nets). A mixed crowd gathers till late, running full on the basketball courts while handball enthusiasts swing and dive on the two lit handball walls adjacent to the courts. This is one of the few places on the Island where the lights stay on after Labor Day, so the joint is hopping on fall evenings.

NEW YORK STATE

All the good basketball in the state of New York isn't located within New York City's confines, it just seems that way sometimes. In fact, they play all across the state, though not with the fervor that can be found in N.Y.C.

BUFFALO AREA

Delaware Park
Parkside Avenue and Jewett Parkway
Buffalo

8/4,

Delaware is a bustling outdoor spot where natives Cliff Robinson and Christian Laettner, who's from the southern burb of Angola, grew

TALES FROM THE ROAD:
High Drama in Buffalo

We take advantage of the city's light traffic and cruise to Martin Luther King Park, site of numerous outdoor summer leagues. We happen upon a game between city employees and kids from a youth camp, a sort of end-of-the-camp square-off. An excited guy with a mustache is behind the mike, providing high volume play-by-play. He is doing his best Brent Musberger imitation, treating every play as if it might possibly decide the game. "Little guy gets it . . . He dribbles, He SHOOTS! . . . Nothing! . . . Old-timer brings it up, he passes it to Sally, SALLY SHOOTS IT!! Oh no, she misses, yes folks, she MISSES!"

We endure ten minutes of this commentary and witness a dramatic victory by the youth team, which must have shot at least 15 percent from the field as a squad. They celebrate their victory by running and taunting the counselor bench, as they are taught by their idols in the NBA.

up playing, though not always dominating. "Cliff got schooled just like everybody else out here," one player told us. In the summer there are often four full-court games going on in the late afternoon. When running on the main court, be aware that one of the rims is low.

Also in Buffalo Area

The **Buffalo Athletic Club, 69 Delaware Avenue** (4/1, 🏠 ▣=4 ⚪=4 ⛰ $ ☞ ♀), is an excellent downtown facility with a plentiful crowd of older guys and a ladies' night on Thursdays. Afternoon runs can be highly competitive, with European pros and ex–college guys in the summer.

The **JFK Recreation Center, 114 Hickory Street** (2/1, 🏠 ▣=3 ⚪=3 ⛰ ♀ 🎟), has a women's night on Friday and rough evening

Everyone can be a big man on the low rim at Delaware Park

games in the winter. Tuesdays and Thursdays a noon crowd of firemen and cops play. **Martin Luther King Park, Best Street and West Parade Avenue** (2/1, 🏠 🔲=4 ◐=3 ⛰ ☞ ♨), is busy all summer long.

North of Buffalo in the sleepy suburb of Kenmore, they play at **Crosby Field, Crosby and Colvin** (6/2, 🏠 🔲=3 ◐=2 🏠), while to the east of the city in Cheektowaga, right off the I-190–I-90 interchange, **Dingens Park, Dingens Street and South Colby** (4/2, 🏠 🔲=3 ◐=3 🏠), provides a pleasant setting for an outdoor game. Be mindful of the nearby baseball diamond. As the sign warns, "Be alert, baseballs hurt."

ROCHESTER

Robach Community Center
Ontario Beach Park
Beach Avenue and Estes Street
Rochester

6/3,

Robach Community Center's three courts are enclosed within a latticed stone wall to provide players protection from stray beach balls while allowing a view of bathing beauties on Ontario Beach. Weekday evenings and summer weekends you'll find the best pickup in Rochester at Robach, with hometown boy John Wallace occasionally showing. Nearby, Captain's Cabin Custom Tattoo can give you that Rodman look if that's what you think your game is missing.

A more consistent, though a less scenic, run goes on at **Cobbs Hill Park, Norris and Culver Drives** (4/2, 🏀 ▣=3 ●=4 🏠).

SYRACUSE

Sunnycrest Park
Robinson Street and Teall Avenue
Syracuse

6/2, 🏀 ▣ ▣ ▣ ● ● ● 🏙

You can run all afternoon at Sunnycrest, just don't try to shoot any baseline threes—the arc practically intersects the sideline. The park is in a truly diverse neighborhood; across the street is a British Foods store that flies the Union Jack, down the street is Klub Polski, a Polish-American club, and the Italian American Athletic Club is two blocks away.

Also in Syracuse

For the best games around, head to Flanagan Gym at **Syracuse University.** While playing, don't be surprised if a student decides to sit

TALES FROM THE ROAD:
Where's B.A.?

Our morning consists of a trip to Lake George, an Adirondacks vacation hotspot for New Yorkers and their screaming kids. We drive past the strip in all its minigolf glory in search of a little hoops. Our quest yields **Usher Park, Racawana Road and Highway 9L** (2/1, 🏛 🖼=3 ◒=2 🏚 ♀), a quiet park across the lake from the strip.

When we arrive, two guys are playing one-on-one on the near basket. One is the caricature of rich: a fiftyish white guy with per-

Hannibal unfurls a sky hook at Usher Park

fectly coiffed white hair, a well-kept white mustache, a healthy tan, short aqua-colored polo shorts, and brand-new high-tech, gel-filled, compression-resistant, glaring white cross-trainers. His opponent is younger (possibly a son-in-law) with brown hair reminiscent of the 'do on Face Man from the *A-Team*. He grunts a lot and skips to the basket with nimble feet, looking much as though he should be in a Broadway musical.

The two of them proceed to throw up a lot of hooks and set shots and, from what we can tell, Face Man loses to Hannibal, whom we can almost hear mutter, "I love it when a plan comes together."

courtside and give play-by-play; Syracuse is the alma mater of sports announcers Dick Stockton, Marv Albert, Mike Tirico, and Bob Costas.

ELSEWHERE IN NEW YORK STATE

Albany

The busiest outdoor spot is **Washington Park, Madison and Western Avenues** (4/2, 🖼 🔲=3 ●=3 ⛰ ☂ ☀). Up the street they play indoors at **V.I. Community Center, 844 Madison Avenue and Ontario Street** (2/1, 🏠 🔲=2 ●=3 ⛰ ☂). Women looking for a game head to the campus of **SUNY–Albany.**

Ithaca

Spacious **Barton Hall, Cornell University** is "like being in the damn catacombs" according to one local. In the winter, the place is packed.

9

New England Region

CONNECTICUT, MAINE, MASSACHUSETTS, NEW HAMPSHIRE, RHODE ISLAND, VERMONT

New England boasts numerous attractions: the rocky shores of Maine, the cow-spotted fields of Vermont, the busy streets of Boston, and the coastal views of Connecticut. There are, of course, negatives as well: the industrial towns of Connecticut, the cold winters of Vermont, the challenge of surviving those busy streets of Boston, and the fact that the psycho characters in Stephen King novels always live in Maine.

When it comes to basketball, the Boston area, home of Hah-vard, is the hub of New England. This is the intellectual city that produced the Professor of the Post, Patrick Ewing; the Dean of the Deep Three, Dana Barros; and the Cognoscenti of Clutch-Free Throws, Rumeal Robinson.

Connecticut, with its proximity to the big cities, has produced prodigious talent as well, and is home to New Haven's once-legendary Goffe Street Playground. The other states in the region aren't crazy about basketball; New Hampshire has more lakes than hoops, and the best two-on-two team in Vermont is probably a couple of fellas named Ben and Jerry.

CONNECTICUT

NEW HAVEN

In the 1970s and early '80s the two courts at Goffe Street Park in New Haven were the place to be. College players and occasional pros would show up and throw down at what was once New England's best pickup joint. Now the courts are in the midst of the ghetto, broken glass litters the courts, and few good players visit. "No one messes with this park anymore, dogs don't even run through here," says one local, brown paper bag in hand.

The smart dogs, along with the good players, are now to be found down the road at **Edgewood Park, Whalley and West Rock Avenues** (2/1, ▨ ▣=4 ◉=4 🏠). Centrally located, with a bus stop right out front and plenty of parking, Edgewood is a more convenient, safer destination than Goffe. It also has scenic appeal: trees shade the court and the craggy outline of West Rock Ridge appears behind one baseline.

Also in New Haven

If you can handle the intellectual bickering, you can play with the students at **Yale.**

HARTFORD

NBA stars Michael Adams and Marcus Camby may have grown up in Hartford, but that doesn't mean finding a good run is easy. **Keney Park** and **Pope Park** are for locals only, and the South Arsenal Neighborhood Development gym, where Marcus played his youth ball, isn't a great tourist location. The best bet for a game without the extra baggage is **Wolcott Park, New Britain Avenue and Chatfield Drive** (4/2, 🏀 ⛹=3 ◉=4 🏠 💡) in West Hartford. Good players drive out from the city for weekday afternoon and weekend morning games on the two end-to-end courts.

ELSEWHERE IN CONNECTICUT

Madison
The Surf Club
Surf Club Road (off West Wharf Road)
Madison

4/2,

If you're making the drive up to Providence from New Haven, it's worth your time to stop at the strangely named Surf Club Beach in Madison, Connecticut. Boasting two lit outdoor courts, an idyllic beach, and a breathtaking view across Long Island Sound, this is easily one of the most scenic courts in the country. Unfortunately, it may also be the most exclusive outdoor court in the country. From Memorial Day to Labor Day, to get into the beach area you must have a beach pass ($15 youth, $20 adult). And here's the catch: To get a beach pass you must be a taxpaying resident of Madison.

Since this criterion doesn't apply to many of us, and this is truly a court worth playing on, I suggest the following tactic: Head to the minimart a couple blocks down the road and buy something. Don't forget to pay the tax on the item. Now head back to the Surf Club and sneak in (it's not terribly hard to do). This way you can play without a guilty conscience, seeing as you are an upstanding tax-paying member of the Madison community, at least for the day.

All it takes is a little creativity to join the Surf Club in Madison

As for the courts, they get lots of use from the community (refereed drop-in play for third to eighth grade during the week), so make sure to come on the weekend, when the slabs are open for adult pickup play.

Stamford

The court's older regulars take great joy in talking smack to the up-and-comers at **Scalzi Park, Bridge Street and Washington Boulevard** (2/1, 📋 🔲=4 ⬤=4 🏔 ☀). The area is suburban but the run is urban, with the city's talented high schoolers battling into the night.

Storrs

Students run with current and former Huskies in the old field house on the campus of the **University of Connecticut.**

MAINE

PORTLAND

Ninety percent of Maine is covered with forest, an immediate tipoff that this is not a good state for pickup hoops. The state's largest city, Portland, does provide a couple viable options. **Payson Park, Back Cove Boulevard and Fernald Street** (2/1, 🏀 🔲=3 ●=4 🏔), sits next to the rocky coast and draws good summertime competition. Beware, though—tough rims, slippery asphalt, and buggy nights make playing ball a challenge.

A less buggy environment can be found indoors in the northwest part of town at the **Riverton Community Center, 1600 Forest Avenue** (6/2, 🏀 🔲=3 ●=4 🏔 $). The gym features a slightly Marxist open-gym system; the first thirty-six players to show up are drafted into six teams, which then square off on two courts. Games are run to 11 points, with the sixth man subbing in at combos of five (3–2, 4–1, etc.). If you win two in a row, you sit, the better to allow all to play (and to further the revolution, Comrade). Competitionwise, college players and the occasional USBL Mountain Cat represent the top level.

Pleasant Street Park, Pleasant and Maple Streets (2/1, 🏀 🔲=3 ●=2 🏔), has a great sealife-themed mural on the wall and is a couple blocks from Fore Street, the nightlife section of Portland. **Deering Oaks Parks, Park Avenue and State Street** (2/1, 🏀 🔲=3 ●=2 🏔 ☀), is right off I-295.

MASSACHUSETTS

BOSTON AREA

Malcolm X Park–Shelburne Recreation Center
Washington Street and Martin Luther King Boulevard
Roxbury

8/4, 🏀 🔲🔲🔲🔲 ●●●● 🏙 ☞ 🚫 ☀

In the rough Boston neighborhood of Roxbury, the most brazen of street gangs, the Intervales, wear T-shirts that boast "Betcha We

Getcha." For many young men who live in the area, the best way not to be "gotten" is to stay off the streets and spend their time at the basketball oasis provided by Malcolm X Park and the neighboring **Shelburne Recreation Center** (6/2, 🏀 🔲=3 ●=4♀ 🏀 🏀).

Inside at Shelburne Rec, three courts host nightly pickup games for college-level players and, one night a week, women who have the jones. Outside at Malcolm X Park, also known as Washington Park, a unique step system of four full courts cascades down the hill. On weekends, between constant pickup play and the two quality leagues—including one sponsored by park graduate and ex-Supersonic James Bailey—the outdoor racks get nonstop usage.

The Fens
Park Drive and Jersey Street
Back Bay

4/2,

Just blocks from the Green Monster and the friendly confines of Fenway Park, the Fens teems with hackers, college kids, and a smattering of ex–college players during the summer. The two full courts are in a great location, in the Back Bay Fens and within walking distance of Boston's post–Red Sox party scene, Lansdowne Avenue. On the blacktop, all the action is on the A court—"There might as well not even be two courts," according to regular Alden Romney—so prepare to wait a bit to get in a game. Unfortunately, the Ebony-Ivory league, a top city loop that used to run here, is now defunct.

A few blocks away, tucked behind a Burger King at the corner of Jersey and Peterborough Streets, you'll find a court even closer to Fenway Park that pays homage to Celtic superstars. The court, painted leprechaun green, has the following jersey numbers lovingly painted on its surface: 32, 00, 7, 35, 20, 34, and, of course, 33. Name all of them and congratulate yourself on being a Boston fan mired in the past (Hint: Acie Earl is not one of them).

NEIGHBORLY LEAGUE BALL IN BEANTOWN

Boston is a league-friendly city: Numerous summer circuits, from the Old Timers League in Dorchester to the James Bailey League at Washington Park to the Gang Peace League, provide players with officiated playing opportunities. The city's crown jewel, though, and one of the country's model youth leagues, is the Boston Neighborhood Basketball League. The BNBL, a citywide outdoor youth league, has been providing a forum for the city's best talent for close to four decades now. Teams in three divisions from all across the metro area battle it out at sixteen different city sites for a chance to play in the finals, which are held in front of a raucous crowd on the asphalt at the Fens. The team to beat? Local coaching legend Al Brodsky's Titans are the Russel-era Celtics of the league, having won seventeen BNBL titles in twenty-seven years.

Devotion School
Beals and Stedman Streets (off Harvard Street)
Brookline

4/2,

"Ask not what your team can do for you, but what you can do for your team" is the unofficial motto of the fundamentally sound players on the outdoor courts at the Devotion School, JFK's alma mater. Besides being historically significant, the grammar school, tucked away into the affluent suburb of Brookline, hosts some great hoops action. Whereas playing at Malcolm X and the Fens can mean dealing with a fair amount of, shall we say, "extracurricular activity," it's all ball at Devotion. This atmosphere has led the talented Fens crowd of the mid-eighties to shift to playing here. From mid-April to September, the courts are packed with players from Boston, Newton, Cambridge, and Watertown who come to play at what one local community college coach calls "the best run in the state of Massachusetts."

Also in Boston Area

Every fall, the Boston population spikes an extra 100,000 because of the collegiate population. As a result, games can be found at almost any of the local schools, including MIT and Harvard. The **University of Massachusetts–Boston** campus has good competition and, as a bonus, is open to the community.

For some waterfront action, you can head to the **Carson Beach courts, Columbia Road and Carson Beach** (4/2, 🏀 🔲=3 ⬤=3 ⛰

Boston legend-in-his-own-mind "Handsome" Jimmy Valiant

Beantown's upper crust fight for boards at the posh Longfellow Sports Club

🐂 ☀), where they play three-on-three during the day and full court at night. Check in with "Handsome" Jimmy Valiant, an older white-haired gent, while you're there. You can decide for yourself whether or not the nickname is facetious. In the North End the Boston Common-ers congregate at **Prince Street Playground, Prince between Commercial and Salem Streets** (2/1, 🏚 ▣=4 ◉=3 🏔 ☀), a recently repaved court in an old Italian neighborhood.

Across the Charles River from Boston, Cambridge is home to two riverfront locations. **Riverside Press Park, Memorial Drive and River Street** (4/2, 🏚 ▣=4 ◉=3 🏔), is a well-manicured park that once drew Ewing but now has lost the better players to **Corporal Burns Playground, Flagg Street and Memorial Drive** (4/2, 🏚 ▣=3

◉=4 ⛰ ☞ ☀), where Pearl Washington, a little rounder than in his playing days, still runs on weekends. A couple blocks from Burns, there's a more organized brand of ball at **Hoyt Field.**

The best **YMCAs** are the Cambridge branch, which has good leagues; the Roxbury branch, which has good comp; the Central branch, which boasts a solid noon run; and the Hyde Park Y, which carries the distinction of being the oldest YMCA in the country. The **Reggie Lewis Recreation Center, 1350 Tremont Street** (14/7, 🏛 ▣=4 ◉=4 ⛰ $☞ ♀ ☀), at Roxbury Community College offers an indoor alternative to Shelburne Rec.

In Framingham, west of Boston, you'll find a crowd at the outdoor courts next to **Loring Arena, Fountain Street and Dudley Road** (4/1, 🏛 ▣=3 ◉=2 🏠)—or Loring "Areener," as locals pronounce it. In Natick, on the hardwood inside at the **Longfellow Sports Club, 203 Oak Street** (4/2, 🏛 ▣=4 ◉=4 🏠 $☞ ♀), the pickup is solid and David Wesley, Rick Fox, M. L. Carr, and Doug Flutie have all played in the leagues.

In Lancaster, 45 minutes west of the city, there aren't as many big names, but the **Orchard Hills Sport Club, 90 Duval Road** (2/1, 🏛 ▣=4 ◉=4 🏠 $☞ ♀) has worthwhile leagues. Crafty old guys scout the pickup and then plot draft strategy to snare the talented new members.

SPRINGFIELD AREA

The Origins of the Game

The history of hoops comes alive at the Basketball Hall of Fame in Springfield, the modest city where Dr. James Naismith invented basketball in 1891. The good doctor, needing to come up with a winter sport after his "indoor rugby" idea failed, racked his brain for a non-contact sport and came up with hoops, an ironic solution because, as it's played today, basketball often involves more physical contact than a wrestling match.

Naismith's game evolved its peculiar rules out of necessity. Take the origin of the backboard, for example. The early version of basketball, as many of you probably know, involved only a peach basket affixed to a balcony in an auditorium. To eliminate the necessity of climbing a ladder to retrieve the ball after every made shot, the bottom of the basket was cut out. As the game increased in popularity, fans began to gather to cheer on their teams, watching the game from the balcony and probably chanting things like "Good shot there, Francis!" and "Score one for our team, William." They found they could increase their team's chances of winning by doing a Manute Bol imitation and swatting away would-be shots from their position in the balcony. The solution? A board behind the basket to make it impossible for spectators to reach around and block shots. The rest, including your junior high coach's adage "Always use the backboard," is history.

Forest Park Courts
Sumner and Forest Park Avenues
Springfield

6/3,

The aptly named Forest Park in southeast Springfield contains 735 acres of woods, streams, gardens, zoos, and athletic facilities. Amidst

Few courts provide as scenic a setting as Forest Park in Springfield

all this vegetation, surrounded by towering trees, are three full courts that fill up in the summer. Despite the redwood feel, the majority of the players, an urban group, aren't your typical day hikers. Homeboys in Yosemite, you could call it.

Also in Springfield

Doc J once worked as an intern at the **Dunbar Community Center, 33 Oak Street** (2/1, 🏠 ▣=4 ◉=4 ⛰ ☞ ♀ ⚷), an inner-city

---

TALES FROM THE ROAD:
We'll Never Make Fun of Vinny Again

Vinny Del Negro, a solid if unspectacular two guard in the big leagues, is one of the graduates of Szot Park, a scenic court just north of Springfield in Chicopee. When we visit town, we hear about a different Del Negro than the one we've seen on TV. A park veteran named Jeff (not a bad player himself) tells us about his encounter with Vinny "Del Fuego."

"Well, there was this one game where I had to cover Vinny," Jeff says. "The first time he comes down the court, he pulls up and nails a thirty-footer on me.

"That was pretty embarrassing, so the next time down I guard him real close. Well, then he gives me an up fake and drives right around me. Dunks it two-handed—real hard, too."

At this point, our looks of surprise at this aerial assault are evident.

"Oh yeah," Jeff says, nodding, "Vinny can sky. When he shot a jumper, his knees would be in your chest. Anyway, to top it all off, on the other end, I try to take it back at Vinny, so I drive right and go up for a jumper from about fifteen. Vinny blocks it so hard that I fall backwards, land real funny, and break my foot. I haven't had any urge to play against him since then."

After that tale, we have no urge to get dunked on by Del Nasty, either.

gym with good talent that recently received a $1.2 million state-funded facelift. The collegiate talent checks in from 1 to 3 Monday to Thursday. Travis Best honed his skills at **Van Horn Park, Armory and Miller Streets** (6/3, 🏀 🔲=3 ◉=4 ⛰ 🐟). Over at the more suburban **Greenleaf Community Center, Wilbraham Road and Parker Street** (2/1, 🏀 🔲=3 ◉=4 🏢 ☞ 🚗), there are both indoor and outdoor facilities. Gritty night games can be found on the pavement at the **William DeBerry School, Monroe and Hawley Streets** (2/1, 🏀 🔲=2 ◉=4 ⛰ 🐟 💡), near Dunbar.

North of Springfield in Chicopee, a topflight outdoor league runs on the hardtop at **Szot Park, Front and Academy Streets** (4/2, 🏀 🔲=4 ◉=4 🏢 ☞ 💡). The court attracts a mix of suburban players and city kids.

ELSEWHERE IN MASSACHUSETTS

Amherst

On the campus of U-Mass, the ringers show at the **Horseshoe,** two outdoor campus courts. Every spring the school also hosts Haigis Hoopla, an indoor tourney that attracts over 2,000 Mass. Maniacs.

Worcester

Bob Cousy grew up perfecting his dishing skills in Worcester (pronounced "Wooster"), where the best run in town these days is at **Newton Square, Highland and Pleasant Streets** (2/1, 🏀 🔲=3 ◉=4 ⛰ ☞ 🚗 💡). Leagues rage during the summer, as do the keg parties that local high-schoolers throw in the park behind the court.

NEW HAMPSHIRE

All right, so we didn't devote too much time to locating courts in New Hampshire. But we did look, and though our search was fairly fruitless, we found a few decent games.

Manchester

In a city that talks and feels like "Bawston," the best ball in town is at **Pulaski Park, Pine and Bridge Streets** (2/1, 🖼 🖾=3 ⊜=4 🏔 🐕)), across from St. Joseph's Junior High. The Celtics run summer clinics down the street on the two full courts at **Sheridan Emmet Park.**

Concord

Rollins Park, Broadway and McKinley Streets (2/1, 🖼 🖾=3 ⊜=1 📋 ☼), is a nice little court with wood backboards in a forested area. Serious hicks can be found at at the **public courts, North State and Penacook Streets.** Though none of the players resemble Walt Hazzard, the fashion styles are vintage *Dukes of Hazzard.*

New Ipswich

Players from Mason, Greenville, and surrounding towns gather at **New Ipswich Town Field, Main Street** (6/2, 🖼 🖾=3 ⊜=2📋). The local phrase of choice is "wicked awesome." Apparently, one wouldn't apply this phrase to the athletic ability of the locals. "If you could dunk, you were a god there," says native Guy Daniello.

Center Harbor

You'll feel like your errant jumpers end up *On Golden Pond* at the **Lake Court, Route 25 a few miles off Route 3** (2/1, 🖼 🖾=4 ⊜=1 📋), a sublime slab that sits on a hill fifty yards from the tranquil waters of Lake Winnipesaukee in central New Hampshire. The White Mountains loom behind you and the beach is just down the grassy hill for post-game dips.

RHODE ISLAND

PROVIDENCE

The newest and most impressive of Providence's rec centers, the **West End Recreation Center, Daboll Street and Bucklin Avenue**

(6/2, 🏀 📺=3 ⚫=4 ⛰ ☞ ♀ 🚗), hosts NCAA-sanctioned midnight basketball leagues for both men and women. To find the center, just look for the building that has so much barbed wire that you could mistake it for a maximum-security prison. Michael Stevens, basketball director, calls the games "highly, highly competitive."

If no one's running at West End, you can head to any of the other city centers—including the Davey Lopes Center, named after the Providence native and Dodger hero—for a similar game. A more organized game can be found at the Peterson Rec Center on the campus of **Providence College,** or over at **Rhode Island College.**

In the suburbs, **Kent Heights Park, Clyde and Richfield Avenues** (4/2, 🏀 📺=2 ⚫=2 🏠) in East Providence isn't the greatest court but is perfect for family shootarounds. In Cranston, southwest of Providence, the games continue into the night at **Stebbins Field Courts, 9 Flint Street** (2/1, 🏀 📺=3 ⚫=3 🏠 💡).

VERMONT

BURLINGTON

Pomeroy Park
North and Booth Streets
Burlington

3/1, 🏀 📺📺📺 ⚫⚫⚫⚫ 🏙 🏃

Pomeroy, a peaceful park in the northern part of town, is the best run in Burlington. The court is busy during the summer, attracting a racially mixed crowd, but the competition really heats up during the school year, when players from the University of Vermont (the university's rec courts are also worth checking out) and St. Michael's College are around to upgrade the games. South Park, on Locust Avenue, used to be the place to play, but strong winds have sent the better games up to Pomeroy, where the only breeze you might encounter is from the occasional joint that is passed around on the sidelines.

When you're done playing, head to Nectar's for some famous fries (Phish fans will recognize the joint from the Burlington band's CD *A Picture of Nectar*) or to Rasputin's for a beer or two.

ELSEWHERE IN VERMONT

Barre
Barre Auditorium
South Seminary Street, Seminary Hill
Barre

6/1,

The dream of every schoolgirl ballplayer in Vermont is to make it to the "Aud," site of the girls' state playoffs. For those of us with the Y chromosome (and for women who aren't in high school) the dream to visit the Aud can be fulfilled from 11:30 to 1:30 Monday through Friday from October to March during pickup play, though it will cost you a couple bucks.

Montpelier
The **Recreation Field, North Park Drive and Elm Street** (6/2, =3 =2), is the best spot for outdoor ball in Montpelier, a town full of expatriate Canadians who still speak French. Because of this, if you disagree with a foul call, try screaming "Je m'en fous" or "Va te faire foutre," both of which, roughly translated, mean "I do not agree with you."

Woodstock
Woodstock Recreation Center
54 River Street
Woodstock

2/1,

It was here in the tiny, idyllic Vermont town of Woodstock in 1978 that the idea for the *In-Your-Face Basketball Book* was cooked up by two rec center employees. While playing a game of H-O-R-S-E out on the blacktop one day, Alex Wolff and Chuck Wielgus decided that what this world needed was a book devoted to the pursuit of pickup basketball. The rest, as they say, is history.

With the center's esteemed hoops tradition, it is only fitting that this is still the best court in eastern central Vermont. Starting every May, players from nearby towns make the drive to the 'Stock for the competitive summer league, which has been running for two decades now.

A few improvements have been made to the center since the *In-Your-Face* days, including a fence around the court to keep balls from going into the river and the addition of a water basketball court in the pool, where you can "dunk" the ball on offense and your opponent on defense.

10
The Southeast Coast
FLORIDA, GEORGIA, NORTH CAROLINA, SOUTH CAROLINA

This region has it all: the original stomping grounds of Michael Jordan, the antebellum style and good manners of Charleston, and the antigravity style and nonstop hooping of the Run n' Shoot in Atlanta. Farther down the coast in Florida, the first love is still football (and owing to the number of seniors shuffling around, the second and third loves might very well be golf and bingo), but hoops is starting to catch on, as evidenced by solid runs like Hurley Park in St. Pete's Beach, the Smith Center in Orlando, and the scenic beach courts in Ft. Lauderdale.

FLORIDA

FT. LAUDERDALE—MIAMI AREA

A1A Beach Courts
South Atlantic (Route A1A) and Harbor Boulevard
Fort Lauderdale

4/2,

Fifty yards from the ocean and surrounded by palm trees, white sand, and hard bodies, these courts look like something out of a Club Med brochure. The place feels like a resort too; tipsy bar hoppers watch the action and a warm tropical breeze accompanies players as they jog up and down the sand-strewn court. As for the games, they are often more about looking good than winning; this might be the only court in the country where the victorious team usually chooses to run *into* the sun, the better to tan the pecs. If you run at the A1A courts, don't play too hard; the nightlife in Ft. Lauderdale is worth saving some energy for, especially during the bacchanalian spring-break scene.

Smart players shoot with the ocean breeze at the A1A courts

One thing to be aware of: The courts are not easy to access, and parking near the beach is nearly impossible when it's warm out.

Also in Ft. Lauderdale–Miami Area

The best game in Miami is at the **University of Miami,** with top runs on Sunday mornings. A mostly Latino crowd brings the family to **Tropical Park, Bird Road and S.W. 82nd Avenue** (4/2, ▦ ▣=4 ◉=2 ⚊ ☼), on weekends to throw some at the rim in between throwing some on the barbecue. At **Grapeland Park, N.W. 14th Street and N.W. 37th Avenue** (4/2, ▦ ▣=4 ◉=3 ⚊), next to Miami International Airport, play continues on the concrete through the balmy winters. High above Miami, the **Downtown Athletic Club, 200 South Biscayne Boulevard** (2/1, ▦ ▣=2 ◉=2 ⚊ $), is located on the fifteenth floor of a bank building. The games, unlike the building, are not a high-altitude affair, with business types sweating it out on the extremely short court.

If you want to know what it's like to be rich, head out past the gate cop on Palm Island to the **Palm Island Public Court, Fountain Street and Palm Avenue** (2/1, ▦ ▣=4 ◉=2 ⚲), and play against your shadow in the shadow of millionaires' homes. When you're done, South Miami Beach and its crazy nights (and mornings, for that matter) are just up the road.

In Ft. Lauderdale, the nonbeach competition has shifted from Sunland Park to **Holiday Park, Memorial and Sunrise** (4/2, ▦ ▣=3 ◉=3 ⚊ ᴣ◎), where they run indoors and under the sun with equal fervor. Don't mind the crowds; Holiday is the type of park where people just hang out, no compelling reason needed.

JACKSONVILLE AREA

Bruce Park
Commerce Street and Underhill Drive
Jacksonville

8/4,

Ballers come from all corners of sprawling Jacksonville, the country's largest city by square mileage, for the runs at Bruce Park, the area's best outdoor court. The park, which is down the road about a mile from Jacksonville University (where local boy Dee Brown, the 6'2" slam-dunk champion, played his ball), gets live around 4:30, when four-on-four games start up on the short courts. It's best to show a little earlier though, as waits can be substantial.

Riverside YMCA
Jackson and Riverside
Jacksonville

4/2, 🏀 ⬜⬜⬜ ●●●● 🏙️ $ 🎽

With short courts and low rims, the game at the Riverside Y—which, as the name suggests, is on the river—is geared for little guys. The court next to the weight room is for recreational ball, and the other court fills up with college caliber players, or, as one local said, "On that court you get people who think they should be getting paid to play ball."

One of those guys is ex–Tennessee State player Ronnie "Tennessee" Cage, the local pickup legend. His rep—"He has the sweetest jump shot in the city," says Karl Tatum, Jacksonville Pro-Am director—is such that dropping his name at Jax courts elicits instant respect.

Also in Jacksonville Area

Outdoors at **Klutho Park, Boulevard and West Fifth Street** (12/4, 🏀 ⬜=3 ●=4 🏙️ 🚲 💡), "They don't start playing until five p.m. 'cause that's when everybody wakes up," according to one regular. At Klutho, also known as "the Boulevard," you have to weigh the pros and cons. Pro: Great court. Con: Bad neighborhood. On the other hand, at **Burnett Park, Burnett Park Road** (6/2, 🏀 ⬜=2 ●=3 🏪 🏧 💡), in Mandarin you'll find crappy courts in a good neighborhood. Very short courts, local football players, and slightly low rims produce physical games. Surrounding the concrete are four Little League fields, where parents scream a lot and wear T-shirts that say things like "Kevin's Mom" and "David's Dad."

ORLANDO AREA

James Smith Center
Bruton Avenue
Orlando

6/2,

You may be a star at your local park, but show at the Smith Center, a sweet gym that hosts the pro-am and Orlando's best pickup play, and you've just become a role player. Unless, of course, you think you should be the focal point of the offense when Nick Anderson and Penny Hardaway are on the floor.

Nick and Penny are just two of the guys that Smith Center director James "J.T." Turner, an All-American at Bethune-Cookman and *the* basketball guy in Orlando, rallies for summer pickup games. Of course not just anyone plays with the fellas, but the regular pickup—the best runs are Sunday, Monday, and Wednesday—isn't too shabby, either, consisting of college and overseas talent. J.T. makes sure basketball is the priority at the gym, setting aside lots of time for pickup play. You have to like his attitude too; when we pointed out a sign that said "No Dunking," he responded, "Shit, I don't know why that's up there. I got to take that down."

If you get tired of dunking, or getting dunked on, as the case may be, the center's also got a game room, a weight room, and an outdoor stage where jazz concerts are held. Down the road is the enormous First Baptist Church of Orlando, referred to as Baptist World by players.

San Lando Park
West Highland and Laura Street
Altamonte Springs

4/2,

The top outdoor run in the Orlando area, north of the city in Altamonte Springs, is at picturesque San Lando Park, a well-paved court boxed in by forested parkland. Games run from 3:30 to 10 on week-

Few follow their shots at San Lando Park

days, and in the summer the top competition, including local NBA and ex-NBA players like Scott Skiles, plays sunrise games at seven in the morning on Sundays when no one else is clogging up the court. If you can pull yourself out of bed, the basketball overdose you'll encounter at San Lando will more than make up for the sleep deprivation.

Also in Orlando Area

Lorna Doone Park, Church and Rio Grande (2/1, 🏀 🔲=3 ◎=3 🏰 🗗 🔆), centrally located near the O-Rena and the Citrus Bowl, has mainly rough half-court games that can be a good tune-up for three-on-three tourneys. It's best not to stop by after sunset, though. At scenic **Lake Cain Marsha Park, Conroy and Lake Turkey Road** (4/2, 🏀 🔲=3 ◎=2 🏰 🗗), the talent isn't great but the arguments are entertaining. Locals with nicknames like Boo-Boo, Poppy, and Blackfoot spout off for hours about every call.

Indoors, the spacious gym at the **Englewood Neighborhood Center, 6123 La Costa** (6/2, 🏀 🔲=5 ◎=3 🏰 $ 🗗 🔆), heats up for evenings games. You can also drive up to Winter Park and check out the springy floor at **Rollins College** or stop by the **Winter Park Community Center, 721 New England** (6/2, 🏠 🔲=2 ◐=3 ⛰️ 🎫), where Floyd keeps the downs list for a mainly adolescent run.

TAMPA—ST. PETERSBURG AREA

Hurley Park
Gulf and 15th
Pass-A-Grille, St. Petersburg Beach

3/1, 🏀 🔲 🔲 🔲 🔲 ◐ ◐ ◐ ◐ 🌴 ♀ 💡

At Hurley, no matter which basket you shoot at, you've got an ocean backdrop; the sparkling waters of the Gulf of Mexico are to the west and calm Boca Ciega Bay laps against the shore to the east. This heavenly locale lures players and beachgoers alike out to the court's location on Pass-a-Grille, a peninsula that extends like a skinny tail from the Florida mainland. The talent level is often pedestrian, but on weekends you'll find serious ballers, as well as serious waits to get on. Willie Braxton, St. Pete's top pickup player, as rated by the *St. Petersburg Times*, no less, runs here and ranks it as the best court in the area.

When you're done playing, jump in the ocean across the street to cool down and then buy a Mello Yello (the ultimate southern drink) at the soda machine next to the court. If you're more into watching than playing, head out early on a Sunday, catch a classy breakfast at the Sea Horse restaurant, and bring your lawn chair.

Also in Tampa–St. Pete

In Tampa, rough games and physical play predominate at **Riverfront Park, 1000 North Boulevard** (5/2, 🏠 🔲=3 ◐=3 ⛰️ 🚫 💡), just west of Hillsborough River. If you can play at the Front, you can play anywhere. **Drew Playground, Cordelia and Tampania** (4/2, 🏠 🔲=3 ◐=2 ⛰️ 🎫 💡), near the Big Sombrero, has lit runs into the night and a cool wall mural of a guy dunking.

In Northeast Tampa, the slew of outdoor courts at the **University of South Florida** gets busy every afternoon around 6 p.m., when USF team players mix it up with local talent. In the winter, offseason baseball players like Fred McGriff drop in on the runs as well. In Sadie, just east of Tampa, the USF players also hit the courts at **Sadie Park, 510 East Sadie Street** (8/4,  ▣=4 ●=4 🔊 ☞ 🅰 ☀), a top run that attracts the best local high schoolers. According to locals, Orlando Magic forward-turned-broadcaster Jeff Turner also makes an occasional appearance.

In St. Pete, **Roberts Community Center, 50th and 12th Street N.** (2/1, ▤ ▣=3 ●=3 🔊), and **Southwest Recreation Center, 131st Street and Vonn Road** (4/2, ▤ ▣=3 ●=3 🔊 🅰 ☀), have both indoor and outdoor facilities, but a better indoor run can be found to the north at **Long Recreation Center, 1501 North Belcher** (6/3, ▤ ▣=4 ●=3 🔊 $ ☞ ♀), in Clearwater.

If dunking on people is your thing, check out **Grand Slam USA, Ulmerton and 66th Street** (4/2, ▤ ▣=3 ●=1 🔊 $), where you can rent out courts by the half hour and adjust the rim height on the reinforced baskets. Slamming is not only allowed, it's encouraged. You're best off bringing your own crew to play.

The lights burn till late at Drew Playground

ELSEWHERE IN FLORIDA

The Sixth Man Club

When you have a family and work full time, fitting pickup games into a busy schedule can be a real challenge—you don't have time to wait around an hour to get on, and you don't have time for all the arguing.

Down in Boca Raton, Larry Schner was finding this out the hard way upon moving to town. "When I first came here there was a group of guys who played outdoors at Woodlands Park in the afternoons," Larry says. "The problem was that, when you get older, you can't get out of work to play ball at four-thirty, so I could never get over there. And when I did, the place would already be packed and I couldn't get in a game. So the idea of the Sixth Man Club was born."

The Sixth Man Club, the brainchild of Schner, is a group of Boca ballplayers, aged twenty-nine to forty-five, who gather at local gyms four times a week, all year round, to play no-bullshit basketball. They play games to 140 points by twos and threes, subbing in as they go. The games are fast-paced and competitive—the talent level fluctuates between Division I players like Schner, who played at Northwestern, to devoted pickup players with no organized experience—and there are no disputes or waits for games. Most of the time, the fifteen or so club members who show on any given day (there are 34 total in the club, with others on a waiting list) are in and out of the gym in an hour and a half.

To pay for gym time, club members pay $300 a year in dues, which Schner uses to make "donations" to the gyms. The club, which is set up as a not-for-profit corporation, also holds social events for members and their families. The fraternal atmosphere means that, in between fast breaking and setting picks, the club members can make some valuable connections.

"I never thought basketball was a networking sport," says Sixth Man member Jeff Schner, Larry's younger brother, "but it really is. I make all kinds of connections through basketball." For this wealthy, successful group, these connections are invaluable. "The group started as a place for guys to play ball and it's turned into more than that," Larry says. "Now we have great camaraderie, and we all do business with each other in the area. We've got just about every field covered here in the club."

When the group first started, in 1988, it was easy and inexpensive to rent out gym time. In the ensuing ten years, it's gotten more costly, so the Sixth Man men have found creative ways to deal with the increase. Larry, for example, teaches an "advanced basketball class" at nearby Palm Beach Community College. His "students" consist almost entirely of Sixth Man members, who pay $35 each and get to use the gym twice a week for two hours to play ball. "I've been teaching there so long," Larry says jokingly, "I'm going to be a tenured professor pretty soon."

Boca Raton

In this wealthy coastal community, the well-manicured handle the rock at the **Boca Raton Athletic Club, 1499 Yamato Road** (6/2, 🏠 🔲=4 ●=4 🔒 $ ☞ ♀), where a number of NFL players play in the off-season. The best run is Saturday morning 8–11 a.m., when the competition is a mix of Division I talent, gridiron greats, and lawyers/doctors.

Daytona Beach

In a town whose name is synonymous with spring break, the **Schnebly Recreation Center courts, 1101 North Atlantic Avenue** (6/3, 🏠 🔲=4 ●=3 🌴 ♿), are packed with inebriated college and high school kids during the spring months. The rest of the time they're as deserted as the Chico State library on a Saturday night. Sober studs like Vince Carter and George McCloud, who both grew up in Daytona, used to light up the nets.

For a run that's actually on the beach, head a mile south on Atlantic to the outdoor beach park, where they play half-court on low rims.

Ft. Myers Beach

Take a break from the surf and head to the **Bay Oaks Recreation Center, 2731 Oak Street** (4/2, 🏠 🔲=2 ●=3 🏙 ☞), where they run until 9 p.m. three nights a week.

Gainesville

The two outdoor courts at the **University of Florida** are constantly in use. It's not unusual for forty people to be playing under the lights at 1 a.m.

North Palm Beach

The best players in the area meet for "no blood-no foul" hoops at the **North Palm Beach Community Center, Prosperity Farms and Burns Roads** (6/2, 🏠 ▣=3 ●=3 ⛰ ☞ ♀ 🐾)).

Royal Palm Beach

Regal games run indoors in the spring and summer at **Royal Palm Beach Recreation Center, 100 Sweet Bay Lane** (6/2, 🏠 ▣=4 ●=3 🏢 $ ☞ ♀), one of only a few air-conditioned gyms in the county. The barking you hear is from the Continental Basketball Association's Florida Beachdogs, who practice at the center.

West Palm Beach

The Jewish Community Center, Military and Community Drive (6/2, 🏠 ▣=4 ●=3 $ ☞ ♀) has leagues that range from recreational to college-level, with a circuit for the thirty-six and over crowd as well. Pickup play starts up around five-thirty weekdays. When the weather's too nice to be inside, head to the best local outdoor run, the courts on **Gun Club Boulevard.**

GEORGIA

ATLANTA

Ralph McGill Park
Ralph McGill Boulevard and Butler Street
Atlanta

4/2, 🏀 ▣▣▣▣▣ ●●●● 🏙 🐾 💡

The locals make a day of it at McGill by bringing coolers and their best critiquing skills. If you play, be prepared to argue and be prepared to go hard—this is the best outdoor game in Atlanta. Over the years, Terry Cummings, Dennis Scott, and Magic Johnson have all stopped by.

TALES FROM THE ROAD:
Round the Clock at the Run N' Shoot

Atlanta finds us making a long-awaited pilgrimage to our own personal Mecca, the **Run N' Shoot Athletic Center,** a giant indoor hoops complex in a converted Kmart in south Atlanta that is open twenty-four hours a day. To fully appreciate it, we decide to spend twenty-four hours in a row at the gym.

Monday, 12:00 noon: We arrive, pay our entry fee, throw our stuff in lockers, and head out onto the courts.

Monday, 3:40 p.m.: We finish playing in our first stint of full-court games and sit down with some other players in front of the big-screen TV. Dennis Rodman is the guest on *Oprah* and he is bragging about his carnal knowledge of Madonna. The general feeling among the players present is that he is a fool.

Monday, 4:45 p.m.: After a quick lift in the expansive weight room, we enter our names into the computer list system and play intermittently in full-court games for two hours. The runs are athletic and fast-paced, with plentiful helpings of dunks. The gym hits its peak between 5 and 7 p.m., when approximately 250 players are in attendance; during the daytime, it fluctuated between 75 and 150.

Monday, 8:45 p.m.: After showering, we eat a hearty dinner of Power Bars and Gatorade while watching some of the Sonics-Rockets playoff game on TV (the three of us forced down ten Power Bars during the twenty-four hours). I chat with the guy sitting next to me and he offers some advice on how to clear rebounds. "I tell you, man," he says, "if you put your elbow into the guy's temple when you swing around—well, they won't be grabbing *you* anymore." I smile and make a mental note not to play in any games with this guy.

Tuesday, 1:05 a.m.: Another hour of ballplaying concludes with a game in which my teammates include three Bulls jersey–clad teens representing Rodman, Pippen, and Jordan. Unfortunately, all three shoot like Rodman and we lose badly. Incredibly, there are still close to 200 people in the gym and three full-court games running.

Tuesday, 3:00 a.m.: We shoot around and play some one-on-one. The crowd is starting to thin out, though there's still one full-court game in progress. A man in his twenties approaches me. "Do you know that Christ is your personal savior?" he asks. I look at him and reply, "I'm down with that, but my friend could use some converting," pointing to another member of the Hoops Nation team, in whose direction he heads to harass. At the time, I think this is awfully funny.

Tuesday, 4:15 a.m.: The crowd finally dies down and the gym hits its low point of eight people: the three of us, two guys shooting around, two people on the running track, and a bum sleeping on the bench.

Tuesday, 4:30 a.m.: I talk with one of the joggers, an older black guy with two knee braces who comes in four times a week to run five miles. He says he jogs in the dead of the night because he wants to be able to take his daughter to school in the morning. On the courts, the lone ballplayer is a tall black man with a smooth jumper. I shoot with him and find out that he works at UPS and comes in after working the night shift to get some exercise before sleeping during the day.

Tuesday, 6:49 a.m.: A beautiful orange sunrise glows through the row of front windows, looking much like a giant basketball peering in through the glass panes. The daylight is rejuvenating after a long, dark night.

Tuesday, 9:09 a.m.: The morning games are in full swing. Two women who hope to make the American Basketball League are practicing with a coach on one court while we play groggy, ineffective half-court ball off to the side.

Tuesday, 12:00 noon: We stumble out of the Run n' Shoot after watching the same *Sportscenter* program three times in one morning. The three of us have played a total of 27 hours of basketball. Feeling slightly heroic for surviving the night, we drive to a friend's house and sleep on the floor for a long time, dreams of basketballs filling our heads.

Also in Atlanta

Fulfill all your hooping needs at the **Run N' Shoot Athletic Center, 1959 Stewart Avenue** (15/7, 🏀 ▣=5 ◑=5 🔺 $ ☞ ♀ 🎟).

For rec centers, check out **Adams Park, DeLowe Drive and West Cedar Lane** (4/1, 🏀 ▣=4 ◑=3 🔺 ☞ 🎟), where the court has the NBA three-point line; **Chastain Park, 135 West Weicu Road** (6/1, 🏀 ▣=4 ◑=3 🏠), which was the best pre–Run N' Shoot game in town; and **Grant Park, Park Avenue and Sydney** (4/1, 🏀 ▣=3 ◑=3 🔺 🚫) where a rougher crowd runs using a clock, which has provided the impetus for a routinely ignored sign that declares, "Absolutely no freezing of ball in the last minute of game."

The **Sportslife** chain of athletic clubs has branches all over Atlanta and can satisfy the rampaging ego of any has-been player. Each club with a gym has basketball leagues, and at the conclusion of league seasons there are citywide playoffs and an inter-club All-Star team is chosen. Of the locations, the two best runs are the Stone Mountain club and the Cobb club.

The **Buckhead YMCA, 3424 Roswell Road** (6/2, 🏀 ▣=3 ◑=3 🏠 $ ☞) is near the night life in northern Buckhead (in the summer the area's a continual party) and has good leagues. Saturday mornings at **Oglethorpe University** in north Atlanta a group of ex-collegians play an enjoyable, fundamentally sound pickup game.

Outdoors, **Hammond Park, Hammond and Glenridge Drives,** in north Atlanta gears up on weekends. If the crowd's too noisy, you can head to nearby **Abernathy Park**—just beware of the unfriendly double rims.

SAVANNAH

Lake Mayer Park
Sallie Mood and Montgomery Cross Roads
Savannah

4/2, 🏀 ▣ ▣ ▣ ▣ ◑ ◑ 🏫 🎟 💡

Looking to take the whole family out for the day in Savannah and sneak in some hoops in the process? Look no farther than Lake Mayer.

Skinny-dipping is not recommended in Lake Mayer

Players can get ahead of themselves running the break on the Mayer courts

The basketball courts are in the middle of a recreation area that includes tennis courts, picnic areas, a baseball diamond, a wheelchair-sports court with low rims, a barbecue area, and even a remote-control car racetrack complete with an announcer, electronic timers, and a guy who waters down the track in between races. If you can't interest the kids in any of those activities, then face it, man, you've got some boring kids.

As for basketball, the comp isn't great, but the park atmosphere more than makes up for it. When you're done playing you can jump into the lake to cool off—that is, if you decide not to pay heed to the sign that warns, "Swimming is dangerous, alligators in lake."

Blackshear Complex
Wheaton and Harmon
Savannah

12/6, 🏀 🏀 🏀 🏀 ⚫ ⚫ ⚫ ⚫ 🏙️ 🚫 💡

Players waiting on almost every court contribute to a tournament atmosphere at this aptly named "complex." Locals run full on the court with low rims, and half-court on most of the others. Lazy play is kept to a minimum in the summer by the long waits for games and the swarms of biting sand gnats that fill the air. The bugs have even gained something resembling celebrity status here in Savannah: The local minor-league baseball team is the Savannah Sand Gnats.

ELSEWHERE IN GEORGIA

Athens

The town that produced R.E.M. is home to anything but sleepy games at the gigantic Ramsey Student Activities Center on the campus of the **University of Georgia.** With four full courts to go along with three pools, ten racquetball and squash courts, and a 44-foot climbing wall, if it's the end of the world as we know it, at least the Georgia students will be feeling fine.

Macon

At **Freedom Park, Roff Avenue and Morgan Drive** (2/1🏠=2 ⚫=2 👟 🏀), the runs go from 6:30 p.m. until it gets dark during the summers. A loud German shepherd that lives across the street announces new arrivals.

NORTH CAROLINA

CHARLOTTE

Camp Greene Park
Freedom Drive and Alleghany Street
Charlotte

24/12, 🏀 🔲🔲🔲🔲🔲 ⚫⚫⚫⚫ 🏙️ 🎵

♀ 👟 💡

This sprawling rackfest, erected in 1996, was originally slated to be christened Larry Johnson Park. That changed pretty quick when LJ took his act to New York, so rather than risk naming it George Zidek Park, the city decided on Camp Greene.

Regardless of its moniker, with twelve full courts, one of which is NBA-length and covered, this is the most impressive outdoor park in the country.

Of course, the courts weren't funded just so that pickup players would never have to wait for a game; the complex was built so the city could run summer leagues outside, thereby alleviating the crunch indoors at community centers.

Central Branch YMCA
400 East Moorehead Street
Charlotte

12/5, 🏀 🔲🔲🔲🔲🔲 ⚫⚫⚫⚫⚫ 🏚️ $ 🎵 ♀

YMCAs across the country should aspire to the basketball heights that Charlotte's Central Branch Y has reached. Multiple gyms, a multitude of skilled players, and the occasional visit from pros like Muggsy Bogues and Jeff McInnis, make playing here a joy. And on top of that, one of the regulars is former North Carolina State frequent flyer David Thompson (he's still dunking by the way).

While the top court has a crowd waiting to play and physical runs, the far court, where the older fellas play (including Duffy, a seventy-year-old, goggle-wearing fixture with a mean set shot) has more genteel games. Not a lot of women play, but ex-UNC star Charlotte Smith has been known to stop by.

Also in Charlotte

Before Camp Greene was built, the best, as well as the roughest, outdoor games in Charlotte were at **Tuckaseegee Park, Tuckaseegee Road.** Another good spot for outdoor games is the ingeniously named **Park Road Park, Park Road and Archdale Drive** (8/3, ▦=4 ◗=3 ⛐ ⚑ ☼), where the lights burn for late-night play.

Rather play out of the elements? Head to the awfully sweet gym at **Sugaw Creek Recreation Center, Sugar Creek Road, just north of Hidden Valley Road** (6/2, ▦=3 ◗=3 ⛐ ⚑), in northeast Charlotte. They may be ambivalent about spelling, but there is no confusion about the style of play on the court—take it strong or take it somewhere else. The center also has two outdoor courts.

RALEIGH—DURHAM—CHAPEL HILL

In the Research Triangle, as this area of North Carolina is known, the student centers at **Duke University** and **UNC** have the best ball. If you can infiltrate the Wilbur Card gym at Duke (iron-barred revolving doors from the Dark Ages must be negotiated first) you'll be able to run with alumni and current players during their off-season. If you want a noncollegiate run, check out **Millbrook Exchange Center, 1905 Spring Forest Road** (4/2, ▦=3 ◗=3 ⛰ ⚑), next to the Raleigh fire station, where they have both indoor and outdoor racks. At the **Green Road Community Center,** also in Raleigh, you can attend the Fire and Ice Basketball Camp (remember Chris Corchiani and Rodney Monroe?), held annually in June.

In Durham, woodsy **Morreene Park, Morreene Road and Sherwood Drive** (4/2, 🏠 🔲=3 ●=2 🎒 ☀), is a few minutes from Duke. If you're near Chapel Hill, head to **Carrboro Community Park, Route 54 bypass off Old Fayetteville Road** (4/2, 🏠 🔲=4 ●=2 🎒 ☀), a hidden gem of a court with self-serve lights for night play. Watch out for a smooth white guy they call Mayonnaise.

ELSEWHERE IN NORTH CAROLINA

Wilmington

Michael Jordan grew up in Wilmington playing at the Community Boys Club and the **Martin Luther King Center, 401 South Eighth Street** (2/1, 🏠 🔲=4 ●=3 🏔 ☞ 🔑). When he was young, Mike would sit in a corner at the MLK Center and watch the older guys playing, but by the time he was in high school, the roles were reversed. "Even before he was big, the kids would follow him around, they seemed to sense something about him," said MLK's William Murphy. "I eventually had to ask him to stop playing in the free play, though. Mike played his game above the rim back then as well, and I was afraid he'd get hurt."

In addition to his Airness, Kenny Gattison and Meadowlark Lemon grew up running the floor at the King Center, which still has a top-notch summer league with college and overseas talent. Every August the center hosts the Battle of the Weekend Warriors, a five-on-five tournament that attracts players from South Carolina and Virginia. There's free play at MLK every day year-round, but it's often ratball. For a better game, head to the **University of Carolina–Wilmington,** which has outdoor and indoor courts.

Rocky Mount

The **South Rocky Mount Community Center, 517 Ravenwood Drive** (6/2, 🏠 🔲=3 ●=4 🏔 ☞ 🔑), or "the Gym," as imaginative locals call it, has been a North Carolina proving ground for years, turning out cats like Buck Williams. A rough game, but one that draws college and junior college players.

Greensboro

The noon crew at tiny **Guilford College,** World B. Free's alma mater, runs with near-religious fervor.

SOUTH CAROLINA

COLUMBIA

Xavier McDaniel can be found pushing guys around at the **YMCA, 1420 Sumter Street** (4/2, 🏠 ▣=4 ●=4 ⛰ $ ♀), the best run in town. McDaniel also shows up at **Forest Lake Recreation Center, Wedgefield and Brookfield Roads** (6/2, 🏠 ▣=4 ●=4 ⛰ ☞ 🕯), during the weekday games, as does Tyrone Corbin. If you're not interested in the X-factor, you can check out **Meadowlake Recreation Center, Meadowlakes Drive and Wilson Boulevard** (6/2, 🏠 ▣=3 ●=3 ⛰ 🕯), during the week, or the good Sunday games at North Springs Rec. The outdoor courts at the University of Southern Carolina, which once had the best games in the city, have been torn down. This tragedy caused local boys Hootie and the Blowfish to sing, "I sat back down, had a beer and felt sorry for myself." No time for self-pity fellas, just sneak into the school gym.

The area's best players, including Alex English, used to play full court at **Heathwood Park, Abelia and Cassina Roads** (2/0, 🏠 ▣=3 ●=3 🏚). As has happened in so many places, the noise from the court bothered the residents of this upper-class neighborhood, and they took action. Their solution was to take down one basket on each court, creating two half-courts. Good players still stop by for four-on-four, but the big-time games are gone.

CHARLESTON

The Citadel
Deas Hall
Charleston

12/4, 🏀 ▣ ▣ ▣ ▣ ●●● 🏙 ⚲ 🎟

Crew cuts are mandatory for games here, and you won't find many women playing (as evidenced by those "Save the Males" T-shirts). In theory, Deas is reserved for cadets and their relatives, but about 60 percent of the people who were playing when we swung by weren't from the school. The word is they're pretty lax about letting noncadets get a run in.

Games on the four short courts are played "to twelve if you're with a bunch of Yankees, to eleven if you play with southerners," according to Jeff, the resident gym rat. Gym hours, as they are posted, are "MWF 0600 to 1800 hours, TTh 0730 to 1800 hours, Sat 1200 to 1800 hours, and Sunday 1300 to 1700." At ease.

Also in Charleston

According to etiquette expert Marjabelle Young Stewart, Charleston is the most polite city in the United States. The coastal city has topped her list four times in the last twenty years, and, according to Marjabelle, is "a place of grace and charm and courtesy."

With that in mind, remember to say thank you every time someone dunks on you at the **City Gym, 81 Hagood Avenue** (6/2, 🏀 ▣=3 ●=4 ⛰ $ ⚲ ♀ 🎟), the best run in town. Gym director Wendell Harbour will make sure you follow the long list of gym rules. Fail to comply and you will be reprimanded—the city cannot jeopardize its number one status just because you feel like swearing after making a bad pass.

Over at **James Island Recreation Center, 1088 Quail Drive** (6/2, 🏀 ▣=4 ●=3 🏫 $ 🎟), you'll find an oasis of rudeness amidst all the good manners. The best games are Thursday, Friday, and Saturday afternoons, and they are wonderfully crass trash-talking, brick-shooting affairs.

Abide by the rules of Charleston's City Gym or else

MYRTLE BEACH

Cinema 10 Courts
20th and Kings Highway
Myrtle Beach

2/1,

Bordering Highway 17 and two blocks from the Atlantic Ocean, this court draws a varied mix of locals and tourists slathered in Coppertone. The games are better in the afternoons and at night, when the lights burn late and thirty or forty guys are often still playing at 2 a.m.

Your postgame options are many: You can see a movie at the Cinema 10 across the street, check out the adventure at Safari Golf, or take a dip in the ocean.

Also in Myrtle Beach

When it's cold out, the linoleum at **Pepper Geddings Recreation Center, Oak Street and 33rd Avenue N.** (2/1, 🏠 ▣=2 ◕=3 🏚

$ ☞), is packed. When the sun shines, they move about 50 yards back of the gym to four outdoor racks and two full courts. There's some talent at the **Canal Street Recreation Center, Canal Street** (2/1, 🏛 ⬜=3 ●=3 ⛰ ☞ ♀ 🐕), but as rec center assistant Greg Moody says, "The boys here would rather fight than play sometimes." A midnight basketball league keeps many of these restless youths occupied from May to August.

ELSEWHERE IN SOUTH CAROLINA

Greenville

Park Avenue Gym
Church and Sunflower Streets
Greenville

6/2,

The denizens of the Park Avenue Gym often spend an awful long time above the rim—suspended above the rim that is, climbing imitation rock cliffs with chalk on their hands and ropes attached to carabiners on their belts. The reason for all these Peter Parkers hanging over the hardwood is an outfit called the Upstate Climbing Club, which, with the help of the city of Greenville, has put up indoor rock-climbing walls in the gym.

Not to worry, though, they still ball here on the sweet floor: regular pickup games run at noon on Tuesday and Thursday and there are leagues four days a week. But it's the climbing that sets the gym apart. This might be the cheapest wall in the country ($5 a visit, $3 if you're a member), and it has a couple of climbs with a difficulty rating of 5.12 (climbing ratings go from 1 to 5.15). So if you want to work on your hang time after playing Sunday afternoons (1–4 p.m.), stay and try scaling the wall instead of your opponent's back for a change.

FLAVOR OF THE GAME:
Making the Highlight Reel

Dunks, Swats, and the White Man's Elixir

Dunker's Delight

Once asked to explain dunking, Julius Erving replied, "It's easy once you learn how to fly."

Just fly. Ah, of course, Doc, why didn't we think of that? Well, for those without the benefit of aviation powers, 6'7" frames, and huge hands (Doc had all three), dunking is much more of a challenge. And for those who can already sky, there are always new tricks to learn, because, as Clark Gable said to Claudette Colbert in *It Happened One Night*, "Say, where'd you learn to dunk, in finishing school? Dunking's an art."

UPGRADING YOUR DUNKS

A dunk can be many things. For some players, it is an act of domination; they thunder home a two-handed monster slam on a helpless defender while letting out a Tarzan yell. For others, it's free-form jazz improv in the air; a series of twists and turns concluding in a graceful stuff. Still others see it as their personal Mt. Everest, an unreachable goal they spend years trying to attain.

If you have scaled that mountain and can throw down, you might as well do so with some flair; the whole raison d'etre of the dunk is to add flash. Anyone who's watched an NBA game has seen the usual array of jams—tomahawk, windmill, one-handed punch, two-handed reverse, etc. If you really want to bring down the house, try one of the following rare breeds of dunks.

1. The self-toss. If you get the ball on a breakaway, try tossing the ball to yourself and then pounding it home; it's a risky move but looks awfully smooth if converted. The toss can be done off the backboard or with the under-the-arm scoop (Isiah Thomas used to do this, only he'd lay it in). If you bank it off the board and then dunk it over someone, consider yourself automatically entered into the Dunkers' Hall of Fame. While you're there, say hi to Harold Miner and ask him what happened to the rest of his game.

2. The double alley-oop. This doesn't require a surfeit of jumping ability, just exquisite timing. To execute correctly, the player bringing the ball up the court tosses it from about the three-point line to a player cutting baseline, the same way as a usual alley-oop. Instead of dunking it, the second player catches it and, in the same motion, tosses it back in front of the basket. The initial passer thunders down the lane, takes off, and rams in the still-airborne ball with two hands. Pull it off successfully and fellas will be running out of the gym yelling.

3. The behind-the-back-pass alley-oop. This dunk is more about the pass than the dunk. The passer starts at the top of the key and dribbles to his right. The dunker starts on either side, goes backdoor, elevates, receives the alley-oop and slams it in. This takes not only perfect timing but a truly smooth-passing point guard. It also usually takes about a year

The behind-the-back alley oop: not for beginners

to perfect. If this dunk doesn't sound too realistic, consider this: A Hoop-It-Up employee wrote an article a few years back in which he described a championship game where, on game point, a player threw the behind-the-back alley-oop from the three-pont line to his cutting teammate, who caught it and threw it down on NBAer David Wingate to win the game.

4. The three-point-line takeoff, somersault-above-the-rim dunk. This is easiest to do if you hit the turbo button as you approach the basket. If you're controlling a good player, he might go flying up and come back down with fire trailing from his heels. Of course, this dunk can only be done in the comfort of your own living room using a video game system while playing old-school NBA Jam, but it sure feels good to do it.

DUNKING ETIQUETTE

There are a few rules that should always be followed when dunking:

1. If you can't dunk with no one guarding you, don't try it in the game—few things are as embarrassing as getting hung (when the ball is swung straight into the front of the rim with a resounding thud). Besides almost breaking your elbow, it kills your field-goal percentage.
2. Never dunk on women, unless, à la Lisa Leslie, they just dunked on you. In that case, it's time to hang up your sneakers, smile real big, and offer to be that girl's agent, because she's going places.
3. Do your pull-ups at the gym, not on the rim. It's no fun playing on rims that are bent down at 45-degree angles because kids have been playing monkey bars on them.
4. If you're playing on low rims and you dunk it, don't gloat. Remember, Shawn Kemp can gloat because he can float. If you're rising 20 inches to jam on an eight-foot rim, think of yourself as Gheorge Muresan dunking—do you ever see him gloat? Then again, have you ever seen Muresan rise 20 inches?

TIPS FOR THE DUNKING-IMPAIRED

Scott Skiles, the square-jawed former Magic guard, was once asked why he never dunked in games. He reportedly replied, "Because they don't pay me to dunk." For all those Woody Harrelsons out there who applaud Skiles's statement or have found themselves repeating the mantra "A dunk's worth the same as a layup," take satisfaction in the fact that the dunk has yet to be elevated to more than two points.

Still, if you're interested in making the jam part of your arsenal but, like Woody, can't quite get up high enough to throw down, here are some tips:

1. Take inventory. First off, determine whether you're a better leaper off two feet (think Michael Finley) or one (think Brent Barry). Two-foot dunking is more explosive and easier to do close to the basket, while one-foot dunking is better suited for breakaways and long takeoffs. Once you know your strength, you can practice accordingly. If, after thinking about it real hard for a while, you come to the conclusion that you are neither a one- nor a two-foot jumper, you can skip this section.

2. Use a good ball. Palming the ball makes dunking much easier, and certain balls are easier to palm than others, so get yourself a good one. (The Spalding Ultimate Indoor is just about the easiest.) It's also easier to palm playing indoors, where dirt and dust don't make the surface of the ball slippery. If you're really desperate, volleyballs work well. If you need to go to the tennis ball, well ...

3. Scout the court. Baskets vary in height and some surfaces provide more spring than others—concrete gives no lift, asphalt slightly more, rubber floors very little, wood floors a fair amount, and suspended wood floors are like trampolines. Check for breakaway rims; they make things easier and mean you won't be pulling that tendon in your forearm by hanging on the rim. If you've ever done it, you know what I mean; you can't shoot a ball or eat with a fork for a week.

4. Catch and dunk. If you're close but can't quite get it right, practice dunking starting without the ball. You can do this one of three ways. First, try standing at the three-point line and throwing the ball high in the air with backspin (like they always do in the dunk contest before they miss the dunk real bad) so that it lands about where the dotted line is in the key. The resulting bounce should rise above the rim so that a well-timed jump will allow you to go up and then ram the ball in with one hand. A poorly timed jump will make you look silly, after which you can yell out an expletive. The second technique is to toss the ball underhand off the backboard as you approach so that it bounces up in front of the rim. A third method is to have a friend (preferably one with a lot of patience) throw you alley-oops.

If you need more than tips, you need hops; maybe the following sounds familiar. . . .

White Man's Elixir

Sit up late at night watching cable TV too much and you will see them, their smiling faces and 800-numbers peering out at you from the tube. They will bombard you with fancy claims of how you can make money so fast your wallet will explode, or how you can gain confidence and "personal power" by simply listening to audiotapes. At 3 a.m., when the brain's a bit hazy, you often wonder if this stuff actually works. . . .

Well, in the world of basketball, the equivalent of these get-rich-quick schemes come in the form of the ads in the back of basketball magazines. You're innocently thumbing through, checking out the pictures of nasty dunks, when the headlines grab you by your skinny Caucasian neck and yell at you, "Get your white ass off the couch and order this video so that you can jump 15 inches higher and dunk on your pimply friend all day long!"

These ads, for products with names like "Air Alert II" and "Maximum Rise," promise incredible results. "Increase your vertical jump up to 6 to 12 inches and have monster calves," one promises. "Soar 8 to 12 inches higher. Play high above the rim," another promises. A third, replete with a picture of Spud Webb, who you know has never worn these clunky things, asks, "Who else wants to jump 5 to 10 inches higher?"

One gives personal claims to back up its assertions, though the grammar is questionable (and if A. Haussling is excited about 11 inches of vert, he's in trouble):

I'm writing to tell you that your program works. I have dunked over two of our towns [sic] top players.

—Richard Silva, California

My vertical leap has increased to 11 inches! Thank you very much!   —A. Haussling, Lovettsville, Virginia

With all these beguiling assertions, the question is the same one that plagues you during those info-mercials: "Do these things work?"

Answer: These gizmos and training "secrets" can help you increase your jumping ability, but only if you put in many long, hard hours of training.

The "systems" advertised fall into three categories:

1. Plyometrics. The idea here is to work the leg muscles with exercises such as lunges and box jumps.
2. Platform shoes. By wearing a big platform in the front of your shoe, you transfer all your weight to the calves, which allows you to isolate the jumping muscles.
3. Resistance machines. These are various contraptions that load the body with weight so that jumping is more difficult.

The theory behind all of these systems (besides for their promoters to get filthy rich off of suckers) is that if you make jumping harder than it usually is, the muscle will respond by reacting faster. The glorified "fast twitch" muscle fibers will then fire quicker, propelling you higher.

If you want to jump higher, you can invest in some of these programs or shoes, but none will do diddly-squat for you unless you spend a lot of time jumping around in them. This, it must be stressed, is no fun at all.

Here's a recommendation for those who are interested in work-

Desperately seeking hops

ing on their jumping and dunking and don't feel like clomping around in oversize moccasins: dunk hoops. If you can't dunk on a 10-footer, head down to the low rims at your local elementary school with a couple friends and spend an afternoon playing dunk ball. It's a lot of fun, and it accustoms you to dunking. To increase jumping ability, try drop-stepping and dunking the ball with two hands repeatedly until you can't do it anymore. Then do it again until you pass out or throw up, whichever comes first. Practice this long enough, and you will be able to dunk on your pimply friend as much as you want—especially if you take him down to the elementary school with you.

Swats and Steals—Playground Defense

Defense—it is what makes champions. You always see those quotes from NBA coaches hyping defense—you know, something like "Our focus is on the defensive end of the floor, defense wins championships." This can be loosely interpreted as "I don't have anyone on my team who can shoot outside of four feet, so we better play D or we're gonna get our asses whupped." In some select cases, the coach does have someone who can shoot, and is actually interested in playing defense. This is not a coach you would like to play for.

In pickup ball, defense looks nothing like it does in the organized game. You remember how your high school coach always told you to get in your stance and move your feet? You'd be sliding across the gym floor in practice in that painful bow-legged position ("Like sitting in a chair," Coach would explain), frantically waving your arms in a motion similar to washing windows while Coach barked out commands like "Left," "Right," "Switch," "Shot," and "Get your butt down, Leroy!" Well, don't worry about that on the pickup court. The key to playing defense in pickup ball is to use your hands, not your feet. Besides, if you suddenly get into your stance during a pickup game, your playground teammates will probably think you've heard gunshots.

Here, for the beginning pickup player, are the keys to defense on the playground:

#1. Matador Defense: Pretend Your Man Is a Bull (the Animal, Not the Team).

The key to being a bullfighter is to get that bull to blow right by you without running into you and goring you to death. Use the same theory on the court. When your man makes a crossover and goes around you, don't worry about moving your feet and blocking his path of movement—you could risk pulling a muscle or taking a charge! Instead, allow him to go by you and then reach around from the back with your hand and poke the ball loose through the crook of his elbow. In organized play this strategy is referred to as "reaching in" and often results in a foul being called. On the playground, it can often lead to a layup on the other end. Once you knock the ball loose, sprint the other direction and hope one of your teammates recovers the ball and passes it to you. If you don't knock the ball out of your opponent's hands, don't worry, just sprint to the other end of the court anyway; your teammates can play defense just fine without you. You will then be in great position for the second rule of pickup defense. . . .

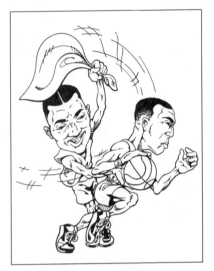

Ole! Matador defense at its finest

#2. The Art of Cherry-picking: Go Searching for Fruit.

Cherry-picking, also known as snowbirding, is the practice of hanging out around the opponent's basket after your team scores or misses a shot. While the other four members of your team hustle back on defense, you can slyly wait at the other team's basket. This way, after they play four-on-five defense, if they are successful in stopping the other team, you can hoist your arms in the air and yell loudly, something like "Throw it," "Down," or "Hey, fellas!" If one of them sees you (and forgives you for not playing defense) he will rifle a one-handed baseball pass to you the length of the court. Easy two points.

Cherry-picking serves three distinct purposes. Number one, it produces some easy layups for your team. Number two, and more important, it allows you to rest and avoid wasting precious energy playing defense. Number three, it makes everyone hate you. But hey, you gotta decide if the benefits outweigh the risk (no one liked Rick Barry, and he was pretty good).

#3. Blocking Shots: Go for the Glory.

Nothing looks more impressive than swatting a shot into the first row of the stands or pinning the ball against the backboard. Dunks are nice and all, but it is the blocked shot that is often the most impressive display in basketball—an emphatic statement on the order of "You might be able to shoot that weak-ass jump hook on your Nerf hoop, but you will *not* be shooting it in my house."

Now, if you play good "fundamental" defense, you will not get many opportunities to spike the ball off your opponent's forehead. Fundamental defense teaches you to stay near your man and to keep your feet on the floor so you won't get duped by pump fakes. Forget that. If you're gonna get some rejections, you need to play continuous help defense and jump around like a pogo stick. Your man is of no consequence—feel free to leave him and chase the ball around. No

The Pancake Swat

one's going to pass the ball on the playground anyway. Coming over on double teams and timing your leap correctly, you can smack away the shot of many an unsuspecting sap.

If you do get your paw on the shot, don't hold back, either, send that thing off the court with authority. Now, it's true that coaches used to praise Kevin McHale because when he blocked a shot, he would do it softly and in the direction of a teammate, allowing the Celtics to retain possession of the ball. This might be effective, but how often have you seen McHale on an NBA highlight video?

#4. The Ample Cushion: No Respect Given.

If you're worried about your opponent driving by you with a quick first step, just give him the Ample Cushion by playing off at least five feet. This prevents the drive to the hoop (and the embarrassment of being dunked on) by giving your man a wide-open outside shot. If he's a bad shooter, you want him shooting that three-pointer anyway. If he's a good shooter who's used to having a hand in his face, it's possible that by not respecting his shot you will throw him off and he will miss the jumper. (Try saying, "Let him shoot it." Nothing is more infuriating to a good shooter than being disrespected this way.) Of course it's also possible that he will nail eleven consecutive wide-open threes and sit your team down, but, hey, at least you didn't get dunked on.

11
The Great Lakes Region

ILLINOIS, INDIANA, MICHIGAN, MINNESOTA, OHIO, WISCONSIN

The grit of the East Coast game and the finesse of the California game meet here in the middle of the country. From physical Detroit street players to fundamentally sound Indiana spot-up shooters, the game is played with an almost religious zeal all across the region. In many parts pickup players even play defense; especially in Hoosier country where half-court games are often played "loser's outs" to put the emphasis on D.

During our travels, we ran at Sprewell's old haunts in Milwaukee, Hooped-It-Up in Minneapolis, visited Larry Legend's hometown of French Lick, Indiana, and battled with Buckeyes in Columbus. Our week in Chicago was the hottest of the year, with shirt-soaking humidity that had us daydreaming of swimming pools and air-conditioning. We might have been sluggish, but the same couldn't be said for the Chicago street faithful, who played right through the sticky heat.

ILLINOIS

CHICAGO AREA

Along with L.A. and New York City, Chicago is one of the country's true basketball meccas. In the summer months you can't drive five blocks without seeing a game in some park or schoolyard, and in the brutal winters players head inside to one of the nearly 200 city recreation centers. Graduates of the Windy City's streets include NBA stars such as Isiah Thomas, Maurice Cheeks, Tim Hardaway, Mark Aguirre, Juwan Howard, and Nick Anderson, but the city also has plenty of playground legends. The first of them was Nat "Sweetwater" Clifton, who was scooped off the schoolyards in 1950 to become the first black NBA signee, as well as the first NBA player to dunk. Clifton was followed by guys like Billy "The Kid" Harris, "Big Art" Hicks, and Lamarr Mondane, a 5′9″ jumpshooter from the West Side made famous by a Reebok commercial in the late eighties (people would yell "Layup" when he'd shoot from outside). He had such a sweet touch that Isiah Thomas, who ran with Mondane on the playgrounds, once said, "He would pass it, but you'd pass it back because his J was better." In the nineties, Bryan "The King" Leach, a lightning-quick point guard, has ruled the streets.

Lake Shore Driving: A Tour of Chicago Pickup Ball

In the movie *Ferris Bueller's Day Off*, the hero, a teenage class-cutter named Ferris Bueller, skips a day of school in affluent Winnetka and drives south with his friends to Chicago. Ferris spends the day checking out a Cubs game, conning his way into a fancy restaurant, and belting out "Twist and Shout" during a city parade.

Now, had Ferris been a ball player, he would have skipped the parade and Wrigley Park and steered Cameron's sweet ride straight down to Lake Shore Drive, the scenic road that follows the coastline of Lake Michigan through Chicago. For there, on either side of the highway, Ferris would have found the best hoops in Chitown; from the laidback beach ball up north to the ultracompetitive runs on the city's south side, the lake courts attract a diverse assortment of players and spectators.

For hoops junkies with a tendency toward truancy, here then is a guide to the Lake Shore courts.

From Winnetka, head down Green Bay Road to Lake Shore Drive. Cruising south, your first stop is . . .

Foster Beach
Foster Avenue and Lake Michigan
Chicago

2/1,

The court at Foster is a hundred yards from the water, sandwiched between the sunbathers on the beach and the bike path. During the summer, the pavement is packed with the best of Chitown. "They got some good talent over there playing," says Orlando Magic guard Nick Anderson. "That's where a lot of guys went to play: me, Tim Hardaway, Kendall Gill, I could go on."

Part of the allure of the court is that, while the games are physical, the court is safe owing to the on-duty cops who patrol the area and the off-duty ones who play in the games. While they might be public servants, even the off-duty badges don't pass the ball here; the style of play on the court is often of the shoot-first, shoot-second,

Gone balling at the Lake: Bueller? . . . Bueller? . . . Bueller?

pass-never variety. If you grab a board you might as well take it to the hole yourself.

Back in the car and south along the shore, your next stop is . . .

Lincoln Park
2045 North Lincoln Park West
Chicago

4/1,

Lincoln, the lake court where the short, white Bueller would have fit in best, is in a pleasant location just a few blocks from Wrigley Field. The free Lincoln Park Zoo is next door, and a racially mixed crowd gathers on the cramped court. While you're waiting to play, you can check out one of the touch football games on the adjacent grass field. Be aware of whom you're lining up against, though; ex-Bears quarterback Mike Tomczak and Big Ten linemen have been known to drop by to toss around the pigskin.

From Lincoln Park, pass the I-55 interchange and continue down Lake Shore Drive to the East Oakwood Boulevard exit and the most scenic of the courts . . .

43rd Street Courts
East Oakwood Boulevard exit
Chicago

8/2,

To your east, Lake Michigan splashes against the rocky shore, while to the north across the water there's an incredible view of the downtown skyline, the Sears Tower jutting up above the rest like Gheorghe Muresan in a Wizards team photo. On occasion the games are good, but it's predominantly hackers playing games of 21. Though it looks like a nice area, be aware that it can be dangerous after dark (as can all the South Side courts).

Next up as you progress south are the **49th Street courts, South Cornell Avenue and East 47th Drive** (2/1, ▦ ▣=2 ◉=2 ⛰ ⤵),

The Chitown skyline looms over the action at 43rd Street

probably the lowest-caliber game of the lake courts. Take the 47th Street exit off of Lake Shore Drive to reach the blacktop.

Heading farther south, get off on the west side of Lake Shore Drive to reach the crown jewel of the lake courts . . .

Jackson Park
South Coast Guard and East Hayes Drive near 67th Street
Chicago

4/2,

July weekends here have that DJ Jazzy Jeff and Fresh Prince "Summertime" feel to them; vendors sell T-shirts, music blares from parked cars, families picnic on the grass, and the venerable "Pops" grills up a storm on his barbecue. On the court, locals get grilled up by studs like Antoine Walker, Tim Hardaway, Nick Anderson, Rickey Green, and members of the Bulls. Every once in a while, though, even the pros feel the heat: "I've seen Scottie Pippen get dunked on out here just like everybody else," claims park veteran Eric "Sky" Walker.

Sorting out the truth from the fiction can be a bit tough at Jackson, but not as tough as getting on the single court used to be. Fortunately, the city installed a second court in 1995 and things are moving quicker now.

Finally, off East 77th Street, two sets of courts await players at **Rainbow Beach, South Shore Drive and East 77th Street** (6/3, =3 =3). The northern courts are used mainly for warming up. The serious games are played on the fenced-in courts at the south end of the park.

Franklin Park Recreation Center
4320 West 15th Street
Chicago

6/2,

Mark Aguirre spent his younger, slimmer days playing at Franklin Park, the West Side's best indoor run. More recently, Kevin Garnett,

Stephon Marbury, and Ronnie Fields could be found getting crazy at Franklin. Garnett and Marbury, who was in town for a tourney, played together for the first time at Franklin Park, executing a thunderously successful alley-oop the first time down the floor. Unfortunately, the games aren't the only craziness in this neighborhood; gangs control the streets and straying from the safe haven of the rec center can be dangerous.

Nevertheless, making the trip can be rewarding; come down to play or watch on weeknights and you're likely to see the type of dunks normally found only on *Sportscenter*. Basketball director Cliff Manning gave us the play-by-play of one such jam when we stopped by. "A couple nights ago in a game a defender had grabbed a rebound above the rim with two hands," Manning said, "and this guy Bink went up, grabbed it with one hand—the other guy was still holding it—and then stuffed it back in. He had like his *elbow* in the rim. People were running out of the gym yelling."

Oz Park
Webster and Lincoln Avenues
Central Chicago

4/1,

You have to box out the Tin Man and stuff the Scarecrow if you want to be the wizard of Oz Park, a solid run in central Chicago. A safe area and competitive games make this a good court for out-of-towners. If you can weasel your way in, the private **St. Vincent DePaul Center** gym next door has indoor facilities.

Hoops—the Gym
1001 West Washington Boulevard
Downtown Chicago

2/1,

Hoops—the Gym is the ultimate in exclusivity, a rental-only facility in downtown Chicago where traders, bankers, and others with heavy wallets can, as the facility motto encourages, "play with who you want, when you want." Opened in July 1992, Hoops provides one skinny court for $90/hour rentals, any time of the day or night you want to reserve it. Those who have stopped by include Mayor Daley, Oprah Winfrey, R. Kelly, Spike Lee (I didn't know diehard Knicks fans even *played* ball in Chicago), Damon Wayans, and even Michael Jordan himself.

The success of Hoops has prompted the management to open a second, larger facility, called Hoops—the Stadium Club, on the near West Side of Chicago at 1380 W. Randolph Street. The Stadium Club, which opened in October of 1996, boasts three full courts, a summer lunch pickup club, and league play.

Also in Chicago Area

For summertime outdoor ball, the lakeshore courts have the most ambience, but there are plenty of other options. The courts at **Washington Park, East 57th Street and Martin Luther King Drive** (16/4, 🏀 🔲=3 ●=3 ⛰ ∅), are impossible to miss—just look for the sixteen bright orange backboards. The park also has a gym that hosts leagues. For a mostly Hispanic run, check out **Wrightwood Park, West Wrightwood and North Greenview Avenues** (8/2, 🏀 🔲=2 ●=2 ⛰), where everybody seems to have good handles and the "big men" are six feet tall. On the northside, a diverse crowd gathers at the **Wrigley Field courts, School Street and Seminary Avenue** (6/2, 🏀 🔲=3 ●=3 ⛰), four blocks south of the Cubs' ivy-covered stadium. If the arguing gets to be excessive, "Coach," an omnipresent old white guy, will intervene.

Across the street from the infamous **Cabrini Green Housing Projects,** strong summer leagues are held on the four lit outdoor courts. Hoop Dreamer William Gates grew up playing here and still plays in the leagues. If you go, stick to the courts, unless you want to risk meeting a real-life Candyman over at the projects.

When the interminable Chicago winter starts up, head to one of the 187 city rec centers. One of the most visitor-friendly, with leagues, is **Sheil Park, 3505 North Southport Avenue** (6/2, 🏀 🔲=4 ●=3 ⛰ ☞), in the residential area of north central Chicago. One of the most competitive men's leagues in the city runs out of the **Southside YMCA, 6330 Stony Island Avenue** (8/3, 🏠 🖥=4 🌓=4 🏔 $ ☞). Both the Southside and the **New City YMCA, 1515 North Halsted** (4/1, 🏠 🖥=3 🌓=3 🏔 $ ☞ ♀) have solid pickup games as well. The Chicago Pro-Am as well as occasional pickup games run out of the **Keating Center** at the **Illinois Institute of Technology, Michigan Avenue and 31st Street.** Celebrities mix it up with business professionals at the **Lakeshore Athletic Club, 441 North Wabash** (2/1, 🏠 🖥=3 🌓=2 🏔 $), across from the Chicago Sun-Times Building in downtown. They've got decent noon runs to 23 points or 13 minutes.

In the northern suburbs, the best runs are in Evanston at **Northwestern University,** and in Deerfield at the **Multiplex, 491 Lake Cook Road** (6/2, 🏠 🖥=5 🌓=3 🏢 $ ☞ ♀), a health club where the Bulls used to practice. There's also a branch, called the Gold Coast Multiplex, in downtown Chicago.

ELSEWHERE IN ILLINOIS

Peoria

At the **Proctor Center, 309 South Du Sable Street** (4/2, 🏠 🖥=2 🌓=3 🏔 $ ♀ 🦅), locals play year-round in the funky gym and outdoors "until there's ice." For a less volatile run, check out Peoria's **YMCA, 714 Hamilton Boulevard,** or the two nights of open gym weekly at West Peoria's **Franciscan Recreation Complex, Heading and Sterling Avenues.**

Springfield

"All the Abe Lincoln you can stomach" should be this city's slogan. Everything Abe is honored here in Lincoln's birthplace, and you can't help but wonder if the big guy had any game. Were he alive today, he would have ample opportunity to show his skills; with the number of people playing in rec leagues, you'd think this was Springfield, Mass., not Illinois. The city-run adult league averages 90 to 96 teams a season, despite having only one city rec center.

For nonleague play, check out **Fairview Park, 19th Street and Griffiths Avenue** (4/2,  ⊡=2 ●=2 🏠), where adolescents predominate, or similar games south at **Lanphier Park, Converse and Michigan Avenues** (4/2, ⊡=3 ●=2 🏙 💡). When it gets cold, play moves inside to the Lanphier High gym.

INDIANA

INDIANAPOLIS AREA

Ben Davis High
West 10th Street and Girls School Road
Indianapolis

8/4, ⊡ ⊡ ⊡ ⊡ ● ● ● ● ● 🏙 🏀 💡

In setting out to write this book, one of my goals was to find the hard-to-find places you wouldn't think to play ball. Everyone knows there are games at the local high school and college, so the emphasis in this book is not on those games. But Ben Davis is different.

The Ben Davis legend is huge. People who aren't from Indiana talk about the games here, and people in Indianapolis mention it as the only place one need go, a sort of Wal-Mart for hoops. I received a court recommendation about Ben Davis that seemed to cross the line from reality to myth. To paraphrase, "The games are incredible. I once saw a six-foot white guy score all twelve points for a team on three-pointers and dunk on a six-foot-eight guy more than once."

If you visit Ben Davis, apparently beware of this white lightning (though I'm still wondering how he scored all the points on threes and still dunked on a guy—did this mini-Sura take off from the arc?), but more important, bring your game. The four lit full courts keep Indy's best Hoopsiers balling all day and into the night.

Also in Indianapolis Area

For indoor ball in Indianapolis, *Jordan rules*. The **Jordan YMCA, 8400 Westfield Boulevard,** (6/2, ⊡=3 ●=5 🏙 $ 🤙 ♀), that is, where the best talent in the city plays, including ex-Pacer Vern Fleming and his brother, Vic. The Y has good leagues, as does the **Indianapolis Athletic Club, Meridian and Vermont Streets** (4/1, ▨ ▣=3 ◓=3 ⛰ $ ☞), an upscale joint where the geezer factor is high. Up north, the Pacers practice at the **Indiana Basketball Academy, Lakeshore Drive E. and Bauer Drive** (9/2, ▨ ▣=5 ◓=4 🏚 $ ☞ ♀). Started by former Indiana University player Tom Abernethy, the gym has top-of-the-line equipment and is used mainly for leagues and youth play, though there is morning and noon pickup play for members. *Hoosiers* was shot at Butler University's stately **Hinkle Fieldhouse,** where during the summer you can play with the Butler players and practice running the picket fence. Off-season, pros such as Alan Henderson and Reggie Miller light it up at the **National Institute for Fitness, 250 North University Boulevard** (4/1, ▨ ▣=5 ◓=3 ⛰ $ ☞), a great run if you can get in.

Outdoors, **Tarkington Park, 39th and Meridian Streets** (2/1, ▨ ▣=3 ◓=3 ⛰ ⊘) is a busy inner-city park. The asphalt heats up in the summer at **North Central High, 86th Street and Cholla Drive.**

In Beech Grove, a south Indianapolis community, spectators come out in droves to watch the high-flying summer action at **Beech Grove Park, Sherman Avenue and Main Street** (4/2, ▨ ▣=3 ◓=4 ⛰ ⛨). Players from nearby colleges do battle against locals like the Hardell brothers, two spring-loaded court legends with reputed 45-inch vertical leaps.

In Zionsville, a northern suburb, the weekend runs are the best at **Lions Park, East Sycamore and South Elm Streets** (5/1, ▨ ▣=3 ◓=3 🏚 ☀).

ELSEWHERE IN INDIANA

Indiana's devotion to basketball is unmatched. Small towns support their high school squads as if they were soldiers going off to war. You can go to a rural Indiana town and ask anyone—the gas station attendant, the gardener, the lady behind the grocery counter—and they'll tell you about the school's team this coming year. It is the dream of every Indiana native that their little Joey or Jane will grow up to be the next great Hoosier high school hero, and the beauty of the state

TALES FROM THE ROAD:
Hoosier Ball and the Birdman

On our way into Indiana we stop in Terre Haute at Indiana State University, where the basketball tradition is strong, or, more accurately, the Larry Bird tradition is strong—Bird led the Sycamores to the 1979 NCAA championship game. His Boston Connection restaurant pulls travelers off the freeway and he's still one of the main topics of conversation around town. While playing some lackluster three-on-three

In Hoosier country, even the hoops have training wheels

with locals at the ISU gym, one of them, a older fellow known as Doc, tells us about playing in pickup games with Bird. "He never stopped to get a drink of water, he was always playing harder than anyone else out there," Doc tells us. "And Larry did stuff I'd never seen before. If he was boxed out, he'd run behind the basket, come out the other side and grab a rebound. I never knew you could do that."

Doc runs over to the basket and acts out this rebounding trick for us, then hurries back to continue his story. "The first time my friend saw him, he came back and told me, 'I saw the best basketball player I've ever seen today. It was this big, slow white guy. He didn't look good at first, but then he stole our first three inbounds passes.' "

A couple days after playing with Doc, we head off into small-town southern Indiana to check out the Hoosier heartland and visit French Lick, the birthplace of that big slow white guy. The fall colors surround us as we cruise down country roads through the small towns, farmland, and wooded terrain of the Hoosier National Forest.

Progressing deeper into southern Indiana, we eventually come around a curve on Highway 56 and enter French Lick. The town looks much like any number of small towns that dot rural America—squat houses line the road, old guys gather at the local diner, and tired baskets adorn garages—but it *feels* like basketball down here.

We head through French Lick toward neighboring West Baden, passing a giant green sign in the shape of a basketball that says LARRY BIRD BOULEVARD. Up the street is Springs Valley High, which serves both French Lick and Springs Valley. The school's impressive gym, the inside of which is plastered with Birds (his three brothers and sister also starred there) is the home court for the Blackhawks. It is evident that the town is proud of Bird, in part because, unlike many superstars, he hasn't left for greener pastures and still spends his summers at his home in West Baden. Around these parts, he's just a regular guy; we talk to people at the local minimart who say things like "Oh yeah, Larry was in here last week. I haven't seen him today, though."

We find out that Larry grew up playing at tiny Kimball Park, often shooting around until the lights went out and then practicing by passing the ball against a wall in the dark. The park is gone now and Springs Valley Community Park serves as a half-court replacement up Ballard Street, though the bulk of the pickup play now goes on outside **Springs Valley High. Larry Bird Boulevard** (4/2, [icon] [icon]=2 [icon]=2 [icon] [icon]).

Unfortunately, we don't run into Larry while in town, though we do loiter at the minimart for a while in hopes that Larry is running low on milk. No such luck.

has always been that any young kid could become that hero, no matter how small the town he or she hails from. (You've all seen *Hoosiers*, the movie detailing Milan's 1954 championship run. If you haven't, I recommend you go do so right now.) Unfortunately, the recent change of the Indiana high school playoffs from an open format to a size-based class system has muted the dream.

As for pickup, all across the state kids are chucking it up in parks and gyms, pretending that they're Damon Bailey, Larry Bird, or Rick Mount. Here are some recommendations for Indiana's smaller cities.

Anderson

Hoosier Hysteria is in full bloom in Anderson. The Anderson High gym, known as **the Wigwam,** seats 8,998 people—that's nine times the enrollment of the high school and makes it the second largest high school gym in the United States. (Another Indiana school, New Castle, seats 327 more, a sore point with Anderson folks.) The town's faithful pack the gym, too; in 1984 Anderson High sold 5,600 season tickets, more than twice as many as the Indiana Pacers did that season. Courtside seats are passed down through generations like valued heirlooms, and the team's coach has a radio show, a cable TV deal, and a shoe contract.

If you'd rather play than watch, head to the **Geater Recreation Center, West 16th and Lincoln Streets** (6/3, 🏙 ▣=3 ◉=2 ⛰ 🎯 ☀️), down the road.

Bloomington

Play ball in the shadow of God (that's spelled B-O-B K-N-I-G-H-T, for non-Indiana residents) in Bloomington. The HPER student rec center on 7th Street at the **University of Indiana** has sixteen, count 'em, sixteen full courts. Another option is straight south of the campus at **Bryan Park** on Park Avenue.

Evansville

At **Wesselman Park, North Boeke Road and East Iowa Street** (9/4, 🏙 ▣=3 ◉=2 👟), the four lit courts are bordered by a bizarre-looking chip-and-putt golf course. Sprouting out of the grass are over fifty towering light standards that look like a herd of giant parking meters huddled on a golf course.

Jeffersonville

The old Jeff High gym is now the **Nachand Field House, 601 East Court Avenue** (4/2, 🏛 ▣=4 ◉=3 🏪 $ 👓 ♀), a great facility with top-drawer leagues and tough weekend runs. Schoolboy legend Damon Bailey, who hails from Heltonville, to the north, runs summer camps.

Greencastle

A solid group of professors and local businessmen gather every day for a good noon run at **Depauw University.** We were told to beware of "the guy who never showers." Who is he? "Oh, you'll know if he's on the court," said one Depauw veteran.

Muncie

One low rim and friendly local unofficial Muncie historian "Lefty" greet you at **Paul J. Cooley Park, South Mock Avenue and 23rd Street** (2/1, 🏙 ▣=3 ◉=2 👟). A more competitive run can be found at **McCulloch Park,** further north at Broadway and Highland. Occasional Ball Staters show, including Chandler Thompson, the guard who had that really sick dunk against UNLV in the Sweet Sixteen in 1990.

South Bend

For three weeks in April every year, the University of Notre Dame goes basketball crazy as it hosts the Bookstore Basketball Tournament, the world's largest outdoor 5-on-5 hoops tournament. Seven hundred teams—sporting creative team names like "Coach [Digger] Phelps: Oxymoron or Just Moron?"—battle through the elements. In past years, even football has taken a back seat; Notre Dame stars like Joe Montana and Ron Powlus have skipped spring practice to compete.

If you're not feeling Irish, but do feel like fighting, the **Martin Luther King Recreation Center, West Linden and College Streets** (4/2, 🕴️ 🖼️=3 ⬤=2 ⛰️ 🚻 💡), has rough-and-tumble games both indoors and out.

Terre Haute

Practice your fadeaway threes in the two gyms at **Indiana State University.** The north one gets more use, but you need a student ID. In town, your options include the **Charles T. Hyte Community Center, 13th Street and College Avenue** (2/1, 🕴️ 🖼️=4 ⬤=3 ⛰️ $ 🚻), and

A vigilant cow guards the barn hoop in southern Indiana

Oakley Park, Eighth Street and College Avenue (2/1, 🏀 🔲=2 ⬤=2 ⛰ 🎟), down the street next to the fire station.

MICHIGAN

DETROIT AREA

Detroit is not really a city anymore; instead a bunch of suburbs have borrowed the city name "Detroit" to apply to their sports teams. The urban decay and white flight (and we're not talking Rex Chapman here) of the last thirty years have turned the city into a wasteland.

Because of the city's problems, business and recreation have moved out to the northern suburbs of Pontiac, Auburn Hills, Rochester, and Shelby Township. As a result, the "Detroit" Pistons play in Auburn Hills and the "Detroit" Lions in Pontiac.

We spent some time scouting Detroit but found very few places to play, in part because city neighborhoods are taking down rims because of violent incidents on outdoor courts. In nearby Dearborn, for example, the city civic center, which had two full courts, tore them down after someone was shot in a dispute, and the city has reduced almost all its outdoor parks to only a single hoop per court.

The Detroit Basketball Gold Rush

With insufficient public facilities in Detroit, where does a Motor City player find a gym? Well, one person's misfortune is another's day at the bank, and in the last ten years a number of pay-for-play facilities have sprung up to fill the void left by deteriorating public parks. Though the going was easy at first, the market has become glutted with competitors for the basketball dollar, and things have gotten sort of nasty. . . .

It all began back in 1988, when then car salesman Gary Rager came up with an idea and taped a motto to his refrigerator: "Build it and they will come." In 1991, his court of dreams, **Basketball City, 16400 Eastland** (12/6, 🏀 🔲=2 ⬤=4 ⛰ $ 🎟), opened its baskets for business in Roseville, a northern community of Detroit. With six courts open all year until midnight for hoops and only hoops, Gary touched a nerve. That first heady year, he would have 150 people waiting in line to pay $6 for two hours of playing time. This despite the fact that the gym had concrete floors, 55-foot courts, and low ceilings that halted any thoughts of alley-oops or shots outside of 20 feet. The low-quality gym did not deter players because they were starved for a place to play. Realizing the market, Gary went ahead with plans to open up two more complexes, one of which, in Southgate, even has a wood floor.

But where there is money to be made and a good idea, you can bet there are others interested. In the space of five years, seven other basketball facilities opened up in the Detroit area. One can't blame Rager if he feels a bit like Apple Computer when Microsoft Windows got big—this was his idea, and now someone with more money has stolen it, repackaged it, and is enjoying more success. "This was the first one in the country," says Rager, a sturdy, blond man in his forties. "You know how I know? Because I couldn't get insurance at first. I had to try as a skating rink, as a health club. They'd never heard of something like this. Now people come in here, look at the place, and then open one up down the street. Yeah, I'm a little mad."

The object of his ire is Joe Dumars Fieldhouse (see "Also in Detroit"), which has sucked up a lot of Gary's business. Within three years of Basketball City opening, the Pistons star had gone in with local investors to open up an impressive complex in nearby Shelby Township. With its six full courts on wood floors, the Fieldhouse not only was higher quality than Basketball City but could also handle more customers. By 1997, while Rager was losing money on all but his original Basketball City gym, Joe Dumars Fieldhouse was already planning to franchise out.

St. Cecilia's
Burlingame and Livernois Avenues
Detroit

2/1,

If you've ever played in a church league, there are certain memories you probably have of the experience. You know—organized games, cordial players, guys who make the JCC run look tough, that sort of thing. What you probably don't remember is being dunked on and then yelled at by Chris Webber, or having George Gervin light you up for 80-something points.

For veterans of the summer leagues held in the gym at St. Cecilia's Catholic Church in Detroit, Webber's slams and Gervin's finger rolls were a routine humbling experience. You see, since its founding in 1969 by the late Sam Washington, the league at St. Cecilia's has been home to Michigan's finest, including Isiah Thomas, Magic Johnson, Derrick Coleman, Jalen Rose, Maurice Taylor, Webber, and the Iceman.

In a drive-with-the-doors-locked area of Detroit, St. Cecilia's stands out, its towering church spires and pristine facade untouched by graffiti vandals. Walk up the imposing stone stairs to the gym and

The holy ground of St. Cecilia's

you'll be greeted by a sign that reads, "Sports Capital of Detroit." The quality, history, and reputation of the league and gym (we heard about it repeatedly all over the country, often referred to as "that church with crazy games in Detroit") make it hard to argue with this boast.

Now run by Central High coach Dott Wilson and Washington's son, Ron, the league is still going strong. They've got a corporate sponsor and four divisions: fifth through eighth grade, high school, girl's high school, and college-pro. There isn't any real pickup ball per se, but if you want a good show, come watch the summer games. You might find yourself sitting next to any number of recruiters or coaches.

Also in Detroit Area

Down the street from St. Cecilia's, serious inner-city talent plays on the courts at Davidson and Dexter avenues. It's a bad neighborhood though, so take care if you brave a visit.

South of the city, in the sleepy suburb of Wyandotte, a talented crowd plays at **Pulaski Park, Oxford Court and 12th Street** (4/2, ▨ ▣=4 ◉=3 ▦). Watch out for a bearded guy from Ohio they call Vlade (in honor of the plodding NBA seven-footer); he has a nice little rep. Rumor has it that the Fab Five once showed up here to play.

North of the city, in Rochester Hills, Barry Sanders zips around the court on the squishy green surface at **Borden Park, Hamlin Road and John R. Road** (6/3, ▨ ▣=3 ◉=3 ▦). Sanders, along with teammate Herman Moore, also surfaces (and rises; according to the locals he "jumps like crazy") in Shelby Township at **Joe Dumars Fieldhouse, 45300 Mound Road** (16/6, ▨ ▣=5 ◉=4 ▦ $ ☞ ♀). The Fieldhouse is like a basketball version of Chuck E. Cheese; they've got everything from indoor sand volleyball to hockey to an on-site restaurant serving Cajun food. Six hardwood courts fill up in the winter, with college talent playing in both pickup and the leagues. One downside: When it's crowded, you pay by the hour.

For lakefront ball, head once again north of Detroit to Mt. Clemens and the courts at **Metro Beach Metropark, 31300 Metro Parkway** (4/2, ▨ ▣=3 ◉=3 ⚡ ☼). The scenic locale attracts a slew of weekend warriors and their families, up for the day from Detroit.

ELSEWHERE IN MICHIGAN

Ann Arbor

Basketball-crazy kids at the **University of Michigan** have two campus options for playing ball: the Central Campus Recreation Building (CCRB) and the North Campus Recreation Building (NCRB). The CCRB has more courts and slightly better competition, but there's also more arguing. Once you're done imitating the Fab Five, head to the Touchdown Cafe, the local sports bar where the actual Fab Five used to hang out.

Grand Rapids

For indoor play, there's **Hoop City,** an indoor complex currently in the process of moving crosstown, as well as the posh **East Hills Club,**

Few heed the backboard's polite pleadings at MLK Park

1640 East Paris, and **Gus Macker Hoops, 3055 Lake Eastbrook Boulevard** (21/5, 🏠 ▣=3 ⬤=2 🏢 $ ☞ ♀). Outdoors, **Fuller Park** and **G.R.-Jaycees Park** get some use, but the best runs have always been at **Martin Luther King Park, Franklin Street and Fuller Avenue** (10/5, 🏛 ▣=4 ⬤=3 ⛰ Ⓧ), though things have gotten rough in the last ten years. A reliable Sunday-morning crowd shows up, but they're more talk than game these days. The backboards all say, "Play fair stay cool—No trash talk or profanity," but players pay this about as much heed as a three-second call on the playground. Loy Vaught and Sonics twelfth man extraordinaire Steve Scheffler both played here while growing up in Grand Rapids.

Lansing

The best games in town are at Magic's alma mater, **Michigan State.** Before leading the Spartans to the national title, Johnson grew up in Lansing playing with his older brother Larry at the Main Street Elementary School playground. Larry used to play full-court defense on Magic as he brought the ball up the court, which Magic hated at the time but now credits with developing his dribbling skills. The two Johnson brothers would even shovel the court in the winter to continue their battles.

MINNESOTA

MINNEAPOLIS—ST. PAUL

The Twin Cities are less than equal when it comes to hoops. In fact, Minneapolis is almost an only child, though a few decent runs can be found in St. Paul.

Mounds View High School
1900 County Road F
St. Paul

6/3,

When Mounds View High throws open its gym doors on summer nights, swarms of local high school and college players are attracted to the hardwood for nightly runs from 7 to 9 p.m. Between this St. Paul high school and the nearby Bethel College, a Division III school that has summer and spring pickup play, there's almost always a good game to be found in St. Paul. Bethel, which is open to nonstudents, also has a noon run three times a week for the older guys and an extensive summer youth league in which over 1,700 kids participate.

Also in Minneapolis–St. Paul Area

Martin Luther King Park, East 40th Street and Nicollet Avenue S. (6/2, 🏠 ▣=4 ◉=3 ⛰ ☞ 🌙), has both indoor and outdoor courts, daily pickup play, and a women's night on Thursdays. The gym also hosts the women's pro-am. **North Commons Recreation Center, 1801 James Avenue** (4/2, 🏠 ▣=2 ◉=3 ⛰ 🚫), likewise has indoor and outdoor racks, with one low rim on the A court outside. Friday and Saturday nights the center does its part to keep kids off the street with open gym from nine to midnight. Across the street at the **YMCA** the runs are more organized.

Linden Hills Park, 42nd Street and Zenith Avenue S. (4/1, 🏠 ▣=2 ◉=2 ⛰ 💡), is in the residential area near Lake Calhoun and caters to mainly mid-level players. Be careful when driving to the hole: The two metal support poles are inbounds on the baseline and can do wonders for the business of your dentist. A less friendly game goes on at **Loring Park, West Grant and Willow Streets** (2/1, 🏠 ▣=3 ◉=3 ⛰ 🌙 💡), where sideline drinking can cause tempers to flare.

The best competition in town is at the **Arena Club, 600 First Avenue N.** (12/4, 🏠 ▣=5 ◉=4 ⛰ $ ☞ ♀), which is located at the Target Center, den of the Timberwolves. The Arena Club is one of eight gym-equipped branches of the **Northwest Racquet Clubs** in the Minneapolis area. The clubs are open 365 days a year and have discount rates for those ages 19 to 25. Call (612) 546-3453 for more information.

Southwest of Minneapolis in the burb of Eden Prairie, members do battle on the expansive gym floor at the **Flagship Athletic Club, 755 Prairie Center Drive** (14/5, ▣=5 ◉=3 🏢 $ ☞ ♀).

TALES FROM THE ROAD:
Playing Ball at the Mall (of America)

While in Minneapolis, we're scheduled to play in a weekend three-on-three tournament being held in the parking lot of the gargantuan Mall of America, ten minutes south of the city. We head to the shopping center on Friday to check in for the tourney and get a look at this mega-mall.

Entering the shopping complex I am impressed, but the building is not as large as I had expected after hearing all the hype—hype effective enough so that there are numerous families at the mall who have driven or flown long distances to vacation at the Mall of America. That says an awful lot about the people in this country; instead of going to a national park or the beach, they take their vacations to malls. Brochures should say, "Come see shoppers in their natural environment, amidst the Mrs. Fields and streams of tourists waiting to go on amusement rides. Commune with nature in authentic fake wood department store displays and scale the escalators to see the padded peaks of Victoria's Secret. Please keep all young children on leashes."

We hike around the mall for a while and eventually find the sign-in. Because of our late check-in, our team name, instead of the intended Hoops Nation, is the Blue Panthers, a creative choice by the tournament staff. "When they don't give us a name, we just name them a color of Panther," the bored lady at the sign-in informs us. As a result, the divisions are peppered with different Panthers. At least we're not the Pink Panthers.

We make our way back through the glass-roofed Camp Snoopy, an indoor amusement park that resembles a giant greenhouse experiment gone awry; roller coasters, water rides, and at least two hundred thousand screaming kids coexist with excessive vegetation and oversize wooden logs. Barely escaping without being attacked by a crazed parent or a 20-foot-high inflatable Snoopy, we head back to our motel and prepare for our first set of games on Saturday.

Saturday morning we arise, throw back some Power Bars for breakfast (not because we're that serious but because we have nothing else in our cooler that's edible), and make it to the tourney on time. The Mall of America parking lot is jumping; the first morning games are already in progress when we arrive. Hundreds of players are shooting, dribbling, pushing, and shoving on the forty different half-courts that are set up. We are early for our game, so to warm up we run through our three plays in an empty part of the parking lot, using an oil slick as our imaginary basket. The oil slick stands no chance against our ingenious plays (which we had drawn up on a napkin the night before).

Our first day at the tournament is a successful one, but day two is a disaster as our outside shooting percentage plummets when the wind picks up. Our complex offense dissolves into a simpler system whereby whoever has the ball shoots it while the other two players yell at him to pass it. We get thrown around in the paint and bow out in the playoffs. To console ourselves, we sit at a restaurant inside the mall and eat Chinese food and big sticky cinnamon rolls.

ELSEWHERE IN MINNESOTA

Mankato

The big news around here is the annual Weir Hooping three-on-three Basketball Tournament. Held in the parking lot of the Weir Insurance Agency (hence the witty tourney title) in downtown Mankato, the one-day event draws over a hundred teams in boys, girls, and men's divisions.

OHIO

CINCINNATI AREA

Baseball used to be the sport of choice in Cincy, but now the diamonds are empty and the courts are full—maybe Marge Schott has soured all the residents on the former national pastime. Though kids are playing lots of hoops, especially in the inner city, the Queen City lacks one central park where players can congregate.

Oakley Recreation Center Courts
Paxton and Taylor Avenues
Cincinnati

4/2,

The best outdoor run in the Queen City is at Oakley, a central hoops hotspot in a middle-class neighborhood that draws players from all over Cincy. Among the top-level players who show is local legend and ex-Xavier star Stan Kimbrough, who takes advantage of the short court (only 58 feet long) and four-on-four format to dominate the games. Oakley has lights, but because of the neighbors, you have to request to have them turned on (call 321-9320 to do so). The hoops were put up in 1981, replacing the tennis courts that had inhabited the park. Now that's urban renewal!

Blue Ash Recreation Center
4433 Cooper Road
Blue Ash

12/4,

At the Blue Ash Recreation Center, twelve miles north of the city of Cincinnati in the exclusive city of Blue Ash, you can play all the ball you want in an incredible facility for $20 a year. If you live in Blue Ash, that is. For the mere 13,000 lucky ones who do, there is access to what may well be the nicest city rec center in the country.

The center has a pool and a full court outside, and inside you could easily mistake the facilities for a ritzy health club; the complex contains a top-of-the-line fitness room, a swimming pool, racquetball courts, and two gyms. Both gyms have wood floors, six baskets, and two full courts. At least one is open all the time, and there are daily runs at noon and starting again around 4:30 p.m. Sounds pretty good? It is, though the competition suffers because of the strict usage rules (translation: the players are mainly upper class and unathletic). The games are clean and friendly, and the leagues are a little better than the pickup, but the center could use a talent infusion.

Got skills and want to donate a few? If you want to play and aren't a resident or a full-time employee in the city (you must work 35+ hours a week and present a pay stub), you must come as a guest and pay a $5 guest fee. Not bad, but you need to have a friend who (1) lives in Blue Ash, and (2) plays basketball. With the senior-citizen, golf-playing upper-class population that is prevalent in Blue Ash, this is not an easy thing to find.

If you can't get into the gym but got excited by that golf reference, check out the nearby eighteen-hole Blue Ash Public Golf Course, rated as one of the country's top seventy-five municipal courses by *Golf Digest.*

Also in Cincinnati Area

An elderly Oscar Robertson still runs at the **Central Parkway YMCA, Central and Elm Streets** (6/3, 🏚 🖵=3 ⬤=4 🏔 $ ☞), "and he still hates to lose," according to one local. For outdoor runs, the second best in the city is **Hartwell Recreation Center, Vine Street and Galbraith Road** (4/2, 🏚 🖵=2 ⬤=3 🏔 🚹), where two courts sit right up the street from the "Hubcap Daddy of Cincinnati."

CLEVELAND AREA

A recent urban renaissance has transformed Cleveland from a city mentioned in the same breath as Detroit to a city mentioned in the same breath as . . . well, not Detroit anymore, at least. The downtown area, with the Rock and Roll Hall of Fame and a new science museum, the Great Lakes Science Center, is impressive, and the pumping clubs in "the Flats" have revitalized the city nightlife. There's no need for a hoops renaissance, though—the city already has a number of hot spots, both indoor and out.

Rocky River
Hilliard Boulevard and Wagar Road
Rocky River

5/2,

Rocky River is a true anomaly: an organized outdoor game. Hoops junkie Mike McLaren, who should be the poster boy for that old ad slogan "You got the love?," runs daily games on the two slabs using a downs list. For the whole story on Rocky River, see its entry in the country's top five courts in Chapter 3 (page 42).

Luke Easter Park
Dickens Avenue and East 116th Street
Cleveland

8/4,

The four colorful courts at Luke Easter fill up with Cleveland ballers during the summer months. College talent, including diminutive former EMU point guard Earl Boykins, squares off against local studs on the asphalt, which is painted in an eye-pleasing mélange of reds, blues, and greens. Come out early (10 a.m.–1 p.m.) or late (after 6 p.m.) to avoid the afternoon heat and get into the best games. When it's warm out, the surrounding park takes on a festive atmosphere as locals come out for picnics. Beware, though, few things on the court are as distracting as the sweet smell of barbecue.

On the courts, you'll find a fair amount of ratball, but "when the good players show, the games are really good," according to one local.

Everyone's a point guard at Luke Easter Park

Also in Cleveland Area

If you've never had a Reggie Miller experience, you can get the next best thing by entering the **Zone Recreation Center, West 65th Street and Lorain Avenue** (6/2, 🏠 🖵=3 ◉=3 ⛰️ ☞ 🐉), a well-equipped gym that hosts a midnight basketball league. The daily pickup play is populated primarily by prepubecents (try saying that fast five times). On the East Side, bordering the suburbs, the shiny new **Gunning Recreation Center, 16700 Puritas Avenue** (6/2, 🏠 🖵=4 ◉=4 🏢 ☞), attracts players from all over the city and is a highly recommended run.

For a taste of New York in Ohio, head to the eastern burb of Brooklyn, where they run outdoors at **Brooklyn Memorial Park, Memphis Avenue and North Amber** (8/4, ▦ 🖵=4 ◉=3 🏢 💡). The park has some low rims mixed in with the 10 footers. South of Cleveland in Middleburg Heights, the **Omni Athletic Club, 6600 West 130th Street** (6/2, 🏠 🖵=4 ◉=3 🏢 $), has the best health club hoops in the area, while those looking for the campus run can head to **Cleveland State** or one of the campuses of **Cuyahoga Community College** (known as

Tri-C). The east campus has women's ball while the metro campus, right next to Jacobs Field in downtown Cleveland, hosts the Cleveland Pro-Am.

COLUMBUS AREA

JFK Park
Main Street and Davidson Drive
Reynoldsburg

4/2,

Columbus's best make the drive east of the city to Reynoldsburg for the games at JFK Park. The park has two courts (referred to as the CBA court and NBA court by the players), but players stick to the far court, where the rims are a touch low and the wait can be thirty deep on summer weekends. Watch out for a guy named Scoot; he may be a little older, but he knows JFK better than Oliver Stone.

Also in Columbus Area

Near the 315 freeway, **Anterim Park, Olentangy River Road and Greenridge Road** (2/1, ▓ ▣=2 ●=3 🏠 ☀), is the second best outdoor run in the area, after JFK. On the campus of the nation's second largest university, Ohio State, they play outdoors at **the Cages, Hunter and 11th Avenues** (6/3, ▓ ▣=4 ●=3 🏙 ㋐ ☀), and indoors at the **Jesse Owens Recreation Center.**

In the wealthy northern suburb of Worthington, there is preregistered fall pickup play on Monday nights at the **Worthington Community Center, 360 Highland Avenue.** The gym used to have open play, but up to eighty guys would routinely show up, creating mass chaos. Now, only the first thirty-five to register for the season get to play.

WISCONSIN

MILWAUKEE AREA

Ahhh, Milwaukee, the only city in the country that can claim beer as its chief industry. The cheese-heads may reside up the road in Green Bay, and Madison may be partial to a different sort of stimulant, but Milwaukee is a veritable suds fest.

For Milwaukee's Best hoops, tap into Lincoln Park in the north part of town, where gravity-defying Latrell Sprewell grew up living the High Life above the rim. The games on the six outdoor courts have a rich yet smooth flavor, with an abundance of hops. For outdoor ball in the summer, to quote one wise advertising slogan, "It doesn't get any better than this."

Lincoln Park
West Villard and Green Bay Avenues
Milwaukee

12/6,

Lincoln's expanse of courts resides in a suburban area, but the brand of ball is strictly urban. "It was fun playing there coming up as a kid," said park graduate Latrell Sprewell. "A lot of the inner-city kids would go there because the competition was better." Over the years, that competition has included fellow native Terry Porter and Milwaukee Bucks like Todd Day and Lee Mayberry.

Occasionally there are games on all six courts, though often you'll find four full court runs and games of 21 on the other courts. There is a court hierarchy as well. "You get the big boys on this court," Steve, an older, rather rotund hoopster told me while motioning with his hand. "Over there you get the intermediates, on that one you got the nobodies, and on that last one you got the good-for-nothings. That's where I go, over with the good-for-nothings."

No matter which category you fit into, you'll find your niche at Lincoln.

Also in Milwaukee Area

The best indoor games in town are at the **University of Wiscon-sin–Milwaukee,** while the serious youngsters play an organized brand of ball at the **Boys and Girls Club, North Sherman Boule-vard and West Locust Street** (6/2, ▦ ▱=3 ◉=3 ⏶ $ ☞). The Hoops Nation Spelling Bee Award goes to the **Kosciuszko Recre-ation Center, 221 South Seventh Street** (2/1, ▦ ▱=3 ◉=2 ⏶ ⇗⏱), where a largely Hispanic clientele plays on a yellow rubber floor that matches the mustard-colored walls.

In the southern burb of Franklin, head to the **Sports Complex, 6000 West Ryan** (6/2, ▦ ▱=3 ◉=3 ⏤ $ ♀), a monolithic domelike facility that houses hoops in addition to volleyball, indoor soccer, and indoor hockey. Just north in Greendale, the **Greendale Community Center, South 76th Street off Parkview Road** (10/3, ▦ ▱=3 ◉=3 ⏤ ☀), host games for a mainly white crowd. Watch out for a kid with glasses who goes by the nickname Big Dog—he's got a nasty spin move.

ELSEWHERE IN WISCONSIN

Madison

The lakefront courts at **James Madison Park, North Blair and East Gorham Streets** (5/2, ▦ ▱=4 ◉=4 ⏶ ⚡ ⇗⏱ ☀) are the place to be in the summer. The tranquil blue waters of Lake Men-dota—a requisite destination for a postgame dip to clean off the bugs and sweat—are just 40 yards away, and a grassy hillside beckons to sunbathers and family picnickers. If you're checking out the Univer-sity of Wisconsin campus area, get in a game at the campus rec centers known as the Shell and the SERF, and stop for grub at La Bamba's on State Street, where the motto is "Burritos bigger than your head." These plentiful portions will come in handy if you partake of the most popular form of local recreation, smoking ganga (the incomparable Hashfest is held here every summer).

If it's too crowded at James Madison, head over a couple blocks to **Orton Park, Rutledge and South Ingersoll Streets** (2/1, ▦ ▱=3 ◉=3), where a more subdued atmosphere prevails.

12

The Great Plains

IOWA, KANSAS, MISSOURI, NEBRASKA, NORTH DAKOTA, OKLAHOMA, SOUTH DAKOTA

All across mid-America, from the Dike West courts in icy Fargo, North Dakota, to a railroader's game in North Platte, Nebraska, basketball has wormed its way into rural areas. The region's best ball is still played in the major cities—at gyms like Woodson in Oklahoma City and Bell in Kansas City—but more and more you can find a good game off the beaten path. Even in the tiny town of Thornton, Iowa, a city so small it doesn't appear on most maps, you can find a solid run at "the Cage."

Among our discoveries in the heartland, we found out that it's best to play indoors in Oklahoma, the better to protect yourself from spontaneous tornadoes, and that few things in South Dakota are more exciting than the legendary Corn Palace.

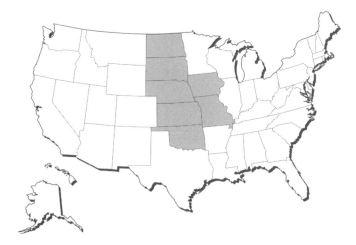

IOWA

IOWA CITY

The Fieldhouse
University of Iowa
Byington Road and Grand Avenue
Iowa City

28/10,

For under- and overage hoopers everywhere, college gyms often seem like forbidden fruit. They have the best facilities and competition in the area, but without an ID card, non students usually can't play. Of course, this rule can always be circumvented with some creativity, but if you want to consistently play at a gym, crawling in through windows or adamantly claiming to be the dean of student affairs can get tiresome.

For this reason, visiting the University of Iowa, where the campus gym is open to all, is a liberating experience. No borrowing of ID cards or entrances through the side door needed—just walk on in to hoops heaven at the Fieldhouse, where two gyms with a total of ten full courts await you. On the courts there is a mix of collegians and area residents and the gym is open from 7:30 a.m. to 10:30 p.m. all week and weekends for basketball only.

The competition encompasses everything from the University of Iowa players who run on the top court to the computer club members who run on court six. Women play with the guys and also have a special "priority for women" rule posted on the wall: If there are eight to nineteen women, they get a court to themselves, twenty to thirty-five women and they get two courts, thirty-six and up, and they get three courts.

So the next time the family is planning a vacation and trying to decide between Disneyland and Hawaii, bring up the stunning beauty of Iowa City. "Iowa City," you can tell your loved ones, "is vastly underrated." Describe to them the benefits of visiting Iowa. "It's near Wisconsin," you can point out, "and, it's in the Central Time Zone."

If that doesn't work, try bribing them—whatever it takes to get yourself to Iowa City for a week of blissful all-day runs.

DES MOINES

Your three basic choices in Des Moines go like this:

Inner-city ball: Hit **Forest Park, Forest Avenue and 16th Street** (4/2, 🏀 📅=4 ◐=3 ⛪ 🎾);
Suburban ball: **Holiday Park, Ninth and Elm Streets** (2/1, 🏀 📅=3 ◐=2 🏢);
Clean indoor ball: **The Riverfront YMCA, 101 Locust** (6/2, 🏀 📅=4 ◐=3 ⛪ $ ☞), its big red sign visible from anywhere in the city

ELSEWHERE IN IOWA

Sioux City

The gym at Division II **Morningside College** is the area's best pickup spot.

Thornton

Weary I-35 travelers take heart, there is something worth stopping for in central Iowa (and it's not those damn bridges down in Madison County). Your tourist destination? Thornton, a tiny town that looks like a rest stop but is home to **the Cage, Main Street and Third Street N. (2/1, 🏀 🔲=3 ●=2 💼 ☞ ☀️).** The aptly named downtown court (fenced in with walls on both sides that are in play during games) hosts a Fireman's Day Tournament every July in addition to daily pickup ball.

KANSAS

KANSAS CITY AREA

For the sake of convenience, both the Kansas and Missouri sides are listed here.

Bell Recreation Center
Rainbow Boulevard and 36th Avenue
Kansas City, Kansas

6/2, 🏀 🔲🔲🔲 ●●●● 🏙️ $ ☞ 👟

In a gym severely lacking in the a/c department, a war takes place every summer in the Bell Recreation Summer Metro League. Jayhawks and local studs go head to head at Bell while players and spectators alike sweat through the stifling heat. Though not a native, NBAer Tony Dumas is a legend around these parts. He went to school nearby at the University of Missouri–Kansas City—where he broke the school record for dunks—and holds the Bell league single-game scoring record, 63 points.

In addition to the summer league, Bell has good pickup games, though be sure to heed the posted rule that states, "No basketball shot may be taken beyond half-court."

Police Station Courts
86th Street and Antioch Road
Overland Park
Kansas City, Kansas

2/1,

Players from all over K.C. converge upon this modest court next to a police station in Overland Park. City players make the drive out to mix with the locals and the "Po-lice" presence keeps everything cool. The result is the best outdoor game in the area.

Also in Kansas City Area

Also in Overland Park, the **Prairie Life Center, 10351 Barkley Road** (6/2, 🏀 ▣=5 ◉=2 🏚 $), a health club that opened in 1995, deserves mention if for no other reason than its street address.

On the Mizzou side, it costs a couple bucks to play at the rec centers, but it's worth it. The **Brush Creek Center, Brush Creek Boulevard and Cleveland Avenue** (6/2, 🏀 ▣=4 ◉=3 ⛰ $ ☞ ♀ 🏃) is close to the city and has leagues for women as well as wheelchair ball. The **Hillcrest Center, 10401 Hillcrest Road** (6/2, 🏀 ▣=4 ◉=3 🏚 $ ☞), a more suburban joint, heats up weekend afternoons. Outdoors, the city kids play at **Parade Park, Truman Road and Woodland Avenue** (4/2, 🏀 ▣=2 ◉=3 ⛰ ⛳ ☀), and **Troost Park, 31st and the Paseo** (3/1, 🏀 ▣=3 ◉=3 ⛰ 🏃 ☀).

ELSEWHERE IN KANSAS

Lawrence

The name of this town might as well be Jayhawk, it is so overrun by **University of Kansas** fever. Obviously, it would behoove you to at least pretend to be a Kansas fan when playing here; it may be hard to get into the gym if you're decked out in Missouri Tigers apparel.

Topeka

Open gym rotates among the city's five rec centers. The **Hillcrest Center, 21st and California** (6/2, 🏀 ▣=4 ◉=4 ⛰ $ ☞ ♀ 🏃), the best of the five, also has leagues galore. Options include women's, over forty, over thirty, 6'2" and under, and a morning league with collegiate talent from nearby Washburn University of Topeka.

Wichita

The best runs in town are at the **Lynette Woodard Recreation Center, 2750 East 18th Street** (2/1, ▓ ▭=3 ◓=3 ☞ ♀ 🐾). The center, which is named after Wichita native Lynette Woodard, the first female Globetrotter, also hosts a top-drawer high school league. Big dogs who've stopped by include Harvey Grant, Xavier McDaniel, and the Big Dog himself, Antoine Carr.

MISSOURI

ST. LOUIS

A. B. Green Middle School
Boland Place and Dale Avenue
St. Louis

4/2, ▓ ▭ ▭ ▭ ◓ ◓ ◓ ◓ 🏠 💡

If you commute home from downtown St. Louis on I-40 west, remember to keep sneaks in the car at all times and be an alert driver. When you come up on the Galleria mall, turn your head left and survey the two lit full courts at A. B. Green (also known as "the forty"), the site of the best summer pickup in St. Louis. If the courts are hopping, you can make a mad three-lane change and take Exit 32 at La Clede Station Road. Drive under the highway, pull up to the school, pop the trunk, and it's "Game on."

You can head down to the sunken court via the wooden steps, or you can make a grand entrance by taking the 50-foot metal slide down (this is a great way to get picked up for nexts). During the summer, both courts are bustling; a mixture of college and top high school players run on one court and hackers and middle school kids play on the other. Players from all parts of St. Louis travel to Green because of the talent, safe atmosphere (it's in the suburban Richmond Heights area), and racial mix. The court load is so high here that nets wear out weekly and many players bring their own. The lights go off at 11 p.m. but devoted souls often keep balling into the night by the erratic illumination of the freeway.

Also in St. Louis

As far as rec centers go, few cities can compete with the wood floors and glass backboards found at most indoor gyms in St. Louis. **West End Recreation Center, Enright Avenue and Union Boulevard** (9/2, 🏠 ▣=4 ●=4 ⛰ ☞ 🎟), has two full courts back to back and stiff comp on Sunday afternoons. **Cherokee Recreation Center, Jefferson Avenue and Wyoming Street** (6/2, 🏠 ▣=4 ●=3 ⛰ ☞ 🎟), has glass backboards and breakaway rims. At the **Dunn-Marquette Recreation Center, 4025 Minnesota** (2/1, 🏠 ▣=3 ●=3 🔒 ☞ 🎟), a peanut gallery of babies watch their baby-sitting dads spring up and down the floor during the afternoon games. **Wohl Recreation Center, North Kings,** and **12th and Park Rec** (which is actually at 12th and Tucker, have grittier games.

The downtown branch is the top **YMCA, 15th and Locust** (4/2, 🏠 ▣=3 ●=3 ⛰ $ ☞), of the fifteen in the area. Suburbanites take to the blacktop at attractive **Willmore Park, Jamieson and Hampton Avenues** (4/2, 🏠 ▣=2 ●=2 🔒), right on the southern boundary of St. Louis. Beware the metal poles between courts—they can Alfred E. Newman unwary players.

ELSEWHERE IN MISSOURI

Columbia

Tigers tussle with local talent and students at Brewer Field House on the campus of the **University of Missouri.**

Jefferson City

Memorial Park, West Main Street and Binder Drive (2/1, 🏠 ▣=2 ●=2 🔒), with its stunning fall colors, is a scenic outdoor spot in

A shadowy showdown at Memorial Park

Missouri's capital. For indoor play, Y not? The **YMCA, 424 Stadium Boulevard** (4/1, 🏛 🖩=3 ●=2 🏭), is right across from the high school.

NEBRASKA

The Pigskin rules supreme here in Huskerland. Driving from Grand Island to Donipher you'll be on the Tom Osborne Expressway, and as you enter Lincoln, it's Cornhusker Highway. In the city of Lincoln alone, there are 66 businesses that use "Husker," "Big Red," or "Cornhusker" in their name. This statewide devotion to one football team is rivaled only by Alabama. Even so, some hoops find their way through the cracks.

TALES FROM THE ROAD:
I've been Balling on the Railroad . . .

Monday morning we leave our motel and make a quick tour of North Platte (city slogan "Live the Adventure!"), a small town in the middle of Nebraska that is dependent on the Union Pacific railroad. "Without Union Pacific," one woman tells us, "we'd be a ghost town."

Not expecting much in the way of hoops, we are pleasantly surprised to find a good run at the North Platte Recreation Center. We enter the gym to see two full-court games in progress, one of which consists of Union Pacific employees, or "railroaders," as they're called. The railroaders receive memberships to the gym courtesy of Union Pacific, and a number of them come in after the midnight–8 a.m. shift to play ball.

The three of us, looking very little like railroaders, watch some of the game from the sideline. Several players eye us suspiciously, possibly thinking we are from management, and one warns us that if we're here for any ulterior motives, "us railroaders stick together." We assure him that we have no devious plans, and that we would never try to come between two railroaders, not even to set a pick.

On our way out, we gather the gym information from the staff at the front desk, who, it turns out, aren't big fans of the railroaders. An older female employee tells us that the Union Pacific crew is, well, a little uncouth. "They're a bunch of potty-mouths," she says emphatically. "Put that in your book."

OMAHA

Somewhere in middle America, the best players participate in the leagues at the **Butler-Gast YMCA, 3501 Ames Avenue** (6/2, 🏠 ▣=4 ◗=4 ⛰ $ ♀), and at **Creighton University.** When both rims are up, **Saddle Creek Park, Saddle Creek Road and Hickory Street** (2/1, 🏢 ▣=2 ◗=3 ⛰ 🚫) gets crowded in the afternoons. At the

Westroads Athletic Club, 1212 North 102nd Street (4/2, 🏠 🔲=3 ●=3 🧺 $), there'll be no free towels acquired—they have those Nordstrom-style plastic antitheft tags on them.

West of Omaha, at West Dodge and 132nd Streets, a daily faculty game persists in the rec gym at **Boys Town,** a home for neglected children made famous by the 1938 Spencer Tracy movie of the same name.

ELSEWHERE IN NEBRASKA

Lincoln
Do your best Jordan at **Air Park, S.W. 46th Street,** or join in Cornhusker fever at the eight courts in the rec center at the **University of Nebraska.**

North Platte
Noon runs are best at the **North Platte Recreation Center, 1300 South McDonald Road** (5/2, 🏠 🔲=3 ●=2 👋 $).

NORTH DAKOTA

FARGO

The Dike West Courts
Fourth Street S. and Fifth Avenue
Fargo

6/3, 🏠 🔲🔲🔲🔲 ●●●● 🏙 ♀ 💡

For a little ice-dishing, take your passing skills just east of downtown to the Dike West courts, frigid Fargo's summer hotspot. Players from North Dakota State and Moorehead State run, as well as the occasional Fargo-Moorehead Bee, the local IBA team that draws big in the winters. The adjustable rims on the main court have definitely been adjusted, to a comfy height of 9½ feet, and the people are "real friendly-like," as the locals would say.

The stifling cold in the winter months sends people indoors to **Courts Plus, 3491 S. University Drive** (12/4, 🏠 ⬜=4 ⚫=3 🛗 $ 🕸 ♀), a pay-for-play facility in south Fargo.

BISMARCK

Family YMCA
1608 North Washington
Bismarck

6/2, 🏀 🔲 🔲 🔲 🔲 🔲 ⚫⚫⚫ 🏙️ $ 🕸

Smack dab in the middle of North Dakota, Bismarck is not much of a tourist destination, but if you do head into town, make sure to find time to play at the top-notch YMCA. The Y has two gyms, the better of which has a regulation-length court, glass backboards, breakaway rims, and a suspended wood floor padded with rubber cushioning. The best games are from 11 a.m. to 1 p.m. daily.

A second, less luxurious, Bismarck option is the **World War Memorial Recreation Center, 215 North Sixth.**

ELSEWHERE IN NORTH DAKOTA

Minot

If you are in town, you can play at the **Minot Family YMCA, 105 First Street S.E.** (6/2, 🏠 ⬜=4 ⚫=2 🛗 $ 🕸 ♀). Pickup play runs daily from 11:30 a.m. to 1:30 p.m.

OKLAHOMA

OKLAHOMA CITY AREA

Woodson Park Gymnasium
3403 South May
Oklahoma City

6/1,

Play on the well-polished hardwood at Woodson and you'll get the chance to run with local college players and pros like Byron Houston and Greg Sutton. Come on the right day, and you might even run with R&B crooner R. Kelly, who stops by when in town.

"When he's here, man, the whole stands, they're filled with ladies," gym director Chris Hamilton says. "I feel like we need security or something, there are so many girls here to watch him."

With this kind of pressure, none of the homies want to get burned by Mr. Kelly, so the defense picks up a notch. "It's funny, all the guys are up on him trying to check him real hard like he's a baller or some-

Shorties making the most of their court time at Chitwood Park

TALES FROM THE ROAD:
Twistin' Through Oklahoma

Ahhh, Oklahoma. For peaceful, relaxing days and nights, you can't beat this state and its completely normal people and beautiful weather. Sarcasm, you say? Read on.

On our first day in Oklahoma we pick up the local paper to see this interesting news tidbit: "Cameron Lee Smith, 33, was arrested at his rooming house in Norman, Okla., on suspicion of first-degree murder after police accused him of beheading his neighbor and walking naked to a trash bin to throw out the head."

You see? Completely understandable behavior. In fact, the three of us agree that were we to decapitate someone, the only really comfortable way to dispose of the messy head would be to do it in the buff.

With this inspiration, we scout courts in Tulsa, playing some outdoor ball at the BC Franklin Recreation Center. Afterward, we watch part of the Sonics-Jazz game, on which there is superimposed a little "tornado watch" graphic. Not thinking much of it, we head south and drive to Oklahoma City in the late afternoon. "I never understand how people get caught in tornadoes," my friend Eric says. "All you have to do is get in your car and outrun the thing—how hard can that be?"

As we approach Oklahoma City around seven o'clock, it starts raining. The rain soon turns to hail and is accompanied by strong winds, which would cause problems for most cars, but not for our formidable Chevy van. By seven-thirty the hail has become dangerous and the combination of precipitation and wind is forcing cars to pull off the road, including our now cowering Chevy van. The hail is threatening to break the windshield glass, water is starting to come in through the door openings, and the trees on the side of the road are whipping around like blades of grass in the strong gusts. We pull over, joining the rest of the traffic underneath one of the concrete overpasses.

Turning on the radio we hear Gary England of the Channel 9 newsroom giving "severe weather coverage." Gary is alerting listeners to tornado watches for the Oklahoma City area while describing "softball-sized" hail and using exciting terminology like "storm walls," "meso-cyclones," and "funnel clouds." He instructs people to proceed to the lowest level of their house, get inside a bathtub, and cover their face with a blanket. Seeing as we are in a van in the middle of the highway, this is not particularly practical advice or comforting news.

While the winds are gusting and Gary is talking, I notice a family in a brown station wagon getting out of their car and hurriedly climbing up into the armpit of the concrete overpass to take shelter. If that sight didn't do the trick, our confidence is shattered for good when Gary warns, "Take shelter immediately and do not, I repeat, *do not* try to get in your car and outrun a tornado."

Eric looks a bit disappointed as we get down on the floor of the van, cover our heads with our hands, and hope for the best.

Ten long minutes later, I peek out the window and see that the clouds are moving the other direction. The tornado decided not to touch down on us, and within a few minutes the sky has cleared and a rainbow fights its way through the smoke-colored clouds. With the storm watch still in effect, we decide it would be neither smart nor fun to check into our campsite right away, so we do the only logical thing and head to a theater to see the movie *Twister*.

---

thing," Hamilton explains. "I mean, he's a'ight, but he's just trying to get some exercise and our boys are all over him making sure they don't get used."

If you miss R. Kelly's ladies, don't fret; big crowds also come out for the center's March tournament, which draws over fifty teams from Oklahoma and neighboring states. For pickup play, the best summer runs are 1–4 p.m. and 6:30–10 p.m. during the week. Saturdays, the fellas play from 10 a.m. to 2 p.m. If no one's balling at Woodson, head to **Municipal Gym** on N.W. Eighth Street, where the same crowd plays.

Also in Oklahoma City Area

North of the city in Edmond, suburban **Chitwood Park, Story and First Streets** (2/1, 🏀 🔲=3 ●=3 🏠), draws a good summer crowd. Check out the funky nets that look like bike locks hanging from a rim.

ELSEWHERE IN OKLAHOMA

Ardmore

The white kids play at the **YMCA, 15th Avenue N.W. and Meadow** (12/4, 🏀 🔲=4 ●=2 📭 $), while the brothers rip it up outdoors on Friday nights at the **H. F. V. Wilson Community Center, 625 East Main** (2/1, 🏀 🔲=2 ●=3 ⛰️ 🏀 💡).

Tulsa

Big-leaguers like Lee Mayberry, John Starks, Wayman Tisdale, and Anthony "Triple Double" Bowie all played at **BC Franklin Recreation Center, 1818 East Virgin Street** (2/1, 🏀 🔲=3 ●=4 ⛰️ 🏀), while growing up in the area. A bring-the-kids-and-the-Frisbee atmosphere prevails at **McClure Park, 73 East Avenue and East Seventh Street,** which, like all Tulsa rec centers, isn't open on weekends.

SOUTH DAKOTA

SIOUX FALLS

Steady runs can be found at the **Kenny Anderson Recreation Center, 3701 East Third Street** (6/2, 🏀 🔲=4 ●=3 📭 ☞), in Sioux Falls. If you thought Kenny Anderson grew up playing ball in New York, not South Dakota, don't worry, you haven't lost your mind. This gym was named after the Sioux Falls City Council member and community activist Kenny Anderson. Comparable games can be found at the **Downtown Recreation Center, 501 North Main** (4/2, 🏀 🔲=3 ●=2 ⛰️ ☞), right across from Main Avenue Bingo. Both centers have leagues and both are closed during the summer. As usual, the **YMCA, 230 South Minnesota Avenue,** provides a solid run.

Woodlake Athletic Club, 4600 Tennis Lane (8/3, 🏀 🔲=5 ●=3 🏠 $ ☞ ♀), has a full-size court which the local CBA team, the Sioux Falls Sky Force, once used. That means you can shoot layups on the same floor that Chocolate Thunder (a.k.a. Darryl Dawkins) once used as a springboard for his dunks. Sky Force players occasionally run with the members.

For outdoor ball, hit up **McKennan Park, Third Avenue and 21st Street** (2/1, ▨ ▣=4 ◉=3 ▥▥), which a visitor's guide hypes as the "crown jewel in the park system."

ELSEWHERE IN SOUTH DAKOTA

Mitchell

Open gym runs from 6 to 10 p.m. during the week at the **Mitchell Recreation Center, 1300 North Main Street** (12/4, ▨ ▣=3 ◉=2 ▭ $).

When it comes to basketball (or anything else for that matter), the real story in Mitchell is the "world famous" **Corn Palace,** a giant town civic center and gym on Main Street where the Dakota Wesleyan college team and the Mitchell High Kernels (yes, spelled in that corny fashion) play their home games. What sets the Palace apart are the murals depicting farm life—made entirely out of corn cobs—that grace the outside of the building and are changed annually. If you couldn't guess, corn is the main industry in Mitchell.

Some fun facts about Mitchell from a former Mitchell High Kernel who emailed the Hoops Nation web site: their team mascot wasn't some fierce-looking animal but rather a corn cob with a smiley face and the "ears" rolled down; opponent's fans would throw corncobs on the floor to intimidate the Kernels at away games; and the affectionate nickname the players had for the Corn Palace was "the World's Largest Birdfeeder."

Rapid City

Roosevelt Park, East Omaha and East St. Louis Streets (2/1, ▨ ▣=2 ◉=2 ▟▟), is the best game in town, and the Firehouse Brewing Company is the best bar in town. The legendary three-on-three team of Teddy, George, and Abe (Tom usually sat on the bench and provided declarations of support) is glorified in stone a half hour to the south at Mt. Rushmore.

13

The Rocky Mountains

COLORADO, IDAHO, MONTANA, WYOMING

This region is home to some of the nation's most impressive national parks; vast tracts of open wilderness are interrupted only by thundering rivers and towering peaks. This means they are completely devoid of asphalt, and, as you can imagine, it's awful tough to do a crossover on a mountain hillside. With the exception of Denver, which has some good courts, there are no true basketball cities in the Rocky Mountain region. Your best bets for reliable games are the college campuses and YMCAs, though there are some pockets of resistance in the bleak roundball landscape; the Slab, in Coeur d'Alene, Idaho, is one of the best outdoor spots in the country.

We made the best of this basketball dry spell by seeing some of the wilderness and searching for ways to play in even the most dire of straits. Our research yielded the answer to the question: Where does one find a game when on vacation in Yellowstone with the family?

COLORADO

DENVER

Skyland Recreation Center
3334 Holly Street
Denver

Colorado's finest, including Michael Ray Richardson and Chauncey Billups, have faced off over the years at Skyland Rec. Though the top games are now on the rubber floor indoors, back in the day they ran *sans* roof on the neighboring outdoor courts. One of the participants in those games was center director Harry Hollines. Hollines, a tall, pipette-thin man with an easy smile and a genial manner, doesn't play much anymore, but if prodded a bit he'll tell you some great stories. Like the one about Al Dillard, a player who had some strong feelings about respecting the call.

Dillard was a rock of a power forward (6'6", 240 pounds) and one of the top small college rebounders in the nation in the late seventies and early eighties. On one sunny weekend day at Skyland, Dillard was playing in a pickup game outdoors when a dispute broke out about a foul call. "You see, Al figured he got fouled," Hollines says. "But they wouldn't give him the call, so he got all pissed off and said, 'I quit' and started walking off the court."

Dillard made it to the edge of the court before he changed his mind and walked back toward the rest of the players. He kept going right by them, though, toward one of the baskets. "He turned to us and said, 'If I can't play, ain't nobody gonna play,' " Hollines remembers. "He jumped up, grabbed the rim and yanked it down with two hands, just like that. Then he went to the other end of the court and pulled down the other rim. He put them both around his neck and walked off the court."

Also in Denver

The **20th Street Gym, 20th Street and Curtis** (2/1, 🏠 🔲=3 ◉=3 🏙 $ ☞ ♀), downtown has long been a gathering spot for top city players. If you've got four and need some help in the paint, try recruiting one of the champion lifters from the center's Olympic-quality weight room. Monday nights the gym is reserved for the women.

The best run in the Mile High City is at **Glenarm Recreation Center, Glenarm Place and 28th Street** (6/2, 🏠 🔲=4 ◉=4 🏙 ☞ ♀ 🐕), where Nugget players will often stop by and the ladies run on Saturday afternoons. To discourage arguing, director A. B. Maxey brings out the clock. "When they start yapping," Maxey says, "everyone on the side starts going 'Tick, tick, tick' and that gets the game going again."

Much of the crowd from Glenarm and Skyland will also play at **Martin Luther King Recreation Center, Newport and 38th Streets** (6/2, 🏠 🔲=4 ◉=4 🏙 🐕), which has the best facility of the three. A basketball committee scrutinizes new arrivals and drafts players for the leagues at the **Denver Athletic Club, 14th Street and Glenarm** (6/2, 🏠 🔲=4 ◉=2 🏙 $ ☞), a converted gentlemen's club in downtown Denver. To give you an idea of the athletic talent on display, the club used to have a fitness competition in categories like situps, pushups, etc. The record for vertical leap, set in 1982, is an astonishing 29 inches (for those who don't pick up on it, that's called sarcasm).

Glendale Park, East Kentucky Avenue and South Clemont Street (6/3, 🏠 🔲=3 ◉=3 🏙 ☀), has two sets of courts, one for hackers and one for players. The Glendale Police have their headquarters at the park, so don't go stealing anybody's ride.

ELSEWHERE IN COLORADO

Boulder
Canyon Park
21st Street and Canyon Boulevard
Boulder

2/1,

Get the total Boulder experience at Canyon as you play alongside hackeysackers and bong-toting free spirits who have their own defini-

Working on a Rocky Mountain High at Canyon Park

tion of "shake and bake." The Canyon courts are all about atmosphere; dogs run around, music blares from portables boxes, and the Rockies provide a scenic backdrop. The quality of the court, on the other hand, with baseline drop-offs and large ankle-crunching cracks, leaves much to be desired. One local has a theory, considering the park is next to apartment buildings. "They don't want to fix the court because then even more people will come and park in the apartment parking lot."

He's right about one thing—they don't want you parking in the apartment building's lot, and, as we can attest, they will call tow trucks. Tow trucks aren't the end of it, either; a sign next to the court warns, "If you don't stop parking here and bringing your dogs without a leash, we will remove the court."

If these threats and the prospect of sprained ankles deter you, you can always find a game up at the **University of Colorado–Boulder.**

Colorado Springs

Winter is the best time to hit **Hillside Community Center, Fountain and Institute** (6/2, 🏚 🖼=2 ◐=3 ⛰ ♀), a city gym that unfortunately lacks air-conditioning.

IDAHO

COEUR D'ALENE

The Slab
Sherman Avenue and Northwest Boulevard
Coeur d'Alene

6/3,

During warm Idaho summers tourists flock to the lake resort town of Coeur d'Alene to enjoy its peaceful serenity and natural beauty. Vacationing golfers can play the unique lakeside course—to reach the 18th hole, a floating island, golfers must tee off from the shore and take a boat out to the green—and visiting ballers can visit the Slab, one of the best outdoor courts in the country. The Slab consists of three

waterfront courts that are a summer battleground for players from
the five local colleges. The weekday play is nothing special, but things
heat up on the weekends. "If you lose you're not going to play again all
day," according to one regular who plays college ball. "I come out here
on the weekend and I'm like the worst player."

You want court legends? How about John Stockton, the all-time
NBA assist leader who grew up taking on all comers at the Slab while
starring at Gonzaga Prep and Gonzaga College and still comes back
three or four times each summer. If you run against the Mailman's better half and get run, don't sweat it; the cool waters of the lake are right
there for a postgame dip.

If the outdoor action is rained out, you can head indoors at **North
Idaho College.**

BOISE

For indoor ball in Boise, you've got two options. Your first is the **Fort
Boise Community Center, 700 Robbins Road** (2/1, 🏀 ▣=3 ●=3 🏔
$), where half-court ball dominates. The second is the trusty **Down-
town YMCA, 1050 West State Street** (5/2, 🏀 ▣=3 ●=2 🏔 $ ☞ ♀),
where the businessmen's basketball program starts at noon weekdays.

For outdoor ball, cruise by the two full courts at the **Willow Lane
Athletic Complex, State Street** (4/2, 🏀 ▣=3 ●=2 🏔), which is
conveniently located across the street from the Burger and Brew. If
you're in town during the summer, check out the basketball tournament during the River Festival and hit the Blues Bouquet on Friday
night for live music and beers.

ELSEWHERE IN IDAHO

Riggins
City Courts
Lodge Street and Highway 95
Riggins

4/0,

The central Idaho town of Riggins serves as a launch point for a number of whitewater river rafting outfits with catchy names like the "Canyon Cats" that take day excursions on the Salmon River. If you've ever been whitewater rafting, you are familiar with the group dynamic involved—six tourists sit in a rubber raft and paddle furiously while a young, suntanned guide yells out instructions.

If you do go rafting on the Salmon, don't forget to bring your sneaks (and your Visa card), because after a day of rafting, a different group dynamic gathers on the four half-courts right off I-95 in Riggins. Nightly river guide pickup games start around 7 p.m. After playing, the fish out of water retire to the Broken Branch saloon across the street for beverages.

MONTANA

BILLINGS AREA

The **Billings Athletic Club, 777 15th Street W.** (2/1, 🏠 ⊡=2 ●=3 ⛰ $ ☞), provides little in the way of pickup play but has good leagues that are occasionally frequented by ex–college players. A better, but still unspectacular, run can be found lunchtime and evenings at the **Billings YMCA, 402 North 32nd Street** (10/3, 🏠 ⊡=4 ●=3 ⛰ $).

In the Area

South of Billings on the Crow reservation, the best pickup games are on the blacktop at the **Crow Agency courts, off I-90** (2/1, 🏠 ⊡=3 ●=3 🖐), or down at the outdoor racks at **Lodge Grass High School** (4/2, 🏠 ⊡=3 ●=3 🖐 ☼). Because of summer heat, the games don't usually start until late afternoon.

ELSEWHERE IN MONTANA

There's little in the way of hoops in Big Sky country, so those looking for competition are best served visiting one of the state's two large colleges, the **University of Montana** in Missoula and **Montana State**

THE OTHER MICHAEL JORDAN

Native Americans have always succeeded at basketball on the high school level—Indian high schools won ten Montana state titles between 1980 and 1990, even though only 7 percent of the state's population is Native American—and the game is played passionately on reservations across the country. But although a number of talented players have come from the reservations, no Indian has ever made it to the NBA. For many, life off the reservation was too foreign and the adjustment to playing the game in the white man's world too difficult. For others, alcohol abuse cut short their playing careers.

But there was one man who almost made it, the greatest Indian player ever. His name, ironically, is Michael Jordan, though he played a decade before his NBA namesake. "Mike" Jordan was a 6'7" forward who played for Colville High in Washington in the

The hoops take center stage at Crow Agency

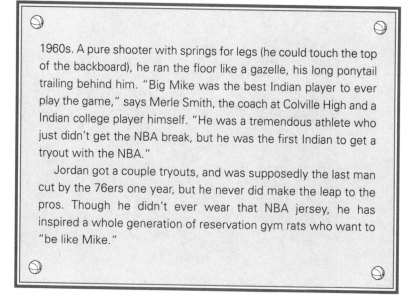

1960s. A pure shooter with springs for legs (he could touch the top of the backboard), he ran the floor like a gazelle, his long ponytail trailing behind him. "Big Mike was the best Indian player to ever play the game," says Merle Smith, the coach at Colville High and a Indian college player himself. "He was a tremendous athlete who just didn't get the NBA break, but he was the first Indian to get a tryout with the NBA."

Jordan got a couple tryouts, and was supposedly the last man cut by the 76ers one year, but he never did make the leap to the pros. Though he didn't ever wear that NBA jersey, he has inspired a whole generation of reservation gym rats who want to "be like Mike."

University in Bozeman, where the sultan of sarcasm, Craig Kilborn, played his college ball.

Wyoming

Finding a Game, Even in the 'Stone

Remember those family trips to Yellowstone? You got to enjoy the natural beauty of the park through the car's side window, watching other tourists watch sedentary bison as they went about their business of staring into space—oh, the excitement of it all! Whether you were the kid or the parent, you pretty much wrote off the trip as a hoops-less one. Never again, sayeth Hoops Nation.

Yellowstone Park processes 2.8 million visitors each year and occupies more land than the states of Delaware and Rhode Island combined, but for some reason, everyone seems to want to go camping. Well, even amidst the lovely terrain of Yellowstone, if you keep an eye out, you can find a court. There are four Yellowstone options

Who needs Old Faithful: one-on-one at Yellowstone

(see listing). In theory, three of them are for employee use only (Mammoth, Lake, and Canyon), but as long as you are respectful and don't tear down the rims, they don't mind the occasional tourist launching some J's.

YELLOWSTONE PARK

Lake Lodge
Yellowstone Lake

2/1,

A full court hides in the employee lounge in a wing off the giant central room at the far end of the Lodge. The conditions aren't perfect—a piano sits on one baseline and the wooden rafters overhead limit the range and arc on outside shots—but the view of Yellowstone Lake behind the far basket is tough to beat.

Park Service Housing Court
Yellowstone Grand Canyon Village

1/0,

Playing outdoors at Canyon allows one to appreciate the full beauty of Yellowstone; the asphalt is surrounded by forest land and bison often lounge in the grassy clearing near the court. The basket support and backboard, in keeping with the outdoor theme, are made of wood. If you feel yourself getting up especially well, it's not due to some "natural high" but rather to the slightly low rim.

Directions: If you're coming from Old Faithful, turn left before Canyon Village at the "Canyon Village" sign, then pull over and park when you see a sign that says "Service road only do not enter." Walk in and make your first left. The hoop is behind the building.

Employee Recreation Center
Mammoth Hot Springs
Yellowstone Park

2/1,

The Mammoth gym, unlike its Lake counterpart, is of high school quality, with glass backboards and a three-point line. The gym has the best park employee games, and non-Yellowstone players occasionally drive down from north of the park to play. For a meal after the game, try a Mammoth burger at the grill around the corner.

Gardiner High School
510 Stone Street
Gardiner, Montana

Five minutes north of the park and just over the state line in Gardiner, Montana, the locals will gather at the school gym on Tuesday and Thursday nights in the summer.

ELSEWHERE IN WYOMING

Jackson
Miller Park
Jackson Street and West Deloney Avenue
Jackson

2/0,

No one's too serious about their ball in laid-back Jackson, a resort town that rests in the shadow of the Grand Tetons, an hour away from Yellowstone. For postgame grub, you can't beat the gooey cheese at Mountain High Pizza, a block from the court.

Laramie
Civic Center
7th Street and Custer
Laramie

8/3,

Head to the Civic Center in downtown Laramie for all your needs, from drivers licenses (only $20) to the United Way to pickup games. During the fall, University of Wyoming students moving back into their dorms come down to play in the archaic gym. Also watch out for the lunch-break crew from the Albertson's grocery store across the street. While you're there, check out the unique floor in the main gym, which is made of two-by-fours stacked vertically on top of concrete.

Summertimes, you'll also find good games on the red surface at Laramie's **Washington Park, South 20th Street and Rainbow Avenue** (2/1, ▣=3 ◉=3 ▐), across from the Fox Theater. For the best indoor comp in town, hit up the plethora of indoor courts at the **University of Wyoming.**

Cheyenne

In late July every year Cheyenne is invaded by tourists in town for Frontier Days, a celebration of everything that is Cowboy. If you tire of line dancing and horses, head to **Holiday Park, Morrie Avenue and 17th Street** (4/2, ▦ ▣=2 ◉=2 ▐), and play a western brand of ball.

FLAVOR OF THE GAME:
Playing Past Forty

The Tricks of "Old Guy Basketball"

Head to the local Y for a noontime run with the over-forty crowd and a group of men will be playing a game they call basketball, but it will look nothing like the game you see on TV. There will be no follow-dunks, no forceful blocked shots, no high-elevation jump shots, and most definitely no goaltending. What you will see is Old Guy Basketball at its finest, described using verbs such as "grunting," "balding," "sweating," and "hobbling." Missing from the vocabulary are verbs like "dunking," "sprinting," "rebounding," and "wearing" less than one knee brace.

Unfortunately, the sport of basketball has no sympathy for aging bodies; more than any other sport, playing basketball requires athletic ability. As time goes by, the rim starts to seem a little farther away on those finger rolls, the quickness has been drained from the rocker step, and the knees ache just a little more after each game. That old "killer crossover" you could always count on has now converted to pacifism, and your "patent" has expired on that double pump layup. When this time comes in your life—when gravity latches ahold of your sneakers and won't let go—the smart player adjusts by developing a repertoire of ground-based moves that rely on experience and treachery. If gravity can no longer be defied, at least it can be accommodated and even put to good use every once in a while.

Once you arm yourself with an assortment of trick shots and strategies, you will be able to play Old Guy Basketball. If you're young, there's no law that says you have to be over forty (the tender age when basketball players become "old") to use these moves; learn them now and you'll be one step ahead of other future Old Guys (hey, it worked for Bill Laimbeer). So here they are, the moves and trade secrets your dad doesn't want you to know about, the bread and butter treachery of all Old Guys, starting with the old standby:

THE HOOK SHOT

A highly effective Old Guy shot, the hook has the added benefit of instantly earning you the nickname Kareem (if your prescription goggles haven't already done so). Like the Laker center, you too can take advantage of the fact that, because the ball is extended away from the defender and looped toward the basket, the hook is a very hard shot to block. What made it even tougher in Kareem's case was the fact that he's about nine feet tall.

Since most of us measure in at Kareem's waist, there are a couple other tricks to shooting the hook that can make it virtually indefensible. First, when shooting your hook, fend off your opponent with your free arm, using your elbow much as a lion tamer uses a chair to keep his growling subject at bay. Second, for maximum effectiveness, set up the shot by faking as if you're going to drive to the basket in the opposite direction (yeah, right, at two mph). Then switch directions and, when you take that step to fire off the hook, put your plant foot firmly on top of the defender's sneaker. Nailed to the ground in this manner, not even Shawn Bradley and his mutant arms are going to reach the ball.

Practice your hook from anywhere out to the three-point line; with the right arc and touch, it has that kind of range. And if you sink a hook shot, be sure to act surprised;

Skyhooking with flair

don't let on that you spend hours practicing at the office using the wastebasket and balled-up company letterhead.

THE UP-AND-UNDER

A complement to the hook, the up-and-under is the Old Guy version of a drop-step dunk—just, instead of throwing it down with authority, you spin it up there underhand with great finesse. (Remember the Old Guy maxim: "Finesse is preferable to authority, unless you're fouling somebody.")

To execute the up-and-under, get the ball in the post with your back to the basket. Now fake one direction as if you're going to shoot a fade-away or a hook. Once your opponent reacts, pivot back the other direction, duck your arm underneath the defender's arm, and shoot the ball from your waist, using the glass to bank it in. The young guy guarding you will be swiping at the air where your hook shot should have been and regarding you as if you're Houdini.

THE SPOT UP

The key to this shot is to find one spot on the floor—15 feet from the basket on the baseline, for example—and work on nailing a set shot from that location. When you play, regardless of what else is going on in the game, jog down and assume a shooting position at your spot, arms up, hands at the ready. Let that young point guard zip around, perform three-spin dribbles and elevate into three guys (one of which is usually your defender) in the lane. When he realizes he has to pass it, he's going to look around desperately for an outlet. When he does he'll see you camped out, wide open, at your familiar spot. With no one guarding you and your feet set, you could knock down this shot in your sleep. After sinking it, remember to say something like "Nice look" to the point guard, the better to make him think he "created" the shot for you.

THE PET SHOT

A pet shot isn't what your pooch gets at the vet; rather, it is the calling card of the Old Guy: the one move that, through repetition, he has refined to the point where he rarely ever misses it. It is up to you as an Old Guy to select your own pet shot depending on where your strength lies (the above three shots are all good examples). For some, it is a mechanical jump hook or a fall-away jumper released Larry Bird style from behind the head; for others it is a two-handed push shot or underhand heave.

The more absurd your pet shot is, the more effective it will be. For example, if you start to shoot a running hook from twenty feet out, your defender's reaction will be to turn and prepare to rebound, assuming that there's no way you're going to hit that crazy shot. When you sink it, everyone will react as if you've won the lottery. "Wohoo! Somebody's birthday today," they'll say, and pat you on the back. Your defender will probably even congratulate you—you know, "Be nice to the old guy." The second time you nail that same hook, there will be increased ribbing of your defender. "The old guy's killing you, Jimmy!" they'll say, shaking their heads and laughing. The third time you nail the same shot, swishing it in as if it were a layup, your defender will stop laughing, commence swearing, and start covering you from thirty feet in. His teammates, all traces of amusement gone from their voices, will be saying, "Yo, Jimmy, are you going to cover him or do you want me to?" By this point it's too late, though, you've already scored three buckets and thrown the opposition into disarray.

THE CHANGE-OF-PACE–FAKE-INJURY PLOY

You're already pretty slow when you're old, so one of the keys to scoring is to employ the change of pace. That hesitation dribble you always wanted to master when you were younger? Now it's easy, and, actually, physically impossible for you not to perform. If you ever watched Chris Mullin drive to the hole, you probably wondered how he got there when it looked like he was in slow motion the whole time. Well, Chris was playing Old Guy basketball at its highest level by taking advantage of the change of pace.

For the Old Guy, the ultimate change of pace is attainable by feigning an injury. Hobble up and down the court (if you already hobble, work on pronouncing the hobble) and grimace while clutching a knee. Your defender will most likely pity you, and you can lull him into thinking that you are now the Slowest Guy on the Planet (assuming you didn't already hold this title). Then, when you get the ball on the baseline, take one hobble-dribble and explode past him for a driving layup. Now, I realize that this explosion may be more cherry bomb than atom bomb at this point in your career, but to get past your defender, who's already thinking about blocking your fadeaway jumper to midcourt, it should suffice.

Why You Should Pick the Old Guy Instead of the Young Guy When Choosing Teams

- More shots for you!
- Almost always a better passer and team player than younger guys.
- Might have a mean pet shot.
- Won't hinder your triple-double quest by stealing any rebounds.
- You can blame him for any defensive lapses the team encounters.
- He'll use up his full complement of twenty-five fouls.
- You'll always have a trailer on the break.
- He could be an influential businessman who will hire you someday.

Ways for Old Guys to Dominate the Game

- Set mean picks that take the opponent's best player out of the game.
- Two words: coughing fits.
- Bore the opposing team with stories from your youth ("Back when I was young we didn't have any of this fancy stuff. No glass backboards, no three-point lines, in fact, we didn't even have basketballs back then. In my family we had a tire rim for a basket and we had to use the cat as the ball. . . .")

14

The Middle Atlantic Region

DELAWARE, DISTRICT OF COLUMBIA, MARYLAND, NEW JERSEY, PENNSYLVANIA, VIRGINIA, WEST VIRGINIA

Much of the NBA's new blood has been drawn from the Middle Atlantic states. Rasheed Wallace is a graduate of Sonny Hill's Philadelphia youth programs, Tim Thomas honed his all-around skills in Paterson, New Jersey, and the Virginia coast has turned out Zo, Joe, and the Answer (that's Alonzo Mourning, Joe Smith, and Allen Iverson, respectively). In "Joisey," you're Shore to find some good games on the coast during the Jersey summer season, and in Baltimore, the greatest high school team in history used to spend their off days playing pickup at "the Dome," the city's famous rec center.

During our Mid-Atlantic swing, we got a chance to run with the Doc in Philly, search for the "supreme court" in Washington, D.C., and drop in on the stalwart seniors at the MLK center in Charleston, West Virginia.

DELAWARE

WILMINGTON

Brown Burton-Winchester Park
East 26th Street and Speakman Place
Wilmington

8/4,

Four asphalt courts attract the city's best to this inner-city joint, which is also known as Prices Park. Wilmington's city slogan—"A place to be somebody"—applies if you can hold court; as one older guy with a mean flat-top fade said, "The comp is heavy up there."

Also in Wilmington

The **Central Branch YMCA, 501 West 11th Street** (4/2, 🏠 🔲=3 ⬤=3 ⛰ $ ☞), has a mirror covering one wall of the gym, allowing you to check out your J while somebody blocks it. The **William "Hicks" Community Center, 501 North Madison Street** (6/3, 🏠 🔲=4 ⬤=4 ⛰ ☞ ⚹), hosts an NCAA-sanctioned league and provides sweet air-conditioned relief in the summers. For those who like it hot, Chambers Playground across the street has an outdoor tourney. Up a couple blocks, the concrete provides shade at the under-the-freeway **Adams Street courts, Adams and Third Streets** (6/3, 🏢 ▣=4 ●=3 ⛰ ⚭ ☀).

ELSEWHERE IN DELAWARE

Bethany Beach

Funny that a town with a population of 326 people would be a hoops hotbed, but that's exactly what Bethany Beach is in the summer. Players from D.C. and Baltimore converge on the single court next to the **Christian Conference Center, Garfield Parkway and Pennsylvania Avenue** (2/1, 🏢 ▣=4 ●=4 🌴 ☞ ☀), in this tiny town in southeast Delaware.

Dover

A great example of the average American outdoor court can be found past the grove of trees at **Dover Park, White Oak and Nimitz Roads** (4/2, 🏢 ▣=3 ●=2 🗄).

DISTRICT OF COLUMBIA (WASHINGTON, D.C.) AREA

The physical, contentious style of play in the nation's capital means that the wait for nexts at many D.C. courts can be interminable. Players can be found imitating their Capitol Hill counterparts by engaging in bickering, posturing, stalling, and even the occasional blacktop filibuster. The end result of all this politicking is gridlock on the court. To avoid such an exercise-impeding experience, keep an open mind and move on to a new court if things are looking a little too partisan where you are.

Stead Playground
17th Street and P Street N.W.
Washington, D.C.

3/1,

For aspiring street artists in search of their Mona Lisa, look no farther than Stead Playground. The fenced court at Stead is bordered on
one side by a gray concrete wall on which graffiti artists—and in this
case that phrase isn't an oxymoron—have created a multicolored
urban mosaic. Lyrics from rap songs, written in shaded block letters,
intertwine with psychedelic pink butterflies making their way up the
wall past fat cumulus clouds. To their left, a gnome-like creature with
pupil-less eyes clutches a baseball bat and grins out at the world from
beneath a blue hooded sweatshirt.

As impressive as this artwork is, it is paid absolutely no attention
by the regulars at the court, who get a solid run going on weekday
afternoons and weekends, with plenty of jawing involved. Located
near Dupont Circle, the court attracts a diverse crowd—white, black,
Puerto Rican, everybody just a freakin', as Prince would say.

Art enthusiasts battling for bounds at Stead Playground

Rose Park
26th Street N.W. and O Street
Washington, D.C.

2/1, 🏀 📷📷 ●●●● 🏙 ♀

Stroll by Georgetown's Rose Park and you'll pick up the mouth-watering smell of dogs on the grill and the sound of bricks in the air. The hot dogs are the doing of Claude "Sham" Shamburger, the unofficial court commish and a park veteran who played here when Oscar Robertson, Elgin Baylor, and Wilt Chamberlain would show. As for the bricks, those are courtesy of the double rims, tiny backboards, and swaying hoop supports that would force even Reggie Miller to holster the twenty-five-footer and take it to the bucket.

Marie Reed Learning Center
Kalorama Road and 18th Street
Adams Morgan

4/2, 🏀 📷📷 ●●● 🏙 🚗 💡

Two full courts are stirred into the melting pot of Adams Morgan, one of the most ethnically diverse communities in the country. You never know what language to expect in the area—the nation's first bilingual McDonald's is a couple blocks from the court—or on the court, though physical games mean most have learned how to say "Foul" in addition to some choice expletives.

ALSO IN WASHINGTON, D.C.

Top summer comp can be found at the appetizingly named courts at **Turkey Thicket, 12th Street and Michigan Avenue N.E.** (6/3, 🏀 📷=4 ●=4 🏭 🚗 ☀), in the Northeast. Othella Harrington occasionally ran at the gritty **Watts Courts, 62nd Street and Banks Place N.E.** (6/3, 🏀 📷=3 ●=4 🏭 🚗 ☀), while at G'Town.

For suburban ball, head north to the **Friendship Recreation Center, Van Ness Street and 45th Street N.W.,** (4/2, 🏀 📷=3 ●=3 🏠 ☕), where weekend action is heavy. Waiting players can fool around on the smaller court's fantasy rims. For more dunks, hit up the **Shaw Junior High Playground, Rhode Island Avenue N.W. and Tenth Street N.W.** (2/1, 🏠 ▣=4 ◉=3 ⛰ ♀ 🎒 ☀), where one rim is ten feet and the other is nine.

Holler with some Hoyas at **Georgetown University,** D.C.'s best indoor run, or address the hardwood delegates at the **National Capital YMCA, 1711 Rhode Island Avenue N.W.** (4/2, 🏠 ▣=3 ◉=3 ⛰ $♀), in downtown D.C. The Y has pickup play seven days a week and reserves Thursday nights for the ladies.

If you'd rather watch than play, the best show in the city is Urbo Ball, a venerable summer league run by the D.C. Urban Coalition. Games are held at Dunbar High School, where the gym fills up quickly on game nights (it seats 2,700 but it seems like about 10,000 when you're in there) and fans come out to see local playground heroes and drop-in pros like Sam Cassell and Walt Williams.

VIRGINIA SUBURBS

Arlington

Georgetown players used to commute over the Potomac to school the locals at the **Thomas Jefferson Community Center, Second Street off South Glebe Road** (7/3, 🏠 ▣=2 ◉=3 🔒 $), but that practice came to an abrupt halt when they were discovered by coach John Thompson.

The court is cracked and decaying, but the talent can make a trip worthwhile to **Glen Carlyn Park, Four Mile Run Drive,** the only local outdoor spot where women play.

Pentagon City

In the land of $500 hammers, the runs gear up weekends at **Aurora Hills Recreation Center, 735 South 18th Street** (4/2, 🏠 ▣=3 ◉=3 🔒 🎒 ☀). Chances are you'll run into one of the Pentagon's 23,000 employees, just happy to be escaping ground zero.

Alexandria

Evening runs attract collegiate talent and Wednesdays are ladies' night at the **Charles Houston Recreation Center, 901 Wythe Street** (6/2, 🏀 ▣=3 ●=4 🎽 ☞ ♀ ⚷). Open gym rules state that you must be a guest of or a resident of Alexandria County, but sneaking in isn't like breaking into Fort Knox. The **Alexandria YMCA, 420 East Monroe** (2/1, 🏀 ▣=4 ●=2 🎽 $ ☞), a brand-spanking-new Y put up in 1996, has a beautiful facility that can be used by nonmembers for a $10 guest fee.

MARYLAND SUBURBS

Silver Spring

An *au naturel* setting, in the north end of the park amidst abundant greenery, belies the *au shit* type of language that predominates amongst the urban players at **Sligo Creek Park, Sligo Creek Parkway and Dennis Avenue** (6/3, 🏀 ▣=3 ●=4 🎽 ⚷ 💡).

Don't let the metropolitan street names fool you; the brand of ball is suburban at **Silver Spring Park, Chicago and Philadelphia Avenues** (4/2, 🏀 ▣=2 ●=3 🎽 ⚷). The older crowd heads to **Woodside Park, Ballard Street and Georgia Avenue** (2/1, 🏀 ▣=3 ●=2 🎽).

MARYLAND

BALTIMORE AREA

The legend of Dunbar High School lives on. The Baltimore school's unreal 1981–83 hoops team, which went 59–0 over two seasons, is widely considered to be the best high school squad ever. The team featured four NBA players: Muggsy Bogues, David Wingate, Reggie Williams, and Reggie Lewis. How deep were they? Consider the fact that as a senior, Lewis didn't even start, playing mostly garbage time behind Williams.

The success of those players has inspired countless young street rats to dream of making it big league. Between the still-powerful Dun-

bar program, a well-run youth loop called the Baltimore Neighborhood Basketball League, and the efforts of the staff of the Madison
Square Recreation Center ("the Dome"), Baltimore youngsters have
some valuable resources at their disposal.

Madison Square Recreation Center ("the Dome")
1401 East Biddle St. at North Eden Street
Baltimore

2/1,

March 1985. Craig Cromwell is watching the Georgetown-
Villanova NCAA championship game at a friend's house in west Baltimore. Craig, a talented high school player, watches as Patrick Ewing
is bewildered by Ed Pinckney and the underdog Villanova Wildcats.
Walking home after the game, visions of his own basketball future
keep him company.

Sadly, Craig would never realize his basketball dreams. On his way
home on that fateful night, Cromwell got caught in the wrong place at
the wrong time and was shot and killed. On the streets of Baltimore,
few teenagers who die in the line of gunfire are remembered, but Bill
Wells wanted to make sure Cromwell was one who was not forgotten.

Wells is the basketball director at East Baltimore's Madison Square
Recreation Center, or "the Dome" as it's known in the basketball com-
munity because of its covered outdoor court. For years, Wells and the
Dome have provided a place for kids to work on their basketball skills
while staying off the streets. Cromwell had been a talented young
player under Wells's tutelage and, more important, a good person.
"Craig got mixed up in the wrong thing and got shot accidentally,"
Wells says. "I thought because he was an outstanding kid that we
should recognize him somehow, so in 1985 I started the Craig
Cromwell League."

The Cromwell League, which is still going strong today, showcases
fourteen of the best high school teams in Baltimore and gives young
players what Cromwell never got—a chance to make it to the next
level. The league complements Midnight Madness, the center's highly

The Dome in Baltimore

successful midnight basketball program that draws the best talent in, and from, Baltimore, including NBA stars like Sam Cassell, Muggsy Bogues, and Reggie Williams. Thousands of fans gather around the outdoor court, blocking the streets to watch the late-night battles between pros and local studs. In addition to providing entertainment, the league keeps participants and spectators off the streets during the late-night hours when it's easy to get into trouble.

"If it wasn't for those games, man, there are a lot of kids that could be other places right now," says NBAer David Wingate, a graduate of the Dome. "A lot of the guys in the league [the NBA] wouldn't even be here. They took time out to successfully run that league *at night*, and that's normally when kids start to get in trouble."

Also in Baltimore Area

Druid Hill Park (4/2, 📋 🖼=4 ◐=3 ⛰ 🎪 💡 **)** has two full courts near the park's lake. A rougher game runs across the street at **Cloverdale Park, McCulloh Street and Cloverdale Road (2/1,** 📋 🖼=3 ◐=3 ⛰ 🚫 💡 **).** If you took an outdoor court and stuck it in a warehouse, you'd have the gym at the **Downtown Athletic Club, 210 East Center Street** (4/2, 🏠 ▣=2 ◕=3 ⛰ $ ☞), a converted railway station with a rubber floor, metal backboards, and lackluster runs. Though the games aren't great, it is one of the few worthwhile indoor places to play in Baltimore.

In Pasadena, to the southeast of Baltimore, suburbanites make use of the breakaway rims on the courts at **Lake Waterford Park, 830 Pasadena Road** (4/2, 🏠 ▣=4 ◕=3 🏢 ☀). Don't expect to test out the lake after playing; only fishing and duck feeding are allowed. Five miles north in Glen Burnie, a higher-caliber game runs on the multiple lit courts at **Sawmill Park, Dorsey Road off I-97.**

ELSEWHERE IN MARYLAND

College Park

D.C. players migrate northeast to the **University of Maryland.** If you're lucky, a couple of the Terrapins might emerge from their shells.

What Streak?

Despite the fact that basketball is the most dangerous sport to play, Cal Ripken, the most durable baseball player of all time, has been jeopardizing the Streak for a decade by playing basketball six days a week in the off-season at his home gym.

From November to January, Ripken invites an assortment of athletes for daily pickup games at his lavish gym, which also has a batting cage, weight set, and a tennis ball machine that spits out grounders. In typical Ripken perfectionist fashion, Cal varies the competition with the aim of improving his game; one day he'll invite local college players to run him into the ground, another day he'll import ex-pro guys who can teach him the tricks of the game, and a third day it'll be his baseball buddies so he can play center with his back to the basket. Does anyone worry about knocking around the most famous body in baseball? "He would be really upset if you slacked off on him," says Tim Kurkjian, a onetime Ripken game regular who wrote about Cal's gym in a 1995 *Sports Illustrated* story. "He takes it, but he also dishes out more punishment than anyone out there. He loves to bang and he's strong—the guy's got the biggest legs in the world."

Besides banging around, the word is that Ripken has improved his game, once limited to post play, so that he's now got three-point range and solid face-the-basket moves. Who knows, maybe the Wizards could use a durable, sure-handed forward. . . .

NEW JERSEY

THE JERSEY SHORE

During muggy East Coast summers, loads of New Yorkers and inland working stiffs head out to the beautiful beaches along the Jersey Shore, spending their weekends soaking up the sun and enjoying the relaxed days and crazy nights. The Shore also attracts droves of ballplayers, who drive out from Philly and beyond to make the summer games along the coast some of the best in the country.

The most organized run is the **Jersey Shore League**, which is held in the air-conditioned confines of the St. Rose gym in sleepy Bellmawr. The chilly gym and hot competition (all the players play either professionally or at Division I schools) entice New Yorkers like Rod Strickland, Lloyd Daniels, and Anthony Mason down to play. "It's a very organized league," Mason says. "You got the crowd, good security, and then you get a lot of competition. You know how you go other places and people have their favorites and they cheer certain people, and they boo others? Out on the Jersey Shore, they just happy you come out to play, they don't care who you play for."

Farther down the coast, games are played by the sea in Ocean City and the quaint coastal town of Avalon, where there are so many college players on the court that you half expect Dickie V to show up and start providing ear-splitting play-by-play. Even down in relaxed Cape May, the ballers take some time to hit the asphalt. One thing to remember if you're headed to the Shore for ball: They play only during the summer. Show up the day after Labor Day and all you'll find is some sand scattered on the blacktop and candy wrappers blowing around the courts. With that in mind, here are the top Shore courts.

Ocean City

The action has subsided since the seventies and early eighties, when the games were all-day affairs featuring Division I and pro players, but Ocean City is still packed with beach rats and high school talent during the summer. The pickup play divides up between the courts at **Sixth Street and Atlantic Avenue** (6/3, 🏀 🔲=4 ●=4 🌴 ☞ 🎽 🔆), and the slabs at **34th Street and Asbury** (4/2, 🏀 🔲=4 ●=3 🏰 ☞ 🎽 🔆). Both have lights for cooler night games and both host strong summer loops. The adult league runs at Sixth Street, the teens at 34th. In general the older players migrate to Sixth Street, which is just off the beach. For indoor play, the Ocean City Sports and Civic Center next door to the Sixth Street courts has winter pickup for teens.

Avalon

Eighth Street Courts
Eighth Street and Ocean Drive
Avalon

4/2,

What Ocean City was twenty years ago, Avalon is today. Local college and pro players like Tim Legler and Matt Maloney make the trek to the southern tip of New Jersey to run early mornings (as in 7:30 a.m.) on the blacktop at Eighth Street. It's smart, tough, competitive ball; there are more picks and backdoor cuts in one game here than you'll see in a whole day at most courts. An annual tournament, the Camaraderie Classic, is held the weekend before Memorial Day and features current and ex-collegians playing on squads with creative names like "the Fartin Irish" and "Wet Dream Weavers."

Cape May

All types play at the **Cape May Court, St. John and Lafayette Streets** (2/1, 🏀 🔲=3 ●=2 🌴 🎽 🔆), in the yuppie retreat of Cape

May at the southern tip of New Jersey. The court is quiet during the week but fills up with locals and tourists come the weekend.

Atlantic City

Once a glittering resort town for the rich and famous that spawned the street names for Monopoly (remember Ventnor, Baltic, and St. James Place?), Atlantic City is now a ghost town, a run-down gambling city full of the wannabe-rich and the infamous.

Atlantic City also once had the best pickup games on the shore, if not in all of New Jersey. One spot in particular, an elementary school yard at Pennsylvania and Arctic avenues referred to as "the Yard," was home to legendary games involving the likes of Chris Ford. The Yard had a strong summer league, and pickupwise, "Games would be going from eight a.m. until the lights went out at two a.m. the next day," according to Atlantic City basketball veteran Rodney Braithwaite. "It was just a little court at an elementary school. I'm not sure what brought people there, but they sure came."

Like much else in the city that was alluring, the court is now gone, torn down and replaced by condos. These days there are a couple AC options—there is year-round open gym from 6 to 10 p.m. five days a week at the **Martin Luther King School Complex, Mamora Avenue and Martin Luther King Boulevard,** (10/2, 🏫 ⬚=4 ●=4 ⛰ ⌚), and a similar run at the **Uptown Complex, Madison Avenue**—but the top players now migrate down to Ocean City and Avalon, leaving Atlantic City quiet. Who knows what the future holds, though; Atlantic City could make a resurgence; as New Jersey's own Bruce Springsteen sang, "Everything dies, baby, that's a fact, but maybe everything that dies someday comes back."

The Rest of the Coast

Toms River isn't really on the coast, but it's close enough. There you'll find a woodsy suburban park, **Skyview Park, Bay and Vaughn Avenues** (8/4, 🏫 ⬚=4 ●=4 ⛰ ⌚ ☀), where high school players from the surrounding area congregate, turning the games into a "nightly dunk fest," according to one regular. Evening runs continue through the fall until the city turns out the lights in October.

Between Normandy Beach and Lavallette, with Silver Bay a couple blocks to the west and the Atlantic Ocean a couple blocks to the east, you can't beat the scenery (even if you can probably beat the competition) at **Chadwick Beach Park, Strickland Boulevard and Route 35 South** (2/1, ), a pleasant court surrounded by the squat vacation homes that proliferate in the area.

NEWARK

Branch Brook Park
Clifton and Seventh Avenues
Newark

4/2,

The place to ball in Newark. A summer circuit draws top college and pro players (Eric Williams, Anthony Avent, and Rod Strickland have played recently) who appreciate the NBA three-point line and the supervision by league honcho Duke. For pickup, the bi-level courts are always busy, though the talent fluctuates.

Also in Newark
For indoor ball, drop by the **Newark YMCA, 600 Broad Street** (6/2,  **$**). There's a daily corporate noon game and big-time runs on Friday nights and Sunday afternoons, when local college studs play. Nonmembers can get in for $7, or $5 if they're under 18.

Some big-name players run at **the Hole,** a sunken housing project court in inner-city Newark, but the dangerous neighborhood isn't worth venturing into unless you're a local or one of those big-name players.

TRENTON

Cadwalader Park
Parkside Avenue and West State Street
Trenton

4/2,

On muggy summer Sunday evenings the cars line up along both sides of Parkside Avenue as hundreds of fans come out to watch one of the country's best summer leagues at Cadwalader. Players from Seton Hall, Georgetown, Rutgers, and other East Coast schools compete three nights a week, to the delight of the vocal crowd.

A less star-spangled outdoor run can be found at **Cooper Field, John Fitch Way** (2/1, 🪙 🖵=3 ◐=3 👑 🎯). The court is across the freeway from the sparkling Delaware River and a giant white sign that proclaims, "Trenton Makes, the World Takes." Guess that means they play loser's outs.

ELSEWHERE IN NEW JERSEY

Jersey City

New Jersey hoops powerhouse St. Anthony's High School, multiple winner of the mythical national championship, practices and plays off-season pickup in cramped **White Eagle Hall, Newark Avenue next to Monaco Lock Company.** Joining the team players are school alums like Terry Dehere and the Hurley brothers (dad Bobby Sr. is the coach at St. Anthony's), who bang bodies with guys like Lloyd Daniels. Playing here is a touchy-feely experience; foul calls aren't allowed and the court is so skinny that the walls are out of bounds.

Parsippany

Players from northwest Jersey do their balling at **Smith Field Park, Route 46 and Baldwin Road** (4/2, 🪙 🖵=4 ◐=3 🍔 ☀). You can check on the competition from I-80, that great artery of America, which runs right by the park. Watch out for local legends Sly and Pepper.

Camden

It's not exactly a tourist location, but Camden has produced loads of talented ball players. If you are in town, you can boost your ego by playing against the team players at the Rutgers University–Camden, who set an ignominious national record by losing 117 in a row between 1992 and 1997. Another option is the **Central Branch YMCA, Third and Federal Streets.**

PENNSYLVANIA

PHILADELPHIA AREA

Top-of-the-Hill Leagues in Philly

In a day and age when young basketball talent is shuttled between All-Star camps, fought over by recruiters, and generally treated like a commodity to be purchased, it's refreshing to see a program like Sonny Hill's in Philadelphia.

For four decades, the Sonny Hill Youth Involvement League, run by William Randolph ("Sonny") Hill, the godfather of Philadelphia basketball, has been grooming the city's best young talent to be not only good players but also good people. Kids from the Philly area enter the program young, in fifth or sixth grade, and are taught discipline through Hill's "my way or the highway" approach.

Players in the youth league, who have included Rasheed Wallace, Hank Gathers, and Pooh Richardson, are separated into four different age divisions and play league games all summer, culminating in an end-of-the-summer tourney in August against other East Coast youth programs. The young players, many of whom don't have stable home lives, are encouraged in their schoolwork and receive some tough love from the coaches. "You either do it our way, or see you later. It's a disciplined program," says Tony Samartino, one of the league's founders and its head of operations for thirty years. "If you need tutoring and you don't go to tutoring, you don't play. And the kids want to play."

The program is different from others across the country in that it emphasizes team skills as much as individual ones. "We're more disciplined. The kids that play in our program know that you put a couple passes on the ball, you don't just own the ball yourself," says Samartino. "Our kids can go anywhere and play because they've already been taught that way. I'll put them against anybody."

If the kids do well, they can aspire to play in Hill's other creation: the Charles Baker Memorial League. Hill started the Baker League in 1960 when he was a 5'9" guard playing semi-pro ball. Early games, held in the basement of a church in North Philly, featured guys like Bill Bradley, Earl Monroe, Walt Frazier, and Wilt Chamberlain.

Today, the Baker league, run at McGonigle Hall on the Temple University campus, still attracts top talent—recently NBA players like Jerry Stackhouse and Lionel Simmons have played against talent from Philly's numerous Division I schools—and serves as a high-profile counterpart to the Youth Involvement league.

The Sporting Club at the Bellevue
1350 Broad Street
Philadelphia

 6/2, $

Playing at the Sporting Club, a luxurious four-story health club perched atop a garage in downtown Philly, can be a bit like going to one of those fantasy sport camps where armchair athletes meet their idols. Case in point: One of the men's league teams here features both

Dr. J operates on a hapless member at the Sporting Club

Maurice Cheeks and Julius Erving. The Hall of Famers match up against local ex-collegians who are careful not to stargaze for too long lest the Doctor should see fit to dunk on their heads (for those who might wonder, he still gets up).

Pickup play, in which Mo participates, is also at a high level, though the good players are mixed in with some lesser-skilled businessmen and professional types. The best games are noontime and from 5 to 7 p.m. weeknights and on weekend mornings.

Hank Gathers Memorial Recreation Center
25th Street and Diamond
Philadelphia

4/1,

Both the late Hank Gathers, for whom the center was renamed in 1993, and point guard extraordinaire Dawn Staley perfected their games at the corner of 25th and Diamond in rough-and-tumble North Philly. The center has something for everyone: women's night (Wednesdays), youth leagues, six-feet-and-under leagues, old-timers leagues, and of course, daily pickup play both indoors and on the two courts outside. Staley, whom you might recognize from the six-story Nike billboard of her downtown at Eighth and Market, still plays in the offseason.

A half mile away, on the outdoor courts at Amos Playground, 16th and Berks Streets, (2/1, ▨ ▣=3 ●=3 ▟ ⚓), near the Temple University campus, city talent mixes it up against occasional college players.

Albert W. Christy Recreation Center
56th Street and Christian
Philadelphia

6/2,

The play at Christy is decidedly above the rim, with directly below the rim being a bad place to be on a two-on-one break. From October to April this inner-city gym is open every afternoon and on Tuesday and Thursday nights. In the summer the locals sweat it out on the adjacent outdoor full court.

Narberth Courts
Haverford and Wynnewood
Narberth

4/2,

Tucked into a suburb near the Main Line, the Narberth courts are the place to go if you want to play half-court. Actually, you have no choice, because, as posted park rules specify, only half-court ball is allowed. Coupled with the four-on-four format, this means that playing defense is a necessity and even the most faithful Dominique Wilkins impersonators have to pass to win.

Games run from 4:30 to 7 p.m. on weekdays and all day on weekends, when upward of fifty players often show. Down the road a bit is Haverford College, where renowned Laker fan Chevy Chase ("6'5", with the afro 6'9'") shot some jumpers at the Alumni field house for a year before moving on to *Saturday Night Live.*

Water Tower Recreation Center
Hartwell Lane and Winston Road
Philadelphia

3/1,

The Water Tower courts, situated just off the cobblestone streets of yuppie Chestnut Hill, provide that rare combination of a relatively safe atmosphere and top inner-city competition. Players from nearby Germantown head up the road to the short outdoor court for summer battles, which start around 5 p.m. Leagues run on the short court indoors in the rec center.

Also in Philadelphia Area

In Center City, **Markward Playground, Pine and Taney Streets** (4/2, 🏚 🖳=3 ◉=3 ⛰ 🎾 💡), attracts a diverse crowd to its location next to the Schuylkill River, while the **Tenth Street courts, Tenth Street and Lombard** (4/1, 🏚 🖳=3 ◉=4 ⛰ 🎾 💡), are just blocks from the heart of South Street, the city's eclectic nightlife area.

At **Villanova,** in du Pont Field House, the better games are upstairs on the Jake Nevin court, while the less serious hoopsters chuck it up downstairs on the rubber floor. Other college gyms worth checking out include **St. Joseph's, Penn** (and the nearby Palestra), **Drexel University** (which also has a pair of outdoor courts at 33rd and Race streets that see a lot of use), **Temple University** (alma mater of the inimitable Bill Mlkvy, a.k.a. "The Owl Without a Vowel"), and **LaSalle.**

At **Shepard Recreation Center, Haverford and 57th** (2/1, 🏚 🖳=3 ◉=4 ⛰ 🎾 🌀), once a battleground for Wilt Chamberlain and Sonny Hill, when the center was known as Haddington, a new gym floor has revitalized the indoor game. Outdoors you'll find eight netless hoops and two slabs where the younger high school crowd hoops it up starting around 4 p.m.

Former college star LeRoy Berry presides over the rim-rockers at the **Mallory Recreation Center, Johnson and Morton** (4/1, 🏚 🖳=3 ◉=4 ⛰ 🎾 ♀ 🎾), in Germantown. Over near the Main Line, the **Belmont Courts, Llandrillo and Belmont** (🏚 🖳=3 ◉=4 🏋 🎾), in Bala Cynwyd, a popular summer spot, are the one-time stomping ground of former Sixer Charles Barkley. The **Roxborough YMCA, 7201 Ridge Avenue** (6/2, 🏚 🖳=3 ◉=3 🏋 $ 🎾), has competitive leagues and a great mix of ages and races. The friendly afternoon run is such an institution that it was featured in the Philadelphia *Inquirer.* (Other Y's worth your time include the Broad Street Y, the Abbington Y, and the Norristown Y). Just outside the city limits in suburban Lafayette Hill, **Myles Park, Germantown and Joshua** (6/2, 🏚 🖳=3 ◉=3 🏋 ♀ 💡), has laid-back summer runs on two courts that overlook sprawling softball and soccer fields.

The Roxborough Y, where defense is often a dirty word

Any visit to Philly would be incomplete without trying a cheese-steak, the local low-fat delicacy. The city's best, as determined by Hoops Nation as well as *Philadelphia* magazine, can be found at Dalessandro's, at the corner of Henry Avenue and Wendover Street in west Philly.

PITTSBURGH

Mellon Park/Reizenstein Middle School
Fifth Avenue and Beechwood Boulevard
Pittsburgh

4/2,

The epicenter of Pittsburgh hoops lies in the eastern part of the city, where the Burgh's two best pickup spots, Mellon Park and the Reizenstein schoolyard courts, are separated by a ball field. For decades, Pittsburgh's best have made the trip out to Mellon because the courts, located between residential neighborhoods like Homewood and East Liberty, provide a neutral site for a good mix of players.

In recent years, the courts have gained in popularity as gang activity in other parts of the city has driven players, worried about their safety, out to the no-man's-land of Mellon Park. Francis Street Playground was *the* run in the early eighties, but is now too dangerous. During the summers, college players come back to play, knowing that what they did at school don't mean nothin' once they're back at Mellon or the 'Stein.

Brookline Recreation Center
Brookline Boulevard and Breining Place
Pittsburgh

2/1,

The summer outdoor basketball leagues are popular at Brookline Rec, a suburban center in Pittsburgh's Southside, but the best competition at the gym is of the pugilistic variety. Diminutive director Chuck Senft (whose basketball claim to fame is that he once "threw a hook over Connie Hawkins's head to win a game") trains local boxers and has racked up forty-three Golden and Silver Glove Championships over the years.

For another good suburban outdoor run, head down to **Moore Park** on Pioneer Avenue at Southcrest Drive.

Also in Pittsburgh

The **Ozanam Cultural Center, 1833 Wylie Avenue** (4/2, 🔲 =3 ◐=4 ⛰ ☞ 🏀 ☀), in the Hill District, has solid leagues and constant pickup play when it's warm out. The **Ammon Recreation Center, 2217 Bedford Avenue** (6/2, 🔲 =3 ◐=3 ⛰ 🏀), is another Hill District option.

It's hard to find a place to park near the **Markethouse Recreation Center, Bedford Square and South 12th Street** (2/1, 🔲 =5 ◐=3 ⛰ ☞), on the Southside, but it's worth the effort to play on the exquisite gym floor. The center has little in the way of open gym but does run adult leagues. **Phillips Park, Spokane Avenue** (2/1, 🔲 =3 ◐=2 🏗), is not a talent magnet but does provide a glorious view from its location atop a hill in the southern suburbs.

HARRISBURG

Before racking up all-purpose yards in the NFL, Rickey Watters took it to the rack at **Brightbill Park, Curvin Drive and Carolyn Street** (4/2, 🔲 =5 ◐=3 🏗 ☀), a great summer spot with slightly low rims. You can also fill it up at **Reservoir Park, Walnut and North 18th Streets** (8/4, 🔲 =4 ◐=3 ⛰ ⚿ ☀), an inner-city court with recently renovated slabs. Old-timers should check out the friendly noon run at the **Salvation Army, Green and Cumberland Streets** (2/1, 🔲 =3 ◐=2 ⛰ $), where they have a civilized way of deciding who plays next when there is an uneven number of people—they draw numbers from a hat.

ELSEWHERE IN PENNSYLVANIA

Hershey

Talk about Chocolate Thunder—you can actually smell the nearby Hershey Chocolate plant while playing at **Brookside Park, Church**

Road and Brookside Avenue (2/1, 📋 ▣=4 ●=2 🏙️), a sweet outdoor court that draws strong Sunday-evening crowds.

Lancaster

Take your horse and buggy and head over to **Brandon Park, 525 Fairview Avenue** (8/4, 📋 ▣=4 ●=3 🏙️ 🏀 🛠️ 💡), for outdoor play in Lancaster. The summer leagues draw local high-schoolers and college players. For indoor play, stop by the Alumni Sports and Fitness Center at **Franklin & Marshall,** where a bevy of rubber-floored courts host student games. If you want to get under the skin of the locals, pronounce the town name "Lan-caster" instead of the preferred "Lane-cu-ster."

Wilkes-Barre

The top schoolboys gravitate to **Miner Park, Old River Road and Richmont** (4/2, 📋 ▣=3 ●=3 🏢), in the southwest part of the city where Bob Sura grew up setting scoring records.

VIRGINIA

HAMPTON-TIDEWATER AREA

Virginia Beach

Kempsville Recreation Center
800 Monmouth Lane
Virginia Beach

6/2, 🏛️ ▣ ▣ ▣ ▣ ● ● ● ● 🏙️ $ ♀

Every day is March Madness at Kempsville Rec, where a unique round-robin open-gym system ensures that everyone gets theirs. From 12:30 to 3 p.m. Monday through Friday, and again from 7 to 9:45 p.m. on Monday and Wednesday nights, the first thirty players to sign up form six teams. Get there early; demand is such that you are allowed to put your name down up to half an hour prior to each session. These six squads then play thirteen-minute games against each other, rotating after each run to play a different team. There is no official champion, but you can be sure the players, who have included local products such as J. R. Reid and Alonzo Mourning, keep track of these things.

Hampton
North Hampton Community Center
1435 Todds Lane
Hampton

6/1, 🏀 🚪🚪🚪 ⚫⚫⚫ 🏙 $ ☞ 🚫

The supervised games run indoors at the gym and the unsupervised games outside are on the courts at Jeff Davis High School, which is attached to the rec center. It was out on the Davis blacktop that Allen Iverson earned his nickname, "The Answer," playing pickup ball. "When we would play pickup games they used to say I was the answer," Iverson told *Sports Illustrated.* "If you wanted to win, I was the answer. If you wanted to score, I was the answer."

Norfolk
Park Place Recreation Center
29th Street and Colonial Avenue
Norfolk

6/1, 🏀 🚪🚪🚪 ⚫⚫⚫⚫ 🏙 ☞ ♀ 🏀

Winter play here is fast and furious, with director Buster Brevard presiding over up to twenty games a night. Because of the number of players who show, including local collegians from Old Dominion and Norfolk State, games are to seven points. In a commendable practice, if two teams argue too much, "I give them both the boot," Buster says.

Joe Smith spent his afternoons perfecting his tomahawk jam here while growing up in the area, and he returns when in town to talk with the kids and give them some tips.

Newport News
Anderson Park
Oak Avenue and 16th Street
Newport News

4/1,

A first-team member of the All-Location Squad, Anderson Park's full court is 30 yards from the shoreline of Chesapeake Bay. Look carefully across the water and you can make out some real firepower at the Norfolk Naval Base, which, for those who care about these things, is the largest naval installation in the world and the headquarters of NATO's Supreme Allied Commander.

To be Supreme Point-Scoring Commander on the court here, you have to take it to the hole, as winds off the bay make outside gunning dangerous.

Doris Miller Rec Center
2814 Wickham Avenue
Newport News

2/1,

Tuesday nights here are for hardcore ballplayers only. In the off-season, Iverson comes back, Reebok contract and all, to play at Miller. If you can't make it on Tuesday night, try coming by on a summer morning, when much of the same crowd plays.

Also in the Hampton-Tidewater Area
Northside Park, Marvin Park and Tidewater Drive (4/2, =4 =3), on, yep, the north side of Norfolk, is the place to be on weekends. Because of the crowds, it costs $1 to drive into the park from 2 p.m. to midnight on the weekend. Save that buck by parking across the street or at the McDonald's.

Norfolk's **Huntersville Recreation Center, O'Keefe and Goff Streets** (6/2, =3 =3), has a ladies' night on Thursdays, midnight basketball, and even a water-basketball squad.

WHATEVER HAPPENED TO . . .
The Arena?

In *the Back-in-Your-Face Guide,* the Arena received the highest competition rating and was described as "the noontime run occasionally patronized by the guy who had a cup of coffee in the pros."

These days you'll still find large men at the Arena, except now, instead of tank tops, they wear tuxes and focus on belting out tunes for the Virginia Opera, which has taken over the building. We managed to find one building employee (apparently with lunch on his mind) who remembered the Arena's glory days. "This place used to be chock-full of basketball players," he said wistfully.

RICHMOND

High school and college zebras officiate the league games at **Robious Sport and Fitness Center, 10800 Centerview Drive** (2/1, 🏠 ⊡=4 ◕=4 🏋 $ ☞), which also has good pickup play. At **Humphrey Calder Community Center, 414 North Thompson Street** (6/2, 🏠 ⊡=3 ◕=3 ⏧ ♀ ⚲), Wednesday nights are set aside for women and Mondays are the top run for the fellas. For Y play, head to the **Tucker Hill** branch. Those looking for a campus game can mosey over to **Virginia Commonwealth University.**

Outdoors, **Randolph Playground, South Lombardy Street and Idlewood Avenue** (4/2, 🏠 ⊡=4 ◕=4 ⏧ ⚲ ☼), in west Richmond is the top blacktop, while trees keep the court shaded at **Pine Camp Park, Azalea Avenue and Old Brook Road** (4/2, 🏠 ⊡=3 ◕=3 ⏧ ⚲), on the northside.

ELSEWHERE IN VIRGINIA

Charlottesville

At the **University of Virginia** you can either head to the student gym or, if it's a nice day, to the two courts known as "the Dell" in the middle of the campus. Charlottesville residents sometimes play, giving it that "townie vs. gownie" feel.

Petersburg

Moses Malone grew up playing at **Lee Park, Johnson Road and South Boulevard** (4/2, 🏀 🔲=4 ●=4 ⛰ 🎯 ☀), a diamond in the rough an hour south of Richmond. And while you may not get a chance to go "fo, fo, fo" like Moses, you can play fo'-on-fo' with the older guys on Sunday mornings. The younger crowd plays afternoons and evenings, when the lights burn until after midnight.

Up the road a bit, in Chesterfield, players make the drive to play at **Iron Bridge State Park, White Pine and Iron Bridge Roads** (6/2, 🏀 🔲=3 ●=3 🏁 🎯), a scenic multipurpose park reached by exiting I-95 onto Route 288 north and following 288 until it intersects Route 10.

Reston

Who said the great ones have to come from the inner cities? Both Grant Hill and Dennis Scott had no problem honing their games on the short court at **Twin Branches Park, Twin Branches and Lawyers Roads** (2/1, 🏀 🔲=2 ●=3 🏠), half an hour west of D.C.

WEST VIRGINIA

CHARLESTON

The best game in Charleston is at the **YMCA,** though the **South Charleston Community Center, 601 Jefferson Road** (4/2, 🏀 🔲=4 ●=3 🏠 $), has a better gym. Duffers will delight in the location of the eight racks of **Shawnee Regional Park, King Street and Fairlawn Avenue** (8/4, 🏀 🔲=3 ●=3 🏠 ☀), right next to a public golf course.

Downtowners play on the linoleum at the **Martin Luther King Community Center, Donnolly and McCormick Streets,** (6/2, 🏀

▣=2 ◉=3 ⛰ ☞). There are afternoon runs, but the hardcore hoopers play at noon (see below).

Bellies, Bald Spots, and Bad Knees

If you're at the **Martin Luther King Community Center** in downtown Charleston and a middle-aged man hustles by you wearing nothing but gym shorts, don't be alarmed; it's just one of the noontime basketball crowd trying to get into the first game.

Starting around 11:30 a.m. every Monday, Wednesday, and Friday, the archaic gym at MLK begins to fill up with archaic hoopsters who huff, puff, and hobble up and down a short court for about an hour before heading back to work. Because they play on their lunch break, these fifty-somethings are serious about getting in their games right away. As a result, there is a longstanding rule that the first ten guys in the gym with their athletic shorts on play in the first game. "You'll see guys walking in with no shirt or shoes, wearing nothing but socks and shorts," one regular says. "As long as it takes guys like us to change, we figure if you've got the shorts on, at least you've got your slacks off."

A group of thirty local businessmen and assorted community figures (the roster includes a lawyer, a judicial officer, a veterinarian, and a Roman Catholic priest) pay $25 a year each to rent out one half of the gym for these noontime runs. Anyone can join, but the group has stayed relatively stable for the last fifteen years. "This is the oldest pickup game in Charleston," a white-haired gent named Steve says. Turns out he could be referring to either the age of the players or the age of the game; this group has been diligently sweating it out at noon since 1966, when they started at the local YMCA. "We're all getting old together," Steve says, stroking his white beard. "It's nice because you can still pretend you're running a fast break; everyone is just moving slower."

In fact, many of these guys still play competitively as part of the Senior Olympic team. Regulars proudly point out that the West Virginia team won the sixty-and-over national tourney in 1994. King's star? Nemo Nearman, maybe the oldest regular at "about seventy," who played at the University of North Carolina in his younger days and anchored that West Virginia Senior Olympic team.

15

The Deep South

ALABAMA, ARKANSAS, KENTUCKY, LOUISIANA, MISSISSIPPI, TENNESSEE

Down South, folks are either basketball-crazy or completely indifferent to the sport. In NBA breeding grounds like Memphis and Jackson, shooting the rock is an essential part of everyday life. In Nashville, on the other hand, you're more likely to find line dancers than rim hangers. This dichotomy is most pronounced in Alabama: the city of Birmingham balls hard but the rest of the state has a different allegiance—the pigskin. A T-shirt we saw in Tuscaloosa summed it up best. On the front of the shirt, in black block letters, it read LIFE AFTER ALABAMA FOOTBALL. On the back of the shirt, in the same letters: DEATH.

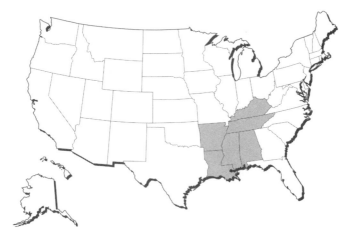

ALABAMA

BIRMINGHAM

At the **Don Hawkins Recreation Center, Roebuck Boulevard and Parkway East** (6/1,🏠 🖼=3 ●=3 🏠 🎯), they have a unique system for deciding who picks teams for the first game. When the gym opens for basketball, all the players present join together in a large game of 21. The first one to 21 is one captain, and the second to reach blackjack is the second captain. Like elitist college stars who skip NBA predraft camps, the better players don't even bother to play, knowing they'll get chosen regardless.

Birmingham's baddest bring their game to **Memorial Park Gym, Sixth Street S. and Sixth Avenue** (4/1,🏠 🖼=3 ●=4 ⛰️ 🎯), on Saturdays. A predominantly teenage crowd gathers at **Ensley Recreation Center, Avenue J and 28th Street** (2/1,🏠 🖼=2 ●=2 ⛰️ 🎯), which director Michael Ainsley refers to, with a touch of hyperbole, as "Hoop City." Other options include the **University of Alabama–Birmingham,** which has the best comp in town, and **Wiggins Park, 31st Street and Parklawn Avenue,** where local ladies play.

The **Downtown YMCA, 321 North 21st Street** (6/2,🖼=3 ●=3 ⛰️ $ ☞ ♀), caters to the business crowd with a CPA League, a corporate league, and a lawyers league. That's an awful lot of briefcases for one gym.

ELSEWHERE IN ALABAMA

Tuscaloosa

Playing at the **University of Alabama** student Rec center can be a disquieting experience. Due to the carpeted floor, balls elicit an eerie *wump* when dribbled instead of the familiar *smack* of leather on wood.

ARKANSAS

If You Build It, They Will Come . . .

There is but one road that winds and dips through the Ozark Mountains in northwest Arkansas, and it is fittingly called the Pig Trail, for there may well be more razorback hogs living in these parts than people. Driving the Pig Trail through the dense forest of the Ozarks, you pass the occasional ramshackle house, but there is little else to disturb the serenity of the wilderness.

That is, until you round a corner and see Dave Ploudre's home—or, more specifically, what sits in Dave's front yard. There, in a clearing bordered by trees, is a 40-by-45-foot slab of concrete painted with the familiar lines and with an adjustable Bison acrylic backboard stationed at one end. The weary traveler, feeling a mite ill from the miles of twisting roadway, could easily mistake the court for a mirage, a hooper's oasis here in the middle of trees and streams. But it is real.

What would inspire Ploudre to haul concrete all the way from Fayetteville, the closest major town, to build this beautiful court? "I love the game," Dave says matter-of-factly.

Love can make one go to great lengths to play ball. Dave, a onetime walk-on player at Southwest Missouri State, is a thirty-eight-year-old traveling salesman who wanted to be able to play ball when at home with his family. Seeing as the only town close to his house is Crosses, which has a grand total of two stores and a population of "about fifty people," Dave decided to build his own court. For competition, he must recruit high school kids from St. Paul High School, eleven miles down the road, to come up on weekends and play half-court ball. The mountain setting, though it provides quite a scenic backdrop, can create complications. The steep hillside that sits behind the baseline, for

Dave Ploudre's court of dreams in the Ozark Mountains

example, posed a serious threat to basketballs, so Dave installed an 11-foot-high net to keep balls from going "down the holler," as he refers to the precipice.

The sight of the 11-foot net, acrylic backboard, and hunk of concrete might lead some to say Dave is detracting from the natural beauty of his location in the Ozarks. Others might argue he has enhanced it.

LITTLE ROCK

Kanis Park
Rodney Parham Road and Mississippi (off I-630)
Little Rock

4/2,

If you're from out of town, getting to Kanis Park is no problem: just get off I-630 at the Rodney Parham exit and the courts are right there, sheltered from the weather underneath the overpass. Getting in a game is a bit harder; on weekends there are often up to thirty players

Rain or shine, the run never stops under-the-freeway at Kanis Park

waiting, and the crowd often includes current and former Razorbacks. To get a jump on things, show up before 2 p.m.

If you do make it on the court, be mindful of the sloped concrete baseline behind one set of baskets; it can turn a strong drive to the hole into a quick ride to the hospital.

Also in Little Rock

Every June, the city goes crazy for the Hoopfest, a local 3-on-3 tourney. To practice up during the winter months, head over to the **War Memorial Fitness Center, Zoo Drive and Monroe Center** (6/2, 🏠 🖼=3 ◉=3 ⛰ **$**), for indoor 4-on-4 games, or hit the **Little Rock Athletic Club, 4610 Sam Peck Road** (10/4, 🏠 🖼=4 ◉=3 🏦 **$ ♀**), which has a separate area with low rims for the young 'uns.

ELSEWHERE IN ARKANSAS

Fayetteville

The best runs in town besides the **University of Arkansas** are on the half-courts at **Wilson Park, Louise Street and Park Avenue**

(2/1, ▨ ▣=3 ●=4 ⛰ ☼). The competition can be excellent, as is the pizza at J.R.'s bar, a local watering hole you can hit up for postgame refreshments.

Another bar on the other side of town, **Cuckoo's, 965 South Razorback Road,** has an on-premise basketball court where lit patrons can play on the lit asphalt at night. Cuckoo's also has TVs in the bathrooms—talk about sports-bar heaven.

Hope

The regulars are generally short and slow of foot at **Fair Park, Park Drive and Mockingbird** (4/2, ▨ ▣=3 ●=1 ▰), in Bill Clinton's hometown, so if you stop by for a game, all you gotta do is believe in a little place called the post. As for Bill, he played in a couple church leagues when young, but said of himself in a *Sports Illustrated* interview, "[I was] a little too chunky and slow to be very commendable on the court."

Hey, that didn't stop Razorback Oliver Miller from making the NBA.

KENTUCKY

Dirt Bowl Bickering

In Kentucky, they take their basketball and their Dirt Bowls seriously. No, the Dirt Bowl is not the latest college football championship to gain a strange sponsor. Rather, it is the name of two strong summer basketball leagues, Lexington's Dirt Bowl and Louisville's Dirt Bowl, that have been hosting the state's best youngsters since the 1960s. Both these grimy leagues derive their names from having started out on clay tennis courts, though they are now played on asphalt.

Both bowls have showcased prodigious talent over the years, including the state's finest high-schoolers and numerous University of Kentucky and U of Louisville collegians, and while both are venerable institutions, there is some contention as to which is the original Dirt Bowl. Those who can remember say that the Lexington version started in 1967 and Louisville's began in 1968. Still, Gil Clark, one of the Louisville league's founding fathers, isn't so sure. "I think you'll find Louisville started before them," he says a bit defensively.

Regardless of who started first, both are still going strong. Lexington's tourney runs out of Douglass Park, where "DIRT BOWL" is painted in large white letters on the concrete court and a wooden announcer's booth sits between two exquisite full courts. The community comes out en masse for games, with the sweet smell of barbecue in the air and well-heeled college recruiters sitting next to barefoot kids with ketchup smeared on their faces. The Bowl is no less of an attraction in Louisville: Up to 3,000 spectators come out to watch the games. The Louisville league is also currently in transition, moving from the four full courts at Shawnee Park to a newly built Shawnee Sports Complex 200 yards away.

Elsewhere in the state there exist smaller Dirt Bowls, and even the occasional Dust Bowl (you get the idea they like their soil in these parts), but although these have some of the tradition of their big-city counterparts, they can't match the competition. The rivalry between Louisville and Lexington is such that when both leagues were younger entities, the winners of the two Dirt Bowls would match up

Douglass Park in Lexington

against each other at the end of the season. That didn't last too long though. "They used to play each other," Clark says. "But there was too much animosity, so they decided it's best if they don't do it anymore."

LEXINGTON

When the Dirt Bowl isn't running, **Douglass Park, Georgetown Road and Howard Street** (4/2, 🗿 🖳=5 ●=4 ⛰ ☞ 🏛), is overrun by local talent out for pickup play. The two full courts over at **Shillito Park,** located off Man O' War Blvd. on Winthrop Road, are almost identical to the ones at Douglass; both have concrete stanchions and trophy stands. You can't miss the team colors at the blue-and-white-painted outdoor courts next to the Boone Tennis Center at the **University of Kentucky.** Three full courts draw big crowds when school's in session.

Head to **Dunbar Community Center, 545 North Upper Street** (6/2, 🗿 🖳=5 ●=3 ⛰), when it gets cold. Watch your tongue, though; posted basketball rules warn, "Arguing causes lights to go out."

LOUISVILLE AREA

What Louisville lacks in charm as a city, it makes up for with solid outdoor hoops. **Shawnee Park, Larkwood Avenue and Southwestern Parkway** (8/4, 🗿 🖳=5 ●=4 ⛰ ☞ 🏛), has full-service outdoor courts equipped with three-point lines, breakaway rims, and nets. Right off I-264 in south Louisville, **Wyandotte Park, Taylor Boulevard and Beecher Street** (6/3, 🗿 🖳=3 ●=4 ⛰ 🏛 ☀), draws kids from the projects and occasional Cardinals players. At **Seneca Park, Pee Wee Reese Road** (4/2, 🗿 🖳=3 ●=3 🏠 ☀ ♀), off I-64, you'll find a run to please everybody. A relaxing park setting, with Rollerbladers zooming by, sets the scene for outdoor games with a diverse mix of people. Women play with the guys, and there's a water fountain present to quench that postgame thirst.

If you don't mind crossing the Ohio River into Indiana, there are good runs in Jeffersonville at the **Nachand Field House, 601 East Court Avenue** (4/2, 🗿 🖳=4 ●=4 🏠 $ ☞ ♀), a converted high school gymnasium.

Seneca Park in Louisville

LOUISIANA

NEW ORLEANS

Shakespeare Park
Washington and La Salle
New Orleans

4/2,

An iron roof keeps Shakespeare's spacious courts cool during the day and dry during downpours. If you like to pull up behind the arc on the fast break to drop three-point dimes, be advised that you will be earning them here—the three is deeper than NBA distance at the top of the key, though it tapers down to a more manageable 19 feet at the baselines.

Lawrence Square
Napoleon and Camp Streets
New Orleans

2/1,

The games at Lawrence Square heat up once the sun goes down and the oppressive southern heat recedes into the dusk. Situated in the nicest area of downtown and across the street from the police precinct, Lawrence is a tidier run than Shakespeare Park. It's also a great place to sweat off that hangover from the previous night's French Quarter revelry by throwing down a couple slam jambalayas.

Also in New Orleans

If you can weasle your way in, the Wellness Center at **Tulane University** has a plethora of hoops. Taking the more conventional route, visitors to the city can get into the downtown **YMCA, 920 St. Charles Avenue** (2/1, ⌂ ⊡=3 ●=3 ▲ $ ☞), for $5 a day if they bring their hotel key with them. The gym is near the Superdome and but nine blocks from the French Quarter, so Mardi Gras visitors will often increase the crowd during February.

ELSEWHERE IN LOUISIANA

Baton Rouge

The **Louisiana Sport and Fitness Center, 3103 Monterrey Boulevard** (2/1, ⌂ ⊡=4 ●=3 ▦ $ ☞), provides an above-average, no-nonsense health club run where the "Absolutely No Dunking" sign gets absolutely no respect. If you'd like to disregard that dunking sign but don't have the requisite ups, head down the street to the low rims at **Vila Del Ray Elementary School, Cuyhanga and Orlando Drives**

(4/2, ▨ 🖿=3 ◉=2 🏋), where anyone can be a rule breaker. Another option is the student rec center at Shaq Diesel's alma mater, **Louisiana State University.**

Lafayette
The rec center at **Southwest Louisiana** is worth checking out. **Red Lerille's Health and Racquet Club, 301 Doucet Road** (8/3, 🖿 🖿=4 ◉=1 🏋 $ ♀), an upscale club with a nice gym, is not. The club won the dubious honor of having the worst full-court game we played in on the whole trip.

Shreveport
On weekdays and Saturdays, the air-conditioned confines of **Airport Park, 6500 Kennedy Drive** (6/1, 🖿 🖿=4 ◉=4 ⛰ 🚲), across the way from the Shreveport airport, are filled with plenty of takeoffs of the non-Boeing type. For those who need a little help with liftoff, the low rims at **Turner Elementary School, West 70th Street,** might help.

MISSISSIPPI

JACKSON

George T. Kurt's Field House
125 Gymnasium Drive (off Bullard Street)
Jackson

2/1, 🖿 🖿 🖿 🖿 🖿 ◉◉◉◉◉ 🏙 🚲

The Field House (also known as the airbase because of a nearby airfield) is a hidden gem of a gym on the outskirts of the city. Jackson's finest, including natives Lindsey Hunter, Othella Harrington, and James "Hollywood" Robinson, play during the summer from 9 to 12 a.m. and again from 2 to 4 p.m. Just about everyone who plays has college or pro experience, so if you put your name on the downs list, you'd better have game; if you're not sure, you're better off not signing the list. You also had better have a quarter, the nominal gym fee at all city rec centers in Jackson.

Also in Jackson

During the week they play four-on-four half-court at **Sykes Gym, Cooper Road and Rickay** (2/1, 🏠 ⬛=2 ⬤=3 ⛰ 🏚). Saturdays it's full court starting at 9 a.m., though it's recommended that you arrive by 8:45 to make sure you get in line. A black crowd that welcomes white guys who can play.

The **Sports Club, 2240 East Westbrook Road** (2/1, 🏠 ⬛=4 ⬤=3 🏢 $ ☞ ♀), has good leagues, whereas basketball-shaped **Battlefield Park, Porter and Walnut** (4/2, 🏠 ⬛=4 ⬤=3 ⛰ 🏚), is hit-or-miss, with an awful lot of 21.

ELSEWHERE IN MISSISSIPPI

Greenwood

Come play dunk ball with the locals at **Martin Luther King Memorial Park, Avenue I and Dr. Martin Luther King Drive** (4/2, 🏠 ⬛=2 ⬤=2 🏁 🏚), just a few miles from where Jerry Rice set a bevy of records at Mississippi Valley State.

Hattiesburg

Fulfill your hoops hankering by playing at the exquisite rec center at the **University of Southern Mississippi,** where Clarence Weatherspoon and Brett Favre were once Big Men on Campus.

TENNESSEE

MEMPHIS

Pine Hill Community Center
973 Alice Road
Memphis

6/1,

The bleachers at Pine Hill fill up in the early afternoon, when the youngsters come out to watch the impassioned play of their elders. "For some of these guys, this is like their job," a regular said. "Wake up at one and come play ball."

Good competition rotates between Pine Hill Mondays through Thursdays, and the East Side's **McFarland Community Center, Pride and Cottonwood** (6/1, 🏠 ⬜=3 ●=4 ⛰ ☞ ⚱), Fridays. The games at McFarland used to lure North Memphis natives Eliot Perry and Penny Hardaway down to test their skills.

Also in Memphis

The Tigers play their games at the imposing Pyramid downtown, but the off-season pickup at the **Elma Roae Field House, University of Memphis,** is as good as it gets. Perry, Hardaway, and another native, Todd Day, are often in attendance.

The city has a multitude of good rec centers in addition to McFarland and Pine Hill, though be careful, as some, such as Lester Community Center in north Memphis, are in very dangerous areas. **North Frayser Community Center, St. Elmo and Edenburg** (6/1, 🏠 ⬜=3 ●=3 ⛰ ⚱), at A. B. Pickett Park is a safer place to park your ride, and the center boasts both indoor and outdoor buckets. An interesting sidenote: At many of the Memphis gyms, hats aren't allowed inside, so dispose of your lid before entering.

Lots of local students work out at the **Alfred Mason YMCA, Highland Street and Walker** (4/1, 🏠 ⬜=3 ●=3 🏋 $ ☞ ♀), a well-equipped Y.

ELSEWHERE IN TENNESSEE

Chattanooga

It's strictly half-court at **Booker T. Washington State Park, Champion Road off Highway 58** (2/1, 🏠 ▣=3 ◉=2 🖐) on the outskirts of town near Lake Chickamauga. For indoor play head down Highway 58 to Oakwood Road and **Washington Hills Community Center,** where Wednesdays are the best runs.

Knoxville

The outdoor courts at the **University of Tennessee,** on campus near the aquatic center, host the best runs in town. **Cal Johnson Recreation Center, 307 Mulvaney Street** (2/1, 🏠 ▣=3 ◉=3 🔺 ☞ 🐾), can heat up when a local stud named Sleepy shows up for the evening games. At **Court South, 207 Walker Springs Road** (2/1, 🏠 ▣=2 ◉=2 🏢 $), a health club on the edge of town, members play four-on-four on a converted racquetball court.

Nashville

In the nation's country music capital you can hear string music of a different kind at the **Downtown YMCA, Church and McLemore Streets** (6/1, 🏠 ▣=4 ◉=4 🔺 $ ☞). A midnight league brings in college talent, and the Saturday-morning games feature some high-fliers (ask b-ball director Adam, and he will recite tales of "guys dunking with their arms parallel to the floor"). The **Green Hills YMCA, 4041 Hillsboro Circle** (6/1, 🏠 ▣=3 ◉=2 🏢 $ ☞), and its rock-hard floor provide a less physical, more suburban run. Games are to 24 on the short courts. For a college run, check out **Vanderbilt,** which has indoor and outdoor hoops. For sweaty Garth Brooks fans, check out Opryland, a gaudy theme park next to the Grand Old Opry.

WHATEVER HAPPENED TO . . .
Dr. Overholt's?

Dr. Robert Overholt's backyard court is still the stuff of legend around Knoxville. Twenty years ago, Doc's full court, equipped with see-through backboards and lights, hosted the state's top players, including Dale Ellis. *The Back-in-Your-Face Guide* featured the court and quoted Ernie Grunfeld, University of Tennessee graduate and New York Knick, as rating it "the best outdoor court I've ever seen."

When in Knoxville we head out in search of Overholt's. At a gas station, a young cashier speaks of it with reverence. "Oh, you guys gotta check out the court this doctor has," he says in between serving up clammy hot dogs. "People come from all over to play there." With this high praise in our ears, we motor out to the affluent West Hills area of town, where we find Doc's. Or what's left of it. The court looks like it hasn't hosted a game in the last decade; there is grass growing up through fissures in the pavement, the opaque backboards are cracked, and an imposing padlock is latched on the gate to the court.

Vowing to get to the bottom of this, I call the good doctor's office. Dr. Overholt is too busy to talk, but his assistant, Jean Greer, explains that Overholt moved out of his house at the end of the eighties and now lives five minutes away, where he has a hoop on his garage but no court. The new owner of his house, a researcher at UT, "put a padlock on the court the day he moved in," Jean explains. "So, Doc Overholt's court is no more."

A tragedy, but at least Doc didn't tear it down to put in a putting green. *That* would have been truly tragic.

16

Is Heaven Still a Playground?

THE CHANGING GAME

Growing up in the Crown Heights section of Brooklyn in the early seventies, Frank Caesar and six of his buddies would travel the city in a van playing basketball. "We would, literally speaking, attack a park," says Caesar, who is now the assistant headmaster at Xavier High in Manhattan. "We'd jump out of the van and our leader, a guy we called Sarge, he'd have us doing some push-ups and jumping jacks. People would be looking at us, like, 'What the hell is the matter with these guys.'"

Caesar, whose long arms and skinny frame earned him the nickname Spiderman during his high school years, would get up early on weekends and spend the whole day driving to parks with his friends. They weren't an organized team, but they played like one: They had informal plays, set picks, and ran the fast break in five lanes. When they won at a new park, "All of a sudden they'd be getting off the court, saying, 'Go get Joe, man, see if Joe's up. See if Mitch's up.' And they'd be running and these guys would come back, and we'd beat them," Caesar says. "They'd be asking if we were coming back next week, ' 'cause we'll make sure that so-and-so will be here.' When we came back the next time, they'd be ready, and we'd stepped up the competition in the park."

They were a neighborhood squad—Schenectady Avenue, they called themselves—and they challenged the best players in other neighborhoods. For them, summertime meant basketball, played purely for the sake of playing basketball.

During our travels around the country we met many people like Caesar who used to live and breathe playground basketball. Although Caesar and his buddies were certainly more devoted than most, they weren't unusual for the basketball scene of the sixties, seventies, and early eighties. Across the nation, the courts were packed all day long, from seven in the morning until after midnight on Saturdays. When Rick Telander wrote a book in 1974 about a summer spent at the outdoor court of Foster Park in Brooklyn, he called it *Heaven Is a Playground*, a fitting title because, for ballplayers two decades ago, basketball bliss could be found down at the local park.

A lot has happened in the world of basketball since then. The game has become a global phenomenon, played by millions worldwide in gyms, leagues, and tournaments. This extraordinary growth has done wonders for the popularity of the sport, but as the times have changed in the last thirty years, the game of basketball has changed with them. Playing ball and talking with players throughout the country, we found that although there are a lot of great courts out there, there are also some disturbing trends affecting the game. Today, for example, Caesar and his friends would be anomalies at many courts: relics playing a team-oriented game in an age of me-first basketball; city schoolyard players at a time when many schoolyards are quiet and the "city game" cannot be played safely in some cities.

The most obvious change in the game is how it is played. One of the great things about basketball has always been the improvisation and the one-on-one showdowns; to see two great players face off in a battle of wills is what makes the game exciting. But these days, both in pickup and at the organized level, it's not just the great ones who face off; it seems that whoever gets the ball often feels compelled to shoot it as soon as possible. To see a group of guys in a pickup game running plays as Caesar did—executing a backdoor cut or setting picks—is a rare sight, and the reaction from the opponents is often one of indignation: "What are these guys doing out here? They're running illegal plays!"

Tom Konchalski, one of the country's premier high school talent scouts, has a theory about this. "People watch *Sportscenter*, and they see sound-bite highlights, whether it be pulling your shirt off, head-butting referees, blocking shots, a guy dunking it—that's what makes *Sportscenter*," Konchalski says from his New York office. "We're living in the age of tabloid excitement, they don't show the great passes. You don't see the Princetons on the highlights, because it might take three or four good passes to set up a shot."

Setting up a shot is a foreign concept to the many players who never learned the fundamentals and feel they don't need to when they have the athletic ability to get off their own shot. Years of watching Michael Jordan take over a game have led them to believe that, even though they lack Mike's skills and abilities, they can do the same. "Guys just come down to the three-point line and shoot. What's that? That's not running an offense—anyone can come down and throw up a three-pointer," says Ken Graham, longtime commissioner of the West Fourth League. "Everybody is out there looking out for themselves. In order to have a successful team, you have got to share the ball and play together."

These shot-happy players are often so intent on achieving personal glory that they hurt their team in an effort to boost their own perfor-mance. Why is this? A number of factors probably contribute—selfish NBA role models, media focus on the individual, increased pressure to succeed—but much of the problem can be traced to one of the oldest evils: money. "It makes it easy for a guy to think about himself when he sees how much money is being tossed around," Graham says. "The sport is ruined simply because there is so much money that guys go in thinking, 'I'm gonna get mine, to heck with everybody else.' They want to be MVP, so they shoot a lot."

"Getting mine" is often pursued these days regardless of the other players on the court. To achieve personal success, players—just fol-lowing the example set by NBA stars and their sneaker ads—feel they have to somehow prove they are the top dog, and they spew forth trash-talk while trying to dominate and intimidate their opponent. As a result, the emphasis on a team winning has been transferred to one person succeeding, and doing so at all costs. This can in turn detract from the camaraderie that makes playing basketball so enjoyable. NBA All-Star Horace Grant has noticed this. "Fifteen years ago, it was just like you'd go out there and you'd play for the love of the

game," Grant says, still wet from his postgame shower in the Orlando Magic locker room. "I think that today, [with] a lot of guys, it has changed from that standpoint of just going out and just having fun."

Although Grant learned the game playing on the streets of Sparta, Georgia, against his brother Harvey, he, like so many other top players, doesn't play streetball anymore. And who can blame them? "There's too much money in the game now," explains New York pickup legend Earl "The Goat" Manigault. "Years ago, guys were only making a hundred thousand, so they could play in the playground games. Today, it's too dangerous for the pros to play [in pickup]."

What this creates is a gap between the guys on the street and the guys in "the league." The segregation starts early, too. It used to be that players would graduate from the playgrounds to college and then maybe to the pros. Now the good players are identified at an early age and sequestered and funneled through youth programs and an endless succession of high-powered summer camps. They are told not to play "streetball" or "ratball." This widens the gap between the guys on the street and the stars, even if these "stars" are only twelve years old. Part of the appeal of pickup ball is never knowing who might show for a game and testing yourself against the best, but that appeal is muted when the best comp never shows up.

The migration of top players away from the playgrounds is also a factor in a second facet of the changing game, the many outdoor courts that are eerily empty. "It's changed, you know, guys don't come out to the park like we did," the Goat says, shaking his head. "For us, it was a seven-day thing, now it's more of a weekend thing."

"Master Rob" Hokett, another New York street legend, agrees. Hokett, who grew up in the Bronx before playing for the University of New Orleans and the Harlem Globetrotters, says he carries a ball with him in his trunk and can get it out and shoot at any park because they're all empty these days. "I don't know why the kids don't play the way they used to play when I was growing up," says Hokett, who has played in the Rucker Tournament for over a decade. "I'm thirty now, but when I was fourteen and fifteen, you go to the park, you couldn't get no run 'cause it was so crowded. And if you wasn't good, you definitely wasn't playing."

Why are there fewer players on the blacktop? Theories abound. Many people play exclusively indoors in gyms, health clubs, leagues,

and tournaments, cutting out outdoor pickup play, in part because of its disorganized aspect. There are also more options these days; kids can watch TV, play video games, or go Rollerblading. In the inner cities, the pull of the streets is often stronger than that of the game. Jon Greenberg, director at the Potrero Hill Recreation Center in San Francisco, has seen the consequences of street life. "Pickup ball has died down in San Francisco," Greenberg says as he looks out across the bay. "I believe the drug scene in the eighties scooped up many of the would-be players, and then when those guys tried to come back out to the courts, they didn't have the skills and were ostracized. Then they were afraid to come back. What happened was, we lost a whole generation of players because the guys who were into other things in the eighties won't take their kids out to the courts in the nineties."

Greenberg touches on what may be the main reason why playgrounds receive less use: the deterioration of cities and a violent aspect that has attached itself to basketball. "When we played, it wasn't about anything else, it was about basketball," Frank Caesar says. "Even back then, there were places we would go to play basketball that I wouldn't go otherwise. There was no way you could get me to go to Breevort [the Breevort Projects, a dangerous Brooklyn area that had good games], but tell me that there's a game there? I'm down."

Great basketball players have always been like sanitation workers. There are areas in the country, like the Bedford-Stuyvesant and Brownsville sections of Brooklyn and South Central Los Angeles, where nonresidents are in danger just driving through the streets. But nobody ever messes with the garbage man. They might mug anyone else who comes through, but you don't mess with the guy who picks up the trash, or the mailman, either, for that matter, because they both provide a community service. Talented basketball players have been viewed the same way—if they came to your neighborhood to play, you didn't mess with them. The last thing you wanted to be known as was the guy who jacked Doctor J. You would've been beat up quicker than you could say "I didn't recognize the 'fro." For this reason, even today there are courts in bad neighborhoods where college and pro guys can play. But, sadly, many courts are now too dangerous for even the basketball players to visit.

Take Pittsburgh, for example. The best talent used to travel all around the city to play at different courts. Now, because of rampant gang activity, the ballers visit only Mellon Park, a no-man's-land, gangwise, in a nice part of the city. Players don't want to risk going to a court where their life is constantly in danger. "The gang situation has changed the game here in Pittsburgh," says Curtis Cureton, who has run leagues out of Ozanam Cultural Center for years. "There used to be a time when you could go to any neighborhood to get a game. Those days are over."

Gang problems go hand in hand with another scourge of the inner cities: drugs. While filming the movie *Hoop Dreams*, Frederick Marx, one of the movie's three creators, saw the pernicious effect crack can have on a neighborhood. The crew filmed at a court on the West Side of Chicago when Arthur Agee, one of the movie's subjects, was a freshman, "When we were first there, the rims were straight, there were nets on the court, there were summer league games happening there," Marx said. "People felt comfortable to bring lawn chairs and just sit out there on a summer evening. And then, just in the course of the shooting of the film, four years later the rims were bent, the nets were gone, there were crack dealers over in the corner, people weren't coming out there anymore, the summer league had been canceled. It was just a dramatic change."

Across the country, cities are crumbling in upon themselves, taking recreational opportunities with them. In Boston, Al Brodsky has been coaching inner-city kids for thirty years. "The younger guys are too involved in gangs and the streets," Brodsky said. "The ones who aren't are too scared to come out to the parks. I can't take a group of kids from one housing project to another without worrying. That's not right."

Why have the cities become unsafe? One can point to the cutbacks in funding of the inner cities; one can point to drugs, gang violence, and a multitude of other factors. That is another discussion, though, one to which a book on basketball is not well suited. What is relevant, though, is that, while basketball has become unsafe in the cities, it is certainly not the problem, as some city planners seem to think. Many cities, such as Detroit, have begun taking down outdoor basketball rims because they believe the courts attract violence. Rather, basketball is one of the most powerful positive forces in the inner cities, as has been proved repeatedly by the success of midnight hoops programs.

The game can provide an outlet for inner-city youths, but not if they are too afraid to go to the playgrounds. Rick Telander, the author of *Heaven Is a Playground*, sees this problem as a philosophically disturbing one. "Play is perhaps the highest order of human activity because when you play it means that all the necessities have been taken care of: food, shelter, meaning in life, perhaps, and prime amongst them, a sense of safety," he said from his Chicago office. "Without a sense of safety, no one can play, it's an impossibility. Your play is not really play, it is some kind of furtive diversion from the terror that surrounds you. And until you can get rid of that fear, whatever it comes from, all games suffer, not just basketball games."

One could argue that, even though our cities are in trouble, the changing face of basketball isn't detrimental to the game at large. So no one passes the ball or sets screens anymore. So fewer people are playing outdoor pickup ball. So there are dangerous city courts. People, 46 million of them in the United States, are playing ball. The game will mutate, survive, and prosper, but what is slipping away is part of the essence of the game. Turn on the TV and you're likely to see some ad that uses the street game to sell a product. An NBA superstar will be out on the blacktop with a bunch of ethnically correct actors portraying pickup players. The ad gives the impression that this All-Star actually spends his Saturday down at the park messing around and drinking Gatorade. The truth is that it's probably the first time he has exposed his $5 million knees to asphalt in years. Ironically, we are celebrating a culture as it is disappearing.

As the culture of outdoor pickup ball vanishes like the vinyl record, the benefits and side effects of pickup ball—the mixing of all types, races, and socioeconomic backgrounds that occurs on the court—are diminished as well. The tendency of some players, and especially white ones, to play exclusively in posh clubs and expensive leagues has become a form of self-segregation. Money is the gate that can be closed to keep out "undesirables," and when this happens, players interact only with others like them, in the process missing out on the benefits of integrated games. "It's kind of analogous to these walled cities we're getting, these suburbs that are gated communities where you have to go past the guardhouse to get in," Telander said. "You know, there have always been subdivisions but now they literally have gates around them, and in certain ways that's what these courts have, gates around them: private membership."

So what can be done? Well, as for the turmoil of city ball, it may be easier to view the situation this way: The problems of our society are reflected in the game of basketball, but they can also be solved in part by the game of basketball.

This is why tearing down basketball rims is not a solution; if kids aren't at the court, it means they're most likely on the streets. Two gentlemen in New York realized this, and are doing their part to keep the playground culture alive. In 1994 Mike Klein and Ed Genesee started the Gabe Valez Foundation with the goal of refurbishing 100 New York City playgrounds. For kids in the Big Apple, where a clean, safe court is a haven from temptations, this generosity is much appreciated.

Basketball is also acting as a repair mechanism through youth programs across the country that use hoops as a means to aid inner-city youngsters. Programs like the Sonny Hill Youth Involvement League in Philadelphia, which teaches kids to be smart players and smart human beings. Programs like Youth Enhancement Support (Y.E.S.), a Pittsburgh organization founded by Curtis Cureton, the coach and educator mentioned earlier. One of the goals of Y.E.S. is to use basketball as a hook, to bring in kids so that they can be taught life skills and kept off the streets. Another goal is to provide racial and economic integration. So far it has succeeded; wealthy sons of attorneys and surgeons from the suburbs go through the program with inner-city kids. Lifelong friendships are developed that cross racial boundaries, and fears are dissolved.

The importance of these types of programs, as well as midnight basketball leagues, cannot be overestimated. "People who say sports aren't important are wrong," writes Baltimore native Muggsy Bogues in his autobiography, *In the Land of Giants*. "Sports are everything in the ghetto. Sometimes it's the only positive thing in a world full of negative things."

Tell this to the politicians who cut funding for midnight basketball leagues. Tell them to go to the Madison Square Rec Center in Baltimore and watch a Midnight Madness League game. It would be hard to leave that experience—thousands of gang members peacefully watching basketball for three hours during prime crime time on weekend nights—still doubting the validity of the program. Even though the 1994 Congress cut out midnight basketball as unnecessary pork—Congressman Lamar Smith, a Republican from Texas, called the program "vague social spending"—cities have continued to run the midnight leagues because of their benefits, but the programs are now underfunded. Mayor's Night Hoops in Kansas City is not federally funded, but the $100,000 program puts 1,200 at-risk adolescents through conflict resolution and job skills development workshops before putting them on the hardwood. Considering it costs $30,000 a year to incarcerate one juvenile offender, the price tag of Mayor's Night Hoops seems like quite a bargain.

As for how the game is played today, basketball is not in trouble—it is just in need of a tune-up. If you have any doubts about whether people are playing ball, just reread the first fifteen chapters of this book. The game is still played with the same passion at many courts—visit Rocky River in Ohio or Avalon in New Jersey for proof of that—and while there are players who are focused on "getting mine," there are also still many team-oriented players focused on "getting the W." Many NBA players may be poor role models, intent on the almighty dollar, but there are also players like Grant Hill and David Robinson, class acts on the court and off who can carry the torch into the next century. The growth of the women's game is encouraging as well, and female players, who traditionally had to look up to male stars, now have their own professional role models.

The new frontier for pickup ball may now be the pay-for-play facilities that are proliferating around the country. Basketball facilities such as the Run n' Shoot in Atlanta, where anyone can come in and play ball for fifteen bucks a month, provide much of the cultural mix that can be found at popular outdoor courts. Players who can't afford the YMCA or the health club can now play to their heart's content at these gyms, and they don't have to feel like second-class citizens, relegated to wait until aerobics is finished to play ball. It's possible that a new culture will emerge on the hardwood of these basketball megaplexes.

As for the playgrounds, things may never be quite *Heaven*-ly again, but if the people who remember those days—the players who used to shovel snow off the court in the winter to play one-on-one, the players who have the love—can instill that love in the next generation, then the playground game will be kept alive. Kids still grow up everywhere shooting at baskets and dreaming basketball dreams; that's not going to change. Little Noah Caesar, Frank's son, is only four years old, but already his professed goal in life is "to be in the NBA." Well, he won't make it there without learning to set screens and run the break in five lanes, and he certainly won't be skipping school or head-butting any referees—not with Frank Caesar on the job.

Appendix

THE CREAM OF THE CROP

The top thirty courts are rated on the basis of recommendations of players everywhere through on-court interviews, mail-in surveys, website surveys, phone interviews, etc. The rest of these ratings are straight from the brains of the four members of Hoops Nation.

COURT BESTS

THE TOP THIRTY NONCOLLEGE COURTS IN THE UNITED STATES, RANKED

The criteria: Quality of the court, quality of the competition, consistency of the competition, availability of the court, atmosphere, location, safety of the surroundings, extracurricular events (leagues, tourneys, etc.), reputation, and the ease of getting into a game.

1. West Fourth Street, New York City
2. Fondé Recreation Center, Houston
3. Venice Beach Courts, Venice, California
4. Run N' Shoot Athletic Center, Atlanta
5. Rocky River Courts, Rocky River, Ohio
6. Jackson Park Courts, Chicago
7. The Circuit (Rogers Park/Westwood Recreation Center/Memorial Recreation Center/Del Aire Community Center), Los Angeles Area
8. Green Lake Park, Seattle
9. The Sporting Club, Philadelphia
10. Eighth Street Courts, Avalon, New Jersey
11. George T. Kurt's Field House, Jackson, Mississippi
12. Rucker Park, New York City

13. St. John's Recreation Center, Brooklyn, New York
14. Smith Center, Orlando
15. Woodson Park Gymnasium, Oklahoma City
16. Charlotte YMCA, Charlotte
17. St. Cecilia's, Detroit
18. Madison Square Recreation Center ("the Dome"), Baltimore
19. Laguna Beach Courts, Laguna Beach, California
20. Lincoln Park, Milwaukee
21. Joe Dumars Fieldhouse, Detroit
22. Mosswood Park, Oakland
23. The Hoop, Beaverton, Oregon
24. The Lost Battalion Recreation Center, Queens, New York
25. Ben Davis Schoolyard, Indianapolis
26. The Slab, Coeur d'Alene, Idaho
27. Malcolm X Park–Shelburne Recreation Center, Boston
28. Mellon Park–Reizenstein Schoolyard, Pittsburgh
29. Hurley Park, St. Petersburg
30. Pacific Beach Recreation Center, San Diego

TOP INDOOR COLLEGE COURTS (NO ORDER)

University of California–Berkeley
University of Iowa–Iowa City
University of North Carolina–Chapel Hill
UCLA (Wooden/Men's Gym/Pauley)
Indiana University at Bloomington
University of Utah–Salt Lake City

TOP OUTDOOR COLLEGE COURTS (NO ORDER)

Clark Field, University of Texas–Austin
The Cages, Ohio State–Columbus
University of Tennessee–Knoxville
University of Kentucky–Lexington
The Horseshoe, University of Massachusetts–Amherst
University of Florida

MOST SCENIC COURTS IN THE UNITED STATES, RANKED

1. A1A Beach Courts, Ft. Lauderdale
2. Laguna Beach Courts, Laguna Beach, California
3. Lake Lodge Court, Yellowstone National Park, Wyoming
4. Hurley Park, St. Petersburg Beach

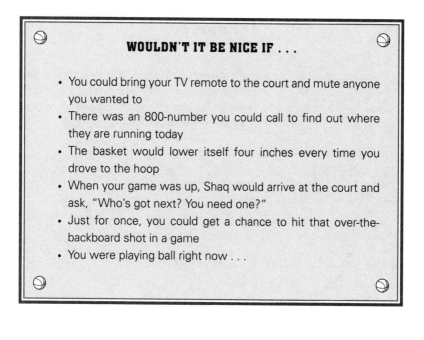

WOULDN'T IT BE NICE IF . . .

- You could bring your TV remote to the court and mute anyone you wanted to
- There was an 800-number you could call to find out where they are running today
- The basket would lower itself four inches every time you drove to the hoop
- When your game was up, Shaq would arrive at the court and ask, "Who's got next? You need one?"
- Just for once, you could get a chance to hit that over-the-backboard shot in a game
- You were playing ball right now . . .

5. The Slab, Coeur d'Alene, Idaho
6. Forest Park Courts, Springfield, Massachusetts
7. Venice Beach Courts, Venice, California
8. James Madison Park, Madison, Wisconsin
9. The Higher Court, San Bernardino, California
10. Foster Beach, Chicago

BEST DUNK HOOPS IN THE UNITED STATES

Whittier Elementary School, Phoenix
Brightbill Park, Harrisburg, Pennsylvania

SPRINGIEST GYM FLOOR

The Sporting Club at Aventine, San Diego

MOST IMPRESSIVE OUTDOOR COURT

Camp Greene Park, Charlotte

BEST GYM NAME

The Sweatbox, University of Texas–Arlington

TRIP BESTS

BEST DUNK WE SAW

A nasty two-hand job on the outdoor courts at Venice Beach. This guy caught it at the free-throw line in a half-court set, took one step, and tomahawked on two guys so hard the backboard was swaying for five minutes. The spectators almost lost their minds screaming.

BEST BURRITO

High-Tech Burrito in Marin County, California

BEST CHEAP MOTEL IN AMERICA

Knights Inn, Columbia, South Carolina. For $27 we checked in three people and got two double beds, a fridge, and a spacious room.

BEST FLAVOR CHEF BOYARDEE MICROWAVE MEAL

Chicken and Noodle all the way

Index of Courts

Index of Hoops Culture